# Admiral Lord Anson

*By the same author:*

WEATHER FORECASTING
AN ABRIDGED VERSION OF LORD ANSON'S VOYAGE

Admiral Lord Anson
*From a mezzotint by J. MacArdell, after Sir Joshua Reynolds*

# Admiral Lord Anson

*The story of Anson's voyage
and naval events of his day*

by

## CAPTAIN S. W. C. PACK

C.B.E., M.Sc.

**Royal Navy**

CASSELL · LONDON

CASSELL & COMPANY LTD.
35 Red Lion Square, London WC1
and at
MELBOURNE · SYDNEY · TORONTO · CAPE TOWN
JOHANNESBURG · AUCKLAND

Made and Printed in Great Britain
by Jarrold and Sons Ltd., Norwich
F.160

Dedicated with admiration and affection to
the First Sea Lord,
Admiral Sir Charles Lambe, G.C.B., C.V.O.

# Preface

ANSON was essentially a man of action. It is said that he wrote little and talked less. Of matters concerning his personal life this certainly seems true, and without contemporary descriptions of the man it is difficult to learn very much about his likes and dislikes or the manner in which he conducted his private life. On naval matters, however, much of his writing is available. His Service letters and orders conform to a pattern of directness and clear purpose, though lacking sparkle or personal interest. In a letter to the Earl of Sandwich, Anson admits to being 'awkward in ceremony and correspondence'. Horace Walpole said he was 'reserved'. Extracts from his letters have been used sparingly in this book. I have preferred to refer to accounts written by his contemporaries, including not only those which concerned Anson directly, but also those of events and conditions closely bound up in his times and the Navy which he loved so well and which he served for fifty years. The story attempts to bring out Anson as the central character, and describes events closely associated with him or with those men who, in his wisdom and judgment, he selected for high command in Britain's crucial days. His greatest claim to fame, after his epic voyage and his successful administration of the Navy, is his selection and training of potential naval commanders.

Richard Walter and Pascoe Thomas wrote graphic accounts of Anson's famous voyage round the world. I have quoted freely from them, using their original spelling and punctuation not only in an attempt to convey atmosphere, but also in order to bring out contrasts in their accounts, particularly where these directly concerned Anson. This is all the more necessary since Walter's account is regarded as being largely inspired by Anson himself. I was fortunate, through the kindness of the Director and staff of the National Maritime Museum, to have access to a narrative by Lawrence Millechamp, who began the great voyage as purser in the sloop *Tryal*, later transferred to the *Gloucester*, and finished the voyage in the *Centurion*. His account is of particular interest when examining the sad wrangle that developed after the voyage, concerning distribution of prize money. It is useful also as a first hand account for comparison with those by Walter and Thomas.

The Seven Years War has been called the Maritime War, since most of the events depended not on the possession of great armies of the continental pattern, as in the War of the Spanish Succession when the great Duke of Marlborough won resounding victories, but almost entirely on the command of the sea. From 1745, when her Navy was at low ebb, Britain suffered repeated threats of full-scale invasion by vast French armies, and although the peace of Aix la Chapelle produced an uneasy lull for some years, the threat later continued and increased. It was mainly due to Anson that Britain's Navy was placed on a firm footing, and reforms and improvements were introduced that paved the way to ultimate victory. Anson must be linked with all the naval successes of this war, not only for building up a Navy that became paramount at sea, but for the great judgment and leadership he demonstrated in selecting for high command men like Hawke, Boscawen, Saunders, Howe, and Keppel. In a work about Anson we should be interested in the operations led by the men of his choice, many of whom were trained by him during his famous voyage, and I have therefore, in a somewhat limited space, endeavoured to follow to the end of Anson's life the naval events directly or indirectly linked with him.

Anson realized full well the importance of competence in his officers and men, and the necessity for education, intelligence, and training. Though possessed of resolute leadership himself, he was aware that this quality alone was not enough and that it was essential to train his officers with effective guidance and stimulation of interest to avoid lethargy, to prepare for the unexpected by the use of foresight and judgment, and to be ahead of the enemy by preparedness and attention to detail in careful planning. Britain is fortunate that the principal direction of the Navy was placed in his capable hands at a crucial time during the two wars with France and Spain that took place towards the end of the reign of George II.

I am indebted to the Earl of Lichfield and to *Country Life* for permission to reproduce the picture of Elizabeth, Lady Anson, and to the National Maritime Museum and the Tate Gallery for permission to reproduce their pictures. I am also grateful for the help given to me by the Admiralty Library, the National Maritime Museum, the British Museum, and the Public Record Office, and for the opportunity provided to copy extracts from letters and journals. I owe much to my wife for encouragement and patience during long hours of toil.

The works I have studied, and which I recommend to those who wish to pursue further reading, are as follows:

At the National Maritime Museum:
>        Officers' Journals and Ships Logs,
>        *Narrative of the Voyage* by Lawrence Millechamp,
>        The Hartwell Collection.

At the British Museum:
>        Anson Correspondence,
>        Newcastle Papers,
>        Hardwicke Papers.

At the Public Record Office:
>        Captains' Letters,
>        Board Minutes,
>        Officers' Journals.

Books to which I have referred are:

*Life of George Lord Anson* by Sir John Barrow.
*Life of Lord Anson* by Captain W. V. Anson.
*Lord Anson's Voyage Round the World* by Richard Walter.
*A True Journal of a Voyage to the South Seas* by Pascoe Thomas.
*Commodore Anson's World Voyage* by Boyle Somerville.
*Roderick Random* by Tobias Smollett.
*From Howard to Nelson* by John Laughton.
*England in the Seven Years War* by Julian Corbett.
*The Navy in the War of 1739–1748* by Sir Henry Richmond.
*Sea Kings of Britain*, Vol. 2 by Sir Geoffrey Callender.
*The Navy of Britain* by Michael Lewis.
*The Nation and the Navy* by Christopher Lloyd.

Anson is often referred to as the Father of the Navy. He could equally well be called the Architect of Victories, or Maker of Admirals, or Creator of British Sea Power. I have given much thought to the use of a catchy title, and although many possibilities spring to mind, I have preferred not to use them. In view of his modesty, humanity, and lack of pompousness, such titles appear to me to be inappropriate, and I prefer to use just his name: a name which for two centuries has excited the interest and quickened the pulse of all seamen and countless others.

S.W.C.P.

Villa Delia,
Malta.
1959

# Contents

# List of Illustrations

## List of Maps

He that commands the sea is at great liberty, and may take as much and as little of the war as he will.

BACON: 1578

*Prayer to be used in the Royal Navy every day*

O Eternal Lord God, who alone spreadest out the heavens and rulest the raging of the sea; who hast compassed the waters with bounds until day and night come to an end; be pleased to receive into thy Almighty and most gracious protection the persons of us thy Servants, and the Fleet in which we serve. Preserve us from the dangers of the sea, and from the violence of the enemy: that we may be a safeguard unto our most gracious Sovereign lady, Queen Elizabeth, and her dominions, and a security for such as pass on the seas upon their lawful occasions: that the inhabitants of our Island may in peace and quietness serve thee our God: and that we may return in safety to enjoy the blessings of the land, with the fruits of our labours, and with a thankful remembrance of thy mercies to praise and glorify thy holy Name: through Jesus Christ our Lord.

Amen

# CHAPTER I

# Background of Anson's Time

ADMIRAL LORD ANSON is remembered primarily because of his remarkable voyage round the world, a voyage which reads like a romance and which lasted four years. The *Centurion*, the ship which bore him home in June 1744, carried the biggest booty that ever returned to England in a single vessel.

Anson is also remembered as a most successful Admiral who became an able administrator in the affairs of the Navy, rising to be First Lord of the Admiralty. This was a political post then as it is now, and is not to be confused with the post of First Sea Lord which was instituted in the nineteenth century. He was elected a Member of Parliament in 1745, and represented Hedon in Yorkshire until 1747, when he was raised to the peerage after the first Battle of Finisterre. He seldom spoke in the House of Commons, and it is not possible to trace his political interest. He was not really interested in politics, and refused to allow promotions in the Navy to be influenced by political interest. After promotion to flag rank his rise was rapid, and in 1761 he became Admiral of the Fleet and the senior naval officer on the active list.

Anson directed Naval policy with such sound judgment and foresight at a critical time in British History that the Royal Navy was placed on a sound footing for all time. He has aptly been called the Father of the Navy. He served for seventeen years at the Admiralty after his famous voyage, and introduced a considerable number of necessary measures for improvement of ships, equipment, and general conditions of service in the Fleet. During the War of the Austrian Succession, Anson,

I

while still retaining his seat on the Board of Admiralty, commanded the Western Squadron and won a resounding victory against the French at the first Battle of Finisterre, in which he captured all the French warships and gave to Britain a much-needed victory. He assisted Pitt greatly in his 'grand system' which led to the building of the British Empire in the Seven Years War, and died still in office shortly before the successful conclusion of the war.

Before dealing with Anson's early life, of which comparatively little is known, it is helpful to look at an impression of the times. It was soon after Anson's voyage began in 1739 that Roderick Random went to sea in the *Thunder* to join Admiral Vernon's fleet in the West Indies. So we have Tobias Smollett's graphic if slightly exaggerated description of the men of the times and the conditions and hazards that existed. The Navy which Smollett saw was suffering a period of eclipse following the long period of peace which ensued after the great successes of the War of the Spanish Succession. The war had ended in 1713 with the accession to Britain of Gibraltar, Minorca, and vast territories in North America, and a recognition that she was paramount at sea.

The great triumphs to be achieved in the Seven Years War of 1756 to 1763 lay far ahead. In the meantime the Navy suffered poverty and neglect. The administration of Sir Robert Walpole from 1721 to 1742 was politically and financially corrupt. Civilian politicians attained and stayed in high office in reward for their support of Walpole, and in spite of professional incompetence. National economy was the watchword; the easiest way to obtain this was to keep the peace and allow the Navy to decay. At the outbreak of the War of Jenkins' Ear, when Anson began his celebrated voyage, and at the moment that Roderick Random was being pressed into the Navy, two-thirds of the ships of the line were unfit for service: many of these were beyond repair. Not only were the seagoing ships in a low state of maintenance, but they were poorly manned and badly provisioned. Conditions of service were appalling, and arrears of pay so great that it is surprising that it was possible to attract any men to serve at all. It is fortunate for Britain that Anson survived his hazardous voyage, fully aware of the disastrous results of long years of corruption and political patronage, resolved to make amends if ever the chance should arise. When the chance did arrive in later years, he wasted no time in bringing about improvements in ships, conditions of service, and fighting instructions, and faced every problem with a resolution to put right the defects from which the Royal Navy had suffered under Walpole's inept régime.

After the death of Queen Anne in 1714 there was a widespread fear of the return of the Stuarts and the revival of Catholic persecution which it was expected would accompany a Stuart restoration. The accession of George I was not popular, but was regarded as preferable to a return of the tyranny which England had suffered under James II, the last of the Stuarts. The 'fifteen' rising and the 'forty-five' rebellion increased the general fear, and their failure did much to establish Protestantism legally if not altogether by the common desire of the people. Smollett was a Scottish Presbyterian and had pronounced views concerning Catholicism which are in great contrast with the religious tolerance we know today. His writing is cynical and exaggerated, but he paints a picture which must have been plausible and acceptable to the public opinion of the day. At a moment when Roderick Random had resolved to remain in France, because England was 'the worst country in the universe for an honest man to live in', he was accosted by a priest who vehemently delivered a sermon, deriding in strong words and curses the Protestant faith. It is Roderick's uncle and companion, Lieutenant Tom Bowling of the Navy, who answers, and in his reply defies 'the Pope, the Devil, and the Pretender'. It is not surprising that 'this association of persons gave great offence to the Friar', but the story emphasizes well the strong feeling of religious intolerance that then existed.

This was a quarrelsome age. Although a superficial courtesy existed, coarseness and rudery were common, and there was a tendency at sea for officers to imitate their social inferiors. Discipline was harsh and was achieved largely by brutality and threat of dire punishment. Corruption and deception bred suspicion in all classes.

Smollett suggests horror when Roderick as a surgeon's third mate in the *Thunder* unexpectedly discovers that his superior,

Dr. Mackshane, the surgeon of the *Thunder*, is a papist. From then on Roderick has the greatest suspicion concerning the integrity of his superior.

In the England of those days the morals of the people were very low. Theft, bribery, debauchery, deceit, brutality, and blackmail were common. Some protection was provided by the law, but the enforcement of the law was difficult. The dangling corpses on view at the gallows at Tyburn might act as a deterrent to crime, but generally speaking the people took the law into their own hands. The desire for revenge at the slightest provocation appears to have been very strong, and honour had to be satisfied. There seems to have been no control over the use of firearms or weapons of any sort. The Bow Street Runners were not instituted until about 1754, to clear the streets of robbers who in most cases were discharged seamen unable to find work. Until that time, a man of substance relied mainly on his own servants and retinue for protection. Those without substance were generally not worth attacking. A traveller would be armed with a good cudgel and possibly a light sword known as a hanger, and would have his money sewn between the lining and waistband of his breeches. Some loose change would be kept handy.

It is interesting to read of the prices of articles. A small bedroom could be hired for one and sixpence a week. Food ashore consisted of bacon, eggs, hashed mutton, boiled beef, tripe, fowl, sausages, bread, and ale, but a frugal meal could be had for twopence halfpenny. A quart of milk cost a penny. There was less variety at sea. Food in ships consisted mainly of hard tack and worm-eaten biscuits, sometimes supplemented by peas and oatmeal infested with mildew. There was, however, a good rum ration every day, and occasionally free wine with meals.

Though the Navy became neglected from 1713 to 1739, there were memorials about the country to remind the people of former greatness, giving evidence that this was an age of achievement. In contrast with the squalor and conditions of poverty to be found in such large measure, there were splendid new buildings. Between 1710 and 1715, Vanbrugh, dramatist and architect, completed Blenheim Palace at Woodstock for the Duke of Marlborough, the victor of Blenheim. The London of this period is a city with many beautiful new churches, built by Sir Christopher Wren after the great fire of London. Seven miles down the Thames from the Tower is Greenwich Hospital, a majestic new series of Wren buildings on the site of an old Tudor palace where Elizabeth I was born. It was built at the instigation of Queen Mary, co-ruler with William III, as a thank-offering after the battle of La Hogue in 1692 to provide a sanctuary for broken seamen. It is now the Royal Naval College, and is complementary to the Queen's House built by Inigo Jones, which houses the National Maritime Museum. Here we may see a portrait of Anson (Frontispiece) painted by Sir Joshua Reynolds in 1761, the year before Anson's death; the year in which Anson received promotion to Admiral of the Fleet, the highest Naval rank, a rank which entitles the holder to fly the Union Flag of the United Kingdom. The flag can be seen flying at the main, in the ship in the background of the portrait.

Alive at this time was Hogarth, who painted in much the same way as Smollett wrote, fearlessly and cynically. There is a picture by him, also in the National Maritime Museum, which gives us a good view of the interior of a naval Captain's cabin in 1745 (facing page 30). The relatively spacious and light cabin are in great contrast with living conditions in the rest of the ship. But probably the best contrast is shown between the figures themselves. The captain and his guest, the chaplain, are seated, the former dressed in a pink silk coat and much finery, the latter in simple neat dress. The captain is Lord George Gordon under whom Smollett served as a surgeon's mate. Hogarth has been skilful in depicting character in his subjects. The face of the purser represents one who would drive a pretty hard bargain.

Reynolds' portrait shows Anson in full-dress naval uniform, a uniform newly introduced by Anson himself. There was no regulation naval uniform until Anson introduced a uniform for officers in 1748, long after the end of the great voyage. A uniform for seamen was not introduced until the middle of the next century. In the time of Anson, the men wore what they pleased, getting their 'slops' from the purser. At sea, they might be barefoot with baggy trousers and an odd shirt or jacket. Ashore, they would wear a round blue jacket, baggy trousers, silver buckled shoes, a spotted shirt, a neckerchief, and a tarred hat worn flat aback over hair formed into a pigtail. Smollett gives us good descriptions of various types of Naval officers' dress which existed prior to Anson's introduction of uniform. Two of these are worth describing here.

The first concerns Roderick Random's uncle, Tom Bowling, lieutenant of a man-of-war.

> His dress consisted of a soldier's coat, altered for him by the ship's tailor, a striped flannel jacket, a pair of red breeches, japanned with pitch, clean grey worsted stockings, large silver buckles that covered three-quarters of his shoes, a silver-laced hat, whose crown overlooked the brims about an inch and a half, a black bob wig in buckle, a check shirt, a silk handkerchief, an hanger with a brass handle, girded to his thigh by a tarnished laced belt, and a good oak plant under his arm.

The second refers to the garb of Captain Whiffle joining his ship with a crowd of attendants, the air impregnated with perfumes.

> A white hat, garnished with a red feather, adorned his head, from which his hair flowed upon his shoulders in ringlets, tied behind with a ribbon. His coat, consisting of pink-coloured silk lined with white, by the elegance of the cut retired backward, as it were to discover a white satin waistcoat embroidered with gold, unbuttoned at the upper part to display a brooch set with garnets, that glittered in the breast of his shirt, which was of the finest cambric, edged with rich Mechlin. The knees of his crimson velvet breeches scarcely descended so low as to meet his silk stockings, which rose without spot or wrinkle on his meagre legs, from shoes of blue Meroquin. A steel-hilted sword, inlaid with gold, and decked with a knot of ribbon which fell down in a rich tassel, equipped his side; and an amber-headed cane hung dangling from his wrist. But the

most remarkable parts of his furniture were, a mask on his face, and white gloves on his hands.

By comparison the uniform we see in Reynolds' portrait of Anson must have appeared modest.

This was the period when Handel was at the height of his fame. It is said that Anson hated dancing, disliked speeches, but loved music. He would therefore have heard the music of Handel's great masterpiece *The Messiah*, completed in 1741, on returning to England after his voyage round the world. It is of interest to learn that 'Rule Britannia' appeared in 1740, and that the British National Anthem was also first heard in its present form at about that time. The great Johannes Sebastian Bach died in 1750, the year before Anson was made First Lord of the Admiralty.

In the field of literature, Nicholas Rowe, the poet considered by some to be next to Shakespeare, died in 1718, the year in which Anson at the age of twenty-one fought at the Battle of Cape Passaro. Henry Fielding and Samuel Johnson were at that time boys of nine, and Oliver Goldsmith was to be born ten years later in 1728, the year in which the *Beggar's Opera* by John Gay was produced.

So much for the background of Anson's time. We see a comparatively leisurely, agricultural England, with both extreme wealth and dire poverty, long before the industrial revolution had brought about its growing social problems. It is an England in which the well-to-do are interested in music and the arts, drama, architecture, and literature, while the less fortunate struggle for an existence. There are peaks of fearful crisis and repeated threats of enemy invasion. It has all happened before and in a short while the threat has been neutralized, the crisis is over, the fear is gone. The need for an effectual Navy once more is forgotten: forgotten except by the provident few on whom Britain has always been able to rely; men such as Anson.

# CHAPTER II

# Anson's Early Life

GEORGE ANSON was the second son of William Anson of Shugborough in Staffordshire, by Isabella, daughter of Charles Carrier of Wirksworth in Derbyshire. He was born on 23rd April 1697, created Baron Anson in 1747, and died on 6th June 1762 without issue, his title becoming extinct. His sister Janette had an only son George Adams who inherited the property and borrowed the name and arms of Anson, and it was his son Thomas who in 1806 was created Viscount Anson. Thomas' eldest son succeeded, and was in 1831 advanced to the dignity of Earl of Lichfield.

George Anson's aunt on his mother's side married Thomas Parker who became Lord Chancellor in 1718, and was created Earl of Macclesfield in 1721. This connexion is regarded by some as being responsible for the early notice that Anson attracted to himself, and indirectly for his rapid promotion. This may well be true, for Anson was not one to call undue attention to himself, and without this influence it is possible that his potential qualities of leadership might never have been encouraged or developed. It is essential to realize, however, that after the reforms in the Navy introduced by Samuel Pepys towards the end of the seventeenth century, influence alone was insufficient. Pepys insisted that officers must possess technical qualifications, and in addition to founding schools of navigation and mathematics on shore, he sent Naval Instructors afloat; an arrangement that was regularized in 1702 by Royal Charter. With the new reforms a midshipman could only qualify for the post of lieutenant by passing an examination after a certain period at sea. If he failed repeatedly as many did, he remained a midshipman all his life.

Following Pepys' reforms, it was permissible to enter Volunteers into the King's Service for service at sea, one for each ship, provided he was over the age of thirteen. He was called a King's Letter Boy and was nominated by the Admiralty, and after a few years at sea, was rated Midshipman. The earlier system whereby the Captain of a ship nominated volunteers who must be over the age of eleven continued, and it is probable that Anson entered the Navy under this scheme as a Captain's Servant or Follower.

Little is known of Anson's early education. At fourteen, in January 1712, he joined the Navy as a volunteer in the *Ruby*, a fifty-four-gun ship with a scratch crew of 185 men, commanded by Captain Peter Chamberlen. His name appears on the ship's pay book between the names of John Baker, ordinary seaman, and George Hirgate, Captain's Servant. He served in this ship for six weeks mainly at the Nore, and the only event worth recording is a court martial of six men, tried for mutiny, theft, disorderly conduct, and desertion of their ship after she had run aground. Under the iron discipline that prevailed within ships, mutinies were practically unheard of, but it was a very different matter after a ship had been lost. Discipline went by the board, and lives and loot became uppermost in mind. The men were found guilty, and received six lashes alongside each ship riding at anchor.

In March 1712, Captain Chamberlen transferred to the *Monmouth* with all his followers, Anson among them, and shortly afterwards sailed for the West Indies in company with three other men-of-war. In the vicinity of Jamaica in late August, a bad time of the year for hurricanes, they encountered a severe tropical storm. The fore-topmast went by the board. The main and mizzen masts had to be cut away. The *Monmouth* shipped so much water that she was all but lost. Pumps were kept going and a chain of men with buckets baled for their lives. She reached Port Royal in Jamaica on 1st September. After several months chasing pirates *Monmouth* returned to Spithead in June 1713.

Anson next followed Chamberlen to the *Hampshire*, where,

9

on 17th May 1716, at the age of nineteen, he was given the acting rank of lieutenant by Admiral Sir John Norris to fill a vacancy. Prior to this event, as a volunteer, he would have no standing on board, and continued in service only at the invitation of Captain Chamberlen who commanded in turn the *Ruby, Monmouth,* and *Hampshire.* It is certain that there would be many candidates for the vacancy in the *Hampshire* and the fact that Anson was selected, and later confirmed for the commission, indicates that he was already highly regarded as a seaman and a leader.

The *Hampshire* paid off in December 1717, and a few months later, in March 1718, Anson was appointed as the second lieutenant of the *Montagu* a sixty-gun ship. He was soon to take part in the Battle of Passaro: a battle famous for the decisive victory gained by the British fleet under Sir George Byng against the Spaniards. England was no longer at war; the War of the Spanish Succession had ended with the Treaty of Utrecht in 1713, and the French-born candidate Philip, grandson of Louis XIV, had succeeded to the Spanish throne as Philip V. But in 1718, in violation of the terms of the Treaty, Philip reoccupied Sardinia and sent a large army of thirty thousand men to Sicily, accompanied by a fleet of eighteen large warships. England at once despatched a fleet of twenty-one large warships under Sir George Byng, who, flying his flag in the *Barfleur,* engaged the Spanish fleet off Cape Passaro on 31st July 1718. His fleet was not greatly superior either in numbers or in armament, but the indecision of the Spanish Admiral whether to fight or run, allowed his ships to straggle into a disordered group. Seizing the situation, Byng did not wait to form an orthodox line, but made the signal for general chase. The English ships in groups thereupon fell upon isolated Spanish ships in turn, and by repeated concentration soon overpowered them with a minimum loss of life.

Anson's ship the *Montagu* and another sixty-gun ship the *Rupert* fell upon and captured a forty-four gun Spanish ship, the *Volante.* Anson must have noted well the tactics employed in this victory, his first battle, and absorbed fully the importance of determination and quick decision, qualities which he himself was to demonstrate in later actions.

The hero of the battle was Captain Walton of the *Canterbury*, who was sent with five ships to pursue Spanish stragglers that were working in towards the coast. He took four ships and burnt six others. His brief report to Sir George Byng a week later off Syracuse is famous for its brevity. It reads: 'Sir, we have taken or destroyed all the Spanish ships upon this coast. The number as per margin.'

Byng was raised to the peerage as Viscount Torrington, and received a tremendous ovation on his return to England. How different was to be the reception of his son John (who also took part in this battle), years later when as an Admiral after the loss of Minorca he returned to England under arrest.

A little over a year after this his first battle, Anson was transferred to the *Barfleur* and remained there until 19th June 1722, when he was promoted at the age of twenty-five to commander and given command of the sloop *Weazle* employed on fishery protection in the North Sea. While in this appointment he captured a number of smugglers from the ports of Holland, laden with brandy and contraband, but otherwise found life uneventful.

In February 1724, at the very early age of twenty-six, he was promoted captain, and given command of the frigate *Scarborough*. His rapid promotion has been ascribed by some to his relationship to Lord Macclesfield, as already mentioned, and if this is true, the Royal Navy is indebted for such interest and discrimination, and for encouragement of a young officer who was later to render such exceptional service.

It became evident about this time that Spain and Austria were in secret collaboration with the intention of restoring Gibraltar and Minorca to Spain, and in return for her assistance Austria would receive Ostend. Squadrons were fitted out in England with the intention of blockading Spanish ships, but orders were somewhat vacillating owing to Walpole's intense desire for peace. Anson, in *Scarborough*, was sent to the coast of South Carolina to protect commerce against pirates and the Spanish guardacostas. Here he remained for six years until 1730, but transferred from the *Scarborough* to *Guarland*, a similar frigate, in July 1728, when the Captain of *Guarland* died. *Scarborough* was in such bad repair that he sent her home to

England. Anson seems to have met with no Spaniards or pirates during his six years off South Carolina, and the only event of note was the capture of a man named Smith who was planning a rebellion in the settlement. In 1728, Captain Peter Warren returning from the West Indies in *Solebay* called on Anson at Carolina, and a close friendship sprang up which ended only with the death of Admiral Sir Peter Warren in 1752. There appears to have been a great resemblance in their characters: they were each men of action but of few words, modest, and imbued with a great sense of duty and humanity. Anson seems to have been very popular with the settlers in South Carolina who gave his name to districts, towns, and mines. The following extract from a long letter written by Mrs. Hutchinson, a lady in South Carolina, to her sister in London, and afterwards printed, gives a description of Anson as a young naval Captain.

He has good sense, good nature, is polite and well-bred; free from that troublesome ceremoniousness which often renders many people, who may perhaps rank themselves among the most accomplished, extremely disagreeable. He is generous without profusion, elegant without ostentation; and above all, of a most tender, humane disposition. At balls, plays, concerts, etc., I have often the pleasure of seeing, and sometimes of conversing with, Mr. Anson, who, I assure you, is far from being an anchorite, though not what we call a modern pretty fellow, because he is really so old-fashioned as to make some profession of religion: moreover, he never dances, nor swears, nor talks nonsense. As he greatly admires a fine woman, so he is passionately fond of music.

I will give you an account of his faults, too, as well as of his virtues; for I have nowhere said he is an angel. In short, it is averred, that he loves his bottle and his friend so well, that he will not be very soon tired of their company, especially when they happen to be perfectly to his taste, which is pretty nice as to both; moreover, if fame says true, he is very far from being a woman-hater, and that now and then his mistress may come in for a share of him.

In view of the flat denial it seems likely that some reference had been made to his being an anchorite. Certain it is that he would shun trivial conversation. He was essentially a man of logical thought and reasoned action.

Soon after his return from America, Anson was appointed to the command of the *Squirrel* on the home station, but in a matter of months was transferred to the command of the *Diamond*, a frigate of forty guns, attached to the fleet under the Command of Sir Charles Wager which went out to the Mediterranean in 1731 with the special object of escorting the Spaniards to Leghorn in accordance with the terms of the treaty recently concluded. This splendid function to set the seal on peace was full of pomp and ceremony, bunting and salutes. It was, however, a peace in no more than name, for in the Spring of 1733 there were rumours of impending Spanish attacks on Georgia. Anson was reappointed to the *Squirrel*, and sent once again to South Carolina, with information of impending attacks by the Spaniard. This information proved false, and in his cruises along the coast of Georgia which continued until 1735, he found the inhabitants under no apprehension of attack. In June 1735 he returned to Spithead, paid off the *Squirrel*, and went on half pay for two and a half years, still a relatively unknown officer and thirty-eight years of age. This was practically his first holiday since joining the Navy.

It is interesting to reflect on these years in the *Scarborough*, *Guarland*, and *Squirrel* spent almost entirely on the South Carolina station. Much time was obviously spent in social activities ashore, but there must have been long periods at sea during which Anson had ample opportunity of studying his men and observing the conditions under which they worked. There was time for examining possible improvements in seamanship, and for carrying out much needed repairs in the ill-found ships of those days. There was scope for an officer of initiative to look into tactical and strategical questions and to carry out drills in readiness for the unexpected. There was need for instruction of the young gentlemen, and for training programmes which would not only improve the ship's fighting qualities but develop morale and interest of the ship's company. And, above all, there was time to realize the gross defects which existed in the administration of the Navy, and to think about the hundred and one improvements which were necessary. Anson, in a letter written to Sir John Norris from the *Squirrel*, refers to the sloop *Happy*, which 'has to be relieved, as she has seven years' pay due'.

Anson was never content to remain just the brilliant seaman that he was. He took the long view realizing that seamanship alone was not sufficient. Education and training in their widest sense were indispensable, and only by particular regard for these, in addition to the planning necessary to establish material efficiency, was he able to provide the Navy that proved Britain's salvation during her critical years. His ideals soon became well known; the confidence later placed in him is adequately expressed in a letter written to him by Admiral Barrett in 1745, on hearing of his appointment to the Admiralty.

> I expect a great deal from you. I am stupid enough to think that we are worse officers though better seamen than our neighbours; our young men get wrong notions early, and are led to imagine that he is the greatest officer who has the least blocks in the rigging. I hope you will give a new turn to our affairs and form a society for the propagation of Sea Military Knowledge.

We know little of what he did and thought during his early years, but we can assume that it was a period when Anson was formulating in his mind what was required of a leader; the role of authority. It was a period of preparation and training which was to stand him in great stead during his voyage round the world, when others were to benefit by his sterling qualities: others who were also to rise to high positions in the Navy and to carry on the splendid tradition and high standards always associated with Anson.

# CHAPTER III

# War with Spain

THE peace with Spain continued to be little more than a hollow truce and came to an end in 1739. For years there had been reports of Spaniards plundering British commercial ships and ill-treating the crews, and there arose in England a feeling of great indignation. Finally an event came to light which fired the public mind. This was a report by Captain Jenkins, master of the brig *Rebecca* of Glasgow, before a Committee of the House of Commons, which stated that after the Spaniards of a guarda-costa had ill-treated his crew, they wantonly cut off one of his ears and insolently told him to take it home and present it to his King. Asked about his thoughts on finding himself in the hands of such barbarians Jenkins replied:

'I recommended my soul to God, and my cause to my Country.'

The declaration of war on Spain on 19th October 1739 was received with a degree of enthusiasm and joy which revealed the general disgust and indignation of the British nation.

In 1737, Anson had been appointed to the command of the sixty-gun ship *Centurion* after his two and a half years ashore on half pay, and sailed for the Guinea Coast with instructions to protect trade. While here he was just in time to prevent the massacre of some Mohammedans by a French ship which was about to open fire upon them. He continued off the African coast, and then, in accordance with instructions, proceeded to Barbados for further orders in the autumn of 1739, when war with Spain was imminent. He returned to Spithead in *Centurion* on 10th November 1739, and received a letter from the First

Lord, Admiral Sir Charles Wager, which ordered him to report immediately to the Admiralty. Anson now heard of a plan for a double blow against Spain. He himself was to be Commander-in-Chief of a squadron of ships which, after embarking troops, would proceed to Manila via the Cape of Good Hope, and take it from the Spaniards. The other blow was to be delivered by a squadron under Captain James Cornewall, another highly esteemed officer who subsequently commanded the *Marlborough* and died in action in 1743, after his legs had been shot off. Cornewall's squadron was to sail round Cape Horn, attack the Spanish Settlements in South America on the Pacific Coast, and then cross the Pacific to join Anson at or near Manila. These were both daring and ambitious schemes, fraught with uncertainties and perils, but it is certain that had they been mounted and launched with full support and without delay, they would have surprised the Spaniards and had far greater chance of devastating success than was to be the case after months of postponement. The enterprise was described as absurd, particularly as it involved the rounding of the Horn or the passage of the Straits of Magellan. The Royal Navy had been neglected, and the King's ships reduced to eighty-four of which half were unfit for service. Out of an establishment of 28,870 seamen only 21,000 could be mustered. Pay had not materially changed since 1651 when the able seaman's wage was settled at twenty-two shillings and sixpence a month: it was not to alter substantially until after the mutinies of 1797. The First Lord, Sir Charles Wager, was close on eighty.

On 21st November 1739, having agitated for years in the House of Commons, Admiral Vernon with a small force of six ships took Porto Bello, a strongly defended Spanish town on the Caribbean Sea side of the Isthmus of Panama. This was a great success and the news was received with rapture in England. It is said that it was at a concert in celebration of the occasion that the National Anthem was first heard in its present form. For the unwarlike prime minister, Walpole, this success probably acted as a spur for reducing the Anson and Cornewall expedition. Anson was informed in January 1740, by the First Lord, that his expedition to Manila was abandoned, but instead he was to carry out the expedition to the South Seas with his squadron.

He now received his commission as Commander-in-Chief of the squadron, with the rank of Commodore, and with great vigour set about manning, storing, and fitting out for the expedition. It was not, however, until 21st June 1740 that he received His Majesty's instructions, dated the previous January, with an additional instruction from the Lords Justices. To gain an idea of what was intended it is necessary to read these in detail, but first it may be interesting to look at the picture of the model of Anson's famous ship, the *Centurion* (facing page 46), which was to serve as flagship to the squadron.

*Centurion* was built in 1732, had a complement of four hundred men, and mounted sixty guns, later reduced to fifty. She was short and beamy, and, as can be seen in the model, carried most of her guns on two decks, the lower gun deck being about a hundred and forty feet long, and only a little above the water-line. She had three masts each carrying three square sails bent on yards. The sails could be controlled by lifts, braces, and sheets. To be able to withstand wind and weather over the years, the canvas and cordage had to be substantial. *Centurion*, being a fighting ship, was not fast. Duties requiring speed were to be left to the sloop or despatch vessel of the squadron, the *Tryal*. The guns were muzzle loaders, their maximum range was of the order of a mile, but action usually took place at close range. The larger guns fired cannon balls weighing twenty-four pounds. The old sailing warships had to be self dependent and self sufficient for months on end. As with present day warships, they required to be fitted out and stored to provide considerable food and drink for their vast crews for long periods, and be certain that they could fight the enemy and keep the sea, in all weather, in a suitable state of maintenance and repair. This called for a vast complement of men in addition to those who manned the yards and worked the ship, and required men or officers each an expert in some craft or profession. The men lived in berths between the guns on the lower gun deck, and kept all their effects here, including chests and mess traps. Here also they slept in their hammocks slung from the beams, and when in port entertained their girl friends as shown in the illustration facing page 47. The officers, among whom were the lieutenants, master, master's mates, midshipmen, surgeon, surgeon's mates, chaplain, schoolmaster, purser, gunner, boatswain, and carpenter, had a little more privacy. The Captain lived in relatively greater comfort in quarters right aft in the ship. A typical picture by Hogarth shows Lord George Graham attended by his cook, chaplain, and purser, and a coloured servant (facing page 30). These were the days of impressment for it was not easy to get men to serve voluntarily under the conditions which then existed. The best men were taken from the merchant service, often on arrival in port after a voyage: the worst were collected from the gaols. Anson therefore found the manning of his squadron no easy task. The prospect of prize money and a daily ration of rum were small inducements for a life of discomfort, privation, and peril, with only an even chance of survival.

Anson's squadron was composed of five men-of-war and one sloop, with two store ships or pinks which were to accompany the squadron until replenishment was completed.

Anson, in addition to serving as commander of the squadron, was to continue to command the *Centurion*. The squadron consisted of:

| Ship | Guns | Men | Captain |
|---|---|---|---|
| Centurion | 60 | 400 | George Anson (Commodore) |
| Gloucester | 50 | 300 | Richard Norris |
| Severn | 50 | 300 | Hon. Edward Legge |
| Pearl | 40 | 250 | Mathew Mitchel |
| Wager | 28 | 160 | Dandy Kidd |
| Tryal (Sloop) | 8 | 100 | Hon. John Murray |

The names of Anson's captains are not particularly striking, but a glance at the list of young officers serving with Anson in *Centurion* at the outset of the voyage, or who subsequently joined him in *Centurion*, reveals many names of officers who later achieved fame or high rank. Here is evidence of Anson's great power of leadership and of his ability to inculcate into his subordinates those qualities of purpose and judgment which led to success. Their journals of each day's events may be seen in the National Maritime Museum. Nearly all seem to have done well but the following reached Flag rank:

Peircy Brett, Admiral of the Blue, Lord Commissioner of the Admiralty. Knighted 1753.

John Campbell, Vice-Admiral of the Red, Governor of Newfoundland and Commander-in-Chief. Refused Knighthood 1759.

Peter Denis, Admiral of the Red. Created Baronet 1767.

The Hon. Augustus Van Keppel, Admiral of the White, First Lord of the Admiralty. Created Viscount Keppel 1782.

Hyde Parker, Vice-Admiral of the Red.

Charles Saunders, Admiral of the Blue, First Lord of the Admiralty. Knighted 1752. Victor with Wolfe at Quebec.

Mention should also be made of Philip Saumarez, lieutenant of the *Centurion*, killed in action in 1747 when in command of the *Nottingham*; and of the great Howe, who, though not in *Centurion*, sailed with Anson's squadron in the *Severn*.

In the *Centurion* with Anson were the schoolmaster, Pascoe Thomas, who wrote a very fine account of the voyage, and the chaplain, Richard Walter, whose three volumes on the voyage have become a classic.

When Anson received his instructions in June 1740 he was still three hundred men short of complement in the squadron, but anxious to waste no further time sailed for Spithead with an Admiralty promise that the balance would be provided by Sir John Norris on arrival. He was met by a point blank refusal from Sir John Norris to supply any men at all, as the latter was in need of men for his own fleet, but later received a hundred and seventy men, of whom thirty-two were discharged from hospital for the purpose, and ninety-eight were newly entered marines who had never been to sea before. Instead of the soldiers he had been promised, Anson was informed at the last minute that he was to receive five hundred Chelsea pensioners: men who had been invalided out of the army. He complained bitterly at this, realizing that few of these men would survive the rigours and privations of a sea journey, let alone an action, and was supported in his complaint by the First Lord, Sir Charles Wager. The military authorities, however, replied that they knew better and that these pensioners were the fittest that could be found for such service. Of the five hundred pensioners that were sent to Portsmouth, only 259 embarked in the squadron: the rest deserted on the way. Of those who joined the squadron, not one survived to return to England and claim his pension. It is said that one man with a wooden leg was sent down to Portsmouth three times, but turned up in London after a short interval. To help fill the gap, 210 raw recruits from various regiments were drafted into the squadron. Walter writes:

> . . . instead of 500, there came on board no more than 259: for all those who had limbs and strength to walk out of Portsmouth deserted, leaving behind them only such as were literally invalids, most of them being 60 years of age, and some of them upwards of 70. Indeed it is difficult to conceive a more moving scene than the embarkation of these unhappy veterans: they were themselves extremely averse to the service they were engaged in, and fully appraised of all the disasters they were afterwards exposed to; the apprehensions of which were strongly marked by the concern that appeared in their countenances, which was mixed with no small degree of indignation, to be thus hurried from their repose into a fatiguing employ, to which neither the strength of their bodies nor the vigour of their minds, were any way proportioned, and where, without seeing the face of an enemy, or in the least promoting the success of the enterprize, they would, in all probability, uselessly perish by lingering and painful disease; and this too after they had spent the activity and strength of their youth in their country's service.

Anson, a man of great humanity and, as was proved later, with a strong sense of moral courage, must have felt greatly moved to resign his appointment, but the country was now at war and his expedition had already suffered grievous delays. The last detachment of marines embarked on the 8th August, and two days later Anson sailed his squadron from Spithead to St. Helen's Roads, there to wait for a favourable wind. Thirty-nine days they had to wait, and it was not until 18th September 1740 that the expedition finally got on its way.

Just before sailing, Anson sent ashore two officers who through age and infirmity considered themselves unfit for further duty. He immediately received an order by the direction of the Lords Justice who seem to have been mainly responsible for the mounting of the expedition, that the officers were to be returned to the Squadron and no more were to be dismissed. The providing of the professional advice by those who had little or none, yet who appear to have had the authority was typical of this age of Walpole, and it must have been a point which Anson noted for the future. Sir Charles Wager, the First Lord, had served at sea upwards of fifty years, had been a Lord of the Admiralty for fifteen years, and First Lord for seven years, and although an officer of great competence, appears to have been no match for the Lords Justices. He died in 1743.

The following extract of instructions signed by George II are of particular interest because of the criticism, subsequently made, that Anson had in some cases exceeded his terms of reference by taking and burning Paita. The absence of the use of rank as a title is worth noting, and is consistent with the idea which then prevailed of the part time nature of an officer's function. It was not until 1860 that the use of rank as a title became general, the appropriate rank of the officer who by that time was regarded as a whole time officer being given in an official Navy List. The term Commodore Anson would not therefore have been in common usage. It would be more correctly Mr. Anson, Commodore of the Squadron. For convenience and brevity it is simpler to use the rank of appointments as a title, as became common in 1860, and this has generally been done in this book.

Signed: George R.

Instructions for our trusty and well-beloved George Anson, Esq., Commander-in-Chief of our ships designed to be sent into the South Seas in America. Given at our Court at St. James's the 31st day of January, 1739–40, in the thirteenth year of our reign.

Whereas we have thought proper to declare war against The King of Spain, for the several injuries and indignities offered to our crown and people, which are more particularly set forth in our declaration of war, we have thought fit to direct that you, taking under your command our ships, should proceed with them according to the following instructions.

You are to receive on board our said ships five hundred of our land-forces, and to proceed forthwith to the Cape de Verde Islands, and to supply your ships with water and such refreshments as are to be procured there; and you are from thence to make the best of your way to the Island of St. Catherine, on the coast of Brazil, or such other place on that coast as you may be advised is more proper, where you are again to supply your ships with water and any other necessaries you may want that can be had there. And when you have so done, you are to proceed with our ships under your command into the South Sea, either round Cape Horn or through the Straits of Magellan, as you shall judge most proper, and according as the season of the year and winds and weather shall best permit.

When you shall arrive on the Spanish coast of the South Sea, you are to use your best endeavours to annoy and distress the Spaniards, either at sea or land, to the utmost of your power, by taking, sinking, burning, or otherwise destroying all their ships and vessels that you shall meet with, and particularly their boats, and all embarkations whatsoever, that they may not be able to send any intelligence by sea along the coast of your being in those parts.

In case you shall find it practicable to seize, surprise or take any of the towns or places belonging to the Spaniards on the coast, that you may judge worthy of making such an enterprize upon, you are to attempt it: for which purpose we have not only ordered the land-forces above mentioned, but have also thought proper to direct that an additional number of small arms be put on board the ships under your command to be used, as occasion may require, by the crews of the said ships, or otherwise, as you shall find best for our service. And you are, on such occasions, to take the opinion of the Captains of our ships under your command at a Council of War.

There follows a suggestion of stirring up a revolt among the great number of native Indians on the coast and suggestions of possible attacks 'to annoy the Spaniards as much as shall be in your power' and attempts to take, burn, or destroy Panama. There is reference to a cipher for secret correspondence with other Commanders-in-Chief both of ships and land forces in order to deny intelligence to the Spaniards. The instructions continue:

> When you shall have proceeded thus far, it must, in a great measure, be left to your discretion, and that of a council of war (when upon any difficulty you shall think fit to call them together), to consider whether you shall go farther to the northward, or remain longer at Panama, in case the place should have been taken by our forces, or you can any way hear that any of our forces may be expected on that side from the north side. But you will always take particular care to consider of a proper place for careening of the ships, and for supplying them with provisions either for their voyage homeward or for their continuing longer abroad.

> If you shall find no occasion for your staying longer in those seas, and shall judge it best to go to the northward as far as Acapulco, or to look out for the Acapulco ship, which sails from that place for Manila at a certain time of the year and generally returns at a certain time also, you may possibly, in that case, think it most advisable to return home by the way of China, which you are authorized to do, or to return home by Cape Horn, as you shall think best for our service, and for the preservation of the ships and the men on board them.

To these instructions, dated 31st January 1740, were attached the additional instructions by the Lords Justices, dated 19th June 1740, the signatories including Lord Hardwicke (whose daughter Anson was later to marry), Holles Newcastle (later Prime Minister, 1754–56, when Anson was First Lord), Sir Robert Walpole, the Prime Minister, and Sir Charles Wager, First Lord of the Admiralty. They seemed to do little except to make excuses for delay and at the same time preclude further delay.

His Majesty having been pleased to suspend your sailing from England till this time, when the season of the year will permit you to make your intended voyage directly to the South Seas (which at some particular seasons is extremely difficult, if not impracticable), you are to proceed forthwith, directly to the South Seas.

Whereas a letter written by the Governor of Panama to the King of Spain has fallen into the hands of some of his Majesty's officers, which letter contains very material advices relating to the situation of the Spaniards, and to the keeping of their treasure in these parts, a copy of the same will, by our order, be herewith put into your hands; and you are to have a regard to the intelligence therein contained in the execution of the orders given you in his Majesty's instructions.

The departure of the squadron was further delayed by contrary winds and the necessity to escort a large convoy of close on a hundred and fifty merchant ships safely out of the Channel. The ships of the convoy were to carry trade for Turkey, the Straits, and America, and already had men-of-war escorts to take them to their destinations. Anson's squadron collected them all in the Channel, the vast fleet now consisting of eleven men-of-war and a hundred and fifty merchantmen. On the morning of 20th September, off Ram Head, Anson hoisted his Commodore's broad pennant and was saluted by all the men-of-war in company. Later in the same day he made a signal for all the captains of the men-of-war to come on board the *Centurion* to receive fighting and sailing instructions, after which the fleet proceeded, and with a fair wind at last stood towards the south-west. It is difficult to picture the beauty and impressiveness of such a scene on a September day in the Channel, or to imagine the thoughts of those in the squadron, particularly the unwilling members, many of whom would never return. But to nearly all must have come the thrill which lies in departure, and the interest and curiosity concerning the next port of call.

When clear of land, Anson ordered the *Pearl* to take station two leagues ahead of the fleet at dawn every morning, and to remain there throughout daylight hours.

On 25th September, that part of the convoy destined for America, together with the *Winchester* as escort, requested leave to proceed, and parted company with Anson, as did the Turkey and Straits convoy escorted by *St. Albans* and *Dragon* on 29th September. There now remained Anson's squadron of five men-of-war, the sloop *Tryal*, and the two supply ships, bound for Madeira and committed at last to the task of 'annoying the Spaniards'. Though hopeful of favourable winds to make up for all the delay recently suffered, the squadron met with contrary winds, and it was not until 25th October 1740, forty days after leaving Spithead, that they anchored in Madeira Roads in forty fathoms of water. The news they had received at Portsmouth three or four days before sailing, that the strength and destination of the squadron were well known in Panama did not make the slowness of the passage any easier to bear.

While at Madeira, Anson wrote to the Duke of Newcastle:

> After a passage of 40 days I arrived here with the Squadron of H.M. Ships under my command, during which time we buried two of the invalid captains. I have given leave to Captain Norris (*Gloucester*) to return to England for the recovery of his health. The ships being all watered I intend to proceed tomorrow to sea.
>
> G. ANSON

# CHAPTER IV

# Scurvy and Storm take their Toll

THE invaliding home of Norris, captain of the *Gloucester*, created a vacancy for a captain in the squadron. Lieutenant Cheap was promoted captain of the sloop *Tryal*, and the following transfers of captains took place:

The Hon. John Murray from the sloop *Tryal* to the *Wager* (28 guns), Dandy Kidd from the ship *Wager* to the *Pearl* (40 guns), Mathew Mitchel from the ship *Pearl* to the *Gloucester* (50 guns). The Hon. Edward Legge remained captain of the *Severn* (50 guns).

The squadron spent a week at Madeira, watering and replenishing with Madeira wine, and weighed and proceeded on 3rd November 1740. The most important event was the Commodore's call on the Governor of Madeira, for it was then that Anson received news of the existence of a Spanish squadron of five men-of-war and a sloop which had appeared for three days off shore to the westward of the island at the end of October. Anson sent the *Tryal* eight leagues to the westward to search, but nothing was sighted. It is certain that the information referred to the Spanish squadron commanded by Don Joseph Pizarro, greatly superior in strength in guns and men, and having on board a Spanish regiment of foot intended for the reinforcement of the garrisons on the Pacific coast of the South Seas. This squadron left Madeira at about the same time as Anson, and proceeded to the River Plate where they arrived on 5th January.

On weighing from Madeira, Anson gave orders that his squadron was to rendezvous at St. Jago in the Cape Verde

Islands in case of separation, but in his determination to push on without further delay, changed the rendezvous the next day to the island of St. Catherine's off the coast of Brazil. Walter, in his account of the voyage, remarks on the fact that the trade winds that were experienced on passage differed considerably from those expected. He was a keen observer of weather, and was advanced in suggesting that deviations existed from the then established rules. The complexity of the problem can best be understood if one realizes that the whole system of tropical and sub-tropical winds is roughly composed of a region of steady north-east trades to the north, and a region of steady south-east trades to the south, separated, but by no means in any regularly delineated way, by the belt of calms known as the Doldrums. The whole system moves irregularly and unsteadily north in the summer of the northern hemisphere, and south during the winter, lagging behind the declination of the sun by two to three months. Anson's haste to round the Horn during the summer of the southern hemisphere on the score that the weather would be better is very much open to question, but it is clear that he was by now full of resolution to press on and pursue the object of the expedition whatever the doubts and perils. He had clear instructions concerning his task and was determined to carry them out if humanly possible.

Nearly two weeks after departure from Madeira, the master of the storeship *Industry*, carrying mainly brandy, made a signal asking to speak to the Commodore. Sail was shortened, and the master went on board *Centurion* to tell Anson that he had complied with the terms of his charter, and wished to be unloaded and dismissed. The ships of the squadron were barely two months out from Spithead and were all found to be still so deep in the water with provisions that it was only with difficulty that they were able to take in more. Nevertheless Anson was keen to comply with the charter. His ships were brought to, and for three days their long boats took off brandy from the *Industry* until she was unloaded, whereupon she parted company after receiving mail for England. She immediately made for Barbados to embark freight for England, and was unlucky enough to be taken by the Spaniards. The other storeship, the *Anna*, continued south with the squadron.

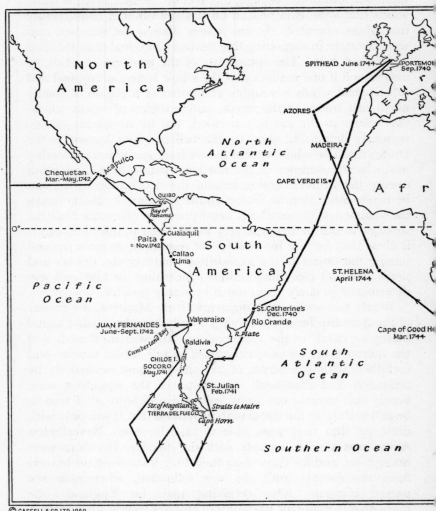

North America

North Atlantic Ocean

SPITHEAD June 1744

PORTSMOUTH Sep. 1740

AZORES

MADEIRA

CAPE VERDE IS.

Afr

Chequetan Mar.-May, 1742

Acapulco

QUIBO

Bay of Panama

0°

Paita Nov. 1742

Guaiaquil

Callao
Lima

South America

Pacific Ocean

ST. HELENA April 1744

JUAN FERNANDES June-Sept. 1742

Valparaiso

St. Catherine's Dec. 1740

Rio Grande

R. Plate

Cape of Good Hope Mar. 1744

Cumberland Bay

Baldivia

CHILOE I.
SOCORO May 1741

South Atlantic Ocean

St. Julian Feb. 1741

Str. of Magellan

Straits le Maire

TIERRA DEL FUEGO

Cape Horn

Southern Ocean

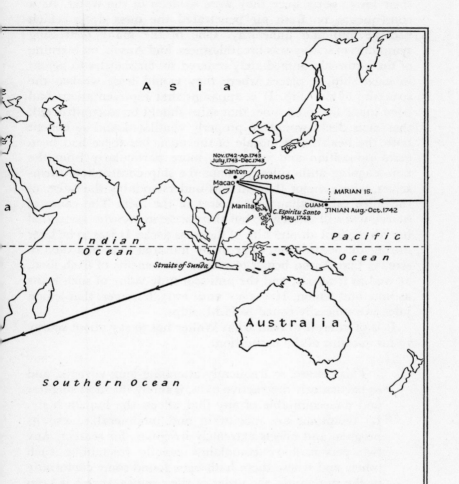

Nov.1742-Ap.1743
July,1743-Dec.1743

Canton

Macao ⟶FORMOSA

MARIAN IS.

Manila

GUAM

C.Espiritu Santo ⟶ TINIAN Aug.-Oct.1742

May,1743

A s i a

I n d i a n
O c e a n

Pacific

Ocean

a

Straits of Sunda

Australia

Southern Ocean

## TRACK OF ANSON'S VOYAGE IN H.M.S. CENTURION

On 20th November 1740, it became evident that scurvy was rife in every ship of the squadron. The ships could not open their lower ports since they were so deep in the water. As a consequence no fresh air penetrated the mess decks which became foul and unhealthy. One of the many distressing symptoms of scurvy was breathlessness, and Anson, on learning of the outbreak, immediately ordered six air scuttles to be cut in each ship in places where they would least weaken the structure of the ship. It is apparent that representations had been made for some time, that ships should be so constructed, that mess decks would be properly ventilated and so benefit both the health and morale of the men, but there had been great opposition and contempt, more particularly from the non-seagoing authorities, perhaps the ship constructors themselves, whose major thought was understandably the safety of the ships rather than the comfort of the men. The cause of scurvy was still unknown, but there were many who associated it with the foul air and filth of the mess decks. It was to be later during this expedition, after many hundred men had died of scurvy, that Anson began to realize the benefits of fresh food, as well as fresh air, and the anti-scorbutic value of such fruits as lime and lemon. It was not until 1793, however, that lemon juice was officially issued to H.M. ships.

It is of interest to read what Walter has to say about scurvy in his account of the expedition.

This disease, so frequently attending long voyages, and so particularly destructive to us, is surely the most singular and unaccountable of any that affects the human body. Its symptoms are inconstant and innumerable, and its progress and effects extremely irregular: for scarcely any two persons have complaints exactly resembling each other, and where there hath been found some conformity in the symptoms, the order of their appearance has been totally different. However, though it frequently puts on the form of many other diseases, and is therefore not to be described by any exclusive and infallible criterions, yet there are some symptoms which are more general than the rest, and, occurring the oftenest, deserve a more particular

A naval captain with his chaplain, purser, cook, and coloured servant

*From an oil painting by W. Hogarth*

Anson
*From an oil painting by an unidentified painter*

enumeration. These common appearances are large discoloured spots dispersed over the whole surface of the body, swelled legs, putrid gums, and, above all, an extraordinary lassitude of the whole body, especially after any exercise, however inconsiderable; and this lassitude at last degenerates into a proneness to swoon, and even die, on the least exertion of strength, or even on the least motion.

This disease is likewise usually attended with a strange dejection of the spirits, and with shiverings, tremblings, and a disposition to be seized with the most dreadful terrors on the slightest accident. Indeed it was most remarkable, in all our reiterated experience of this malady, that whatever discouraged our people, or at any time damped their hopes, never failed to add new vigour to the distemper; for it usually killed those who were in the last stages of it, and confined those to their hammocks who were before capable of some kind of duty; so that it seemed as if alacrity of mind, and sanguine thoughts, were no contemptible preservatives from its fatal malignity.

This last sentence may apply to many illnesses, but it is certain that Walter observed the manner in which in general the officers in the expedition survived better than the men, and the reason for this cannot be attributed entirely to their better living conditions on board.

Walter continues:

But it is not easy to compleat the long roll of the various concomitants of this disease; for it often produced putrid fevers, pleurisies, the jaundice, and violent rheumatic pains, and sometimes it occasioned an obstinate costiveness, which was generally attended with a difficulty of breathing, and this was esteemed the most deadly of all the scorbutical symptoms; at other times the whole body, but more especially the legs, were subject to ulcers of the worst kind, attended with rotten bones, and such a luxuriancy of fungous flesh as yielded to no remedy. But a most extraordinary circumstance, and what would be scarcely credible upon any single evidence, is, that the scars of wounds which had been for many years healed were forced open again by this virulent distemper. Of this there was a remarkable instance in one of the invalids on board the *Centurion*, who had been wounded above 50 years before at the battle of the Boyne, for though he was cured soon after, and had continued well for a great number of years past, yet on his being attacked by the scurvy, his wounds, in the progress of his disease, broke out afresh, and appeared as if they had never been healed; nay, what is still more astonishing, the callus of a broken bone, which had been compleatly formed for a long time, was found to be hereby dissolved, and the fracture seemed as if it had never been consolidated. Indeed, the effects of this disease were in almost every instance wonderful; for many of our people, though confined to their hammocks, appeared to have no inconsiderable share of health for they eat and drank heartily, were cheerful, and talked with much seeming vigour, and with a loud strong tone of voice: and yet, on their being the least moved, though it was from only one part of the ship to the other, and that too in their hammocks, they have immediately expired; and others, who have confided in their seeming strength, and have resolved to get out of their hammocks, have died before they could well reach the deck; nor was it an uncommon thing for those who were able to walk the deck, and to do some kind of duty, to drop down dead in an instant, on any endeavours to act with their utmost effort, many of our people having perished in this manner during the course of this voyage.

It is evident that Anson and his squadron were now alert for a sight of the Spanish squadron under Pizarro, and were particularly keen to get as much information as possible without conceding any. A sail was sighted to the north-west, when in the vicinity of the equator, and the sloop *Tryal* was ordered to chase with the *Gloucester* in support, and shortly afterwards, as Anson was reluctant to separate his ships, the whole squadron joined in the chase, the *Wager* taking the slow storeship *Anna* in tow. They failed to close the sail before dark, but two days later, again seeing what appeared to be the same sail, the whole squadron resumed the chase, for it was now thought that this was a ship from Spain bound for Buenos Ayres with information about Anson's squadron and intentions. Night again fell before she could be overtaken, and she was not seen again.

Crossing the equator was attended by a performance far more arduous than that which is imposed nowadays on the novices, and it is likely that the easy way, of contributing materially to the general fun in the shape of food and drink, was accepted by all but the most spartan and those in extreme poverty. There is a vivid description in a narrative of the voyage by Laurence Millechamp, the purser of the sloop *Tryal*, followed by a colourful description of a dolphin, which is worth recounting.

We crossed the equinoctial line, and there, as it is customary, such Persons as had not cros't it before, were obliged to pay their Bottle and Pound or be Duckt: the Bottle and Pound is a Bottle of Brandy or Rum and a pound of Sugar with which forfeitures the Seamen make Merry: the Ducking which is inflicted on those who either through Poverty cannot, or being able, obstinately refuse to pay the Forfeit: is performed by Hoisting the Man from the Deck to the Main or Foreyard (by Lashings and Tackles prepar'd for that purpose) and letting him fall Sowse over Head and Ears in the Water: this they repeat five or six times till the Offender is as wet as a Drownded Rat: they then take him in, and as he has contributed so much to their Mirth, they suffer him to partake of their Liquor till he is thoroughly Drench'd both inside and out. We crost the line in 27° 03' West Longitude, and have been so Happy as to meet with no Calms Tornadoes or great Rains so usually met with in crossing the Equator.

About this time we caught an abundance of Dolphins, insomuch that many of the ships victuall'd their Men with them. The Beauty of this Fish (while in the Water) is beyond Description, 'tis certain nothing in this World can equal them, but to aim at a Faint representation, their Backs are of a Deep Shining Green, their Finns of a Fine Ultramarine Blew, their Tailes of an Exquisite Bright

Yellow, and their Bellys sometimes of a Silver Colour, at others of a Bright transparent Yellow. They are straight and trim and from Six to two Foot Long.

Although they had been lucky to miss the typical Doldrums weather of storms and calms, they had not been so lucky in escaping disease, for scurvy now increased every day in every ship of the squadron. Great numbers were confined to their hammocks by the disease, many men past all hope of recovery: several died. On 16th December the coast of Brazil was sighted, and on the 20th the squadron anchored in a large sheltered bay in the Portuguese Isle of St. Catherine. Anson at once arranged for each ship to erect two tents on shore for the reception of the sick and for the accommodation of the surgeons. The *Centurion* landed eighty sick and the other ships proportionately the same. The ships were scrubbed and smoked between decks, and every part soaked with vinegar in an attempt to destroy the vermin and remove the foul smells that had developed below. Wooding and watering then proceeded, and masts and rigging were secured. It was now found that the sloop *Tryal*'s masts and yards were in a bad way. A month elapsed before these could be patched up. During that time *Centurion* buried twenty-eight men and found her sick list increased from eighty to ninety-six; other ships were in a comparable state. The squadron sailed from St. Catherine on 18th January 1741, leaving the last friendly port before proceeding to desert or hostile coasts, still unaware of the exact composition or location of Pizarro's squadron. Three days later they ran into a severe gale in which the *Tryal* lost her mainmast and had to be taken in tow by the *Gloucester*. The gale was accompanied by very thick fog during which the *Pearl* disappeared and was not seen again for a month.

The Spaniards had been kept well informed of Anson's movements by the Portuguese governor of St. Catherine. Anxious to get round Cape Horn into the South Seas before Anson, they left the River Plate on 22nd January, four days after Anson's departure from St. Catherine. At one time on passage the *Pearl*, being now separated from Anson, sighted the Spanish squadron, and in the distance mistook Pizarro's flagship *Asia* for the *Centurion*. In poor visibility she approached to within gunshot before discovering her error, and narrowly escaped being taken.

On the 17th February, Anson in the *Centurion* arrived at the rendezvous, St. Julian in Patagonia, and anchored together with the *Gloucester*, *Severn*, and *Tryal*, being soon joined by the *Pearl*, whose lieutenant, Salt, informed the Commodore that Captain Kidd had died at the end of January. He also told Anson of the Spanish squadron he had encountered, two ships of seventy guns, two of fifty guns, and one of forty, the leading ship wearing a broad red pennant which exactly resembled Anson's. He had been chased all day and had slipped the Spaniards at nightfall.

Anson transferred Murray from the *Wager* to succeed to the command of the *Pearl* in place of the deceased Kidd, and moved Cheap from the sloop *Tryal* to the *Wager*. A vacancy for a captain now falling again in the *Tryal*, Anson promoted Charles Saunders his first lieutenant in *Centurion* to the command of the *Tryal*, and promoted Saumarez to the vacancy left by Saunders. Here are two names that became famous, Saunders becoming First Lord of the Admiralty after distinguished service in the Seven Years War, and Saumarez dying gallantly in Hawke's action against the French in 1747 when in command of the *Nottingham*. Saunders being ill of fever, Saumarez was temporarily appointed in command of *Tryal*.

On receipt of the news of Pizarro's squadron Anson ordered that all guns should be mounted for action, and the gun-decks cleared of stores and provisions which were to be returned to the storeship *Anna*. He also held a council of war on board *Centurion*, attended by all his captains and Colonel Mordaunt Cracherode, the commander of the land forces, at which it was agreed that their first assault should be made on the town and harbour of Baldivia in Chile, with the intention of taking it and keeping it as a base for the purpose of refitting and careening their ships while in the South Seas. Since separation might prove fatal, Anson gave orders that no ship was to be at any time further than two miles from the *Centurion*: in the event of any breach of this order the name of the officer responsible was to be reported. In case of separation, ships were to make their way to the island of Socoro where they were to cruise for ten days: thence they were to proceed to Baldivia taking care to keep to the southward of the port, and if not joined by the rest of the squadron after fourteen days off Baldivia, they were to proceed to the island of Juan Fernandez.

By the 27th February, the *Tryal*'s refit was complete, and the squadron weighed from St. Julian in great expectation of meeting Pizarro, but bent on rounding the Horn as soon as possible. Winds were light for several days, and the weather hazy with some rain. The only excitement was an explosion in the *Gloucester*, caused by a spark from a fire igniting some gunpowder. The fire was extinguished, and little damage sustained. On the 7th March, the squadron passed through the Straits Le Maire, regarded by many as the boundary between the Atlantic and the Pacific Oceans, and were now faced with a long tack to the south-west against the westerly storms and currents, over vast areas of ocean in a high latitude unprotected by land of any description to windward. We can picture the squadron with *Tryal* and *Pearl* in the van, *Severn*, *Centurion*, and *Gloucester* in the centre, and *Wager* and the little *Anna* bringing up the rear. Hopes were still high. The weather was fair, the wind brisk; and although scurvy was still rife, there was a feeling on board that they were at last approaching their goal. A haven of wealth and opulence would be the next stop; a plum ripe for picking.

Walter says of the occasion:

> ... the morning of this day, in its brilliancy and mildness gave place to none we had seen since our departure from England. Thus animated by these flattering delusions, we passed these memorable streights, ignorant of the dreadful calamities which were then impending, and just ready to break upon us; ignorant that the time drew near when the squadron would be separated never to unite again, and that this day of our passage was the last chearful day that the greatest part of us would ever live to enjoy.

No sooner were they through the straits than they met the most violent squalls and a strong current which set them to the eastward. Anson, in his report of proceedings, said that he was 'obliged to reef courses, which continued reefed fifty-eight days.'

The prospect now entered some of their minds that they might not be able to round the Horn after all. They met a succession of storms and mountainous seas of such a size that even the old hands confessed that what they had hitherto called storms were moderate gales compared with these. Many men were filled with terror. There was constant danger from the violent rolling and pitching. Some lost their hold and were dashed to death. One was forced overboard. At times the sails were split to ribbons. The little *Anna* parted her fore-stay, and broke her bowsprit. The *Centurion* parted her main shrouds, and sprung her yards. The *Gloucester* broke her main yard. The *Wager* lost her mizzen-mast and main topsail yard. The little *Tryal* made so much water that she was scarcely able to keep afloat. During a brief lull, Anson sent over a pump to the *Tryal*. There must have been few, even among the resolute, who would not willingly have turned back home at this juncture. To realize more fully how shocking were conditions on board, and the melancholy outlook, we must read Purser Millechamp's account, as viewed from the *Tryal* on 10th March 1741, in latitude 60° South:

> Sometimes lying to, at others flying to Windward under our courses, Pincht with cold, have no refreshments even for our Sick Men, but Salt Meat, which in some of the ships could not be Boiled for many Days together, but a Pursers quart of Water—(which is seven-eights of a Wine Quart) for one Man a day. Our men almost all sick, and those that were Dying as well as many of the rest almost devoured by Vermine insomuch that I have frequently seen by a modest Computation above a Peck of Lice on a Man even after he was dead.

Imagine Anson's bitter disappointment more than a month later. According to their reckoning they had made a westing of almost 20° of longitude, so that they thought themselves to be well to the westward of land and therefore now able to stand to the northward to the more pacific waters of the lower

37

latitudes. It was a hazy moonlight night. Suddenly the haze cleared, and all the lookouts received the shock of their lives. There, but two miles distant, was land, bright in the moonlight; the squadron making for it and destruction. Swiftly the alarms were given. Slowly they altered course together; and by a miracle, the wind shifted to a favourable quarter, as they made once again to the southward, and began again their long toil to clear the land. They now realized that they had sighted Cape Noir, the westernmost point of Tierra del Fuego. To this discouraging episode was now added the disappearance of both the *Severn* and *Pearl*, never to be seen again by the squadron. It seemed to many that fate was against their survival, yet favourable wind and bright moon had come to their salvation. Anson was thankful. Disappointment and melancholy, however, seemed to augment the ravages of scurvy, and Millechamp in the *Tryal* wrote:

> Our seamen now almost Despairing of ever getting on shore Voluntarily gave themselves up to their fatal distemper, and only used to Envy those whose good Fortune it was to die first. Nothing was more frequent than to Bury Eight or Ten Men from each Ship every Morning.

On 8th May, the *Centurion* alone arrived at the rendezvous off Socoro, and after cruising for a fortnight without seeing the others, sailed for Juan Fernandez. It is worth recording that it was on the 28th May that the *Centurion*'s reckoning placed her at the island of Juan Fernandez. Land however was not in sight, and because there was a strong opinion that they were much too far to the west of the island it was decided to stand to the eastward, running along the parallel of latitude of the island until they hit it off, or at the worst could make a landfall on the mainland from which they would correct the reckoning and make a new departure. In those days the chronometer had not been perfected and the determination of longitude was unreliable. The determination of latitude, however, provided the sky were clear, could be obtained with accuracy by a sextant altitude of the sun at noon. Anson was fairly certain that he had sighted the Island, but the weather was hazy, and in view of strong persuasion, he agreed to the change to an easterly course. They sighted the mainland on 30th May, and confirmed by their reckoning to the landfall that they had needlessly altered course. They were now getting short of water and had the added misfortune of meeting calms and contrary winds to make their westing to the Island; this cost them a further nine days. It was not until 9th June that *Centurion* arrived there, her ship's company now in a parlous state, the men dying four, five, and six in a day. So few seamen were available that the ship had to be worked with the assistance of the officers. She had lost forty-three men in April and almost double that number in May. There remained but two hundred odd men of the five hundred who had left England. Those who yet lived were dispirited by the setbacks and disheartening circumstances, the considerable loss of life, and above all by the thought that the rest of the squadron had perished. Soon after *Centurion* berthed, however, a sail was seen approaching, and there was tremendous joy when this proved to be the sloop *Tryal*. Captain Saunders of the *Tryal* informed Anson that out of his small complement of a hundred men he had buried thirty-four. Of those who lived, only he and his lieutenant and three men were able to work the ship. The arrival of the *Tryal* was heartening, and Anson had hopes of seeing his other vessels soon. The *Tryal* also reported that she had fallen in with the storeship *Anna* on 9th May off Chile, and had kept company with her for four days before they were parted in a strong gale.

Anson speedily arranged for tents to be set up ashore, and he and his officers assisted in the work of carrying the sick in their hammocks to the tents on shore. The stench and filth between decks was by now unbelievably loathsome, and the work of carrying was extremely fatiguing. Many of the sick died as soon as they were moved, others died in the boats on the way to the shore. Deaths continued for several days among the sick on shore, but the fresh air and the fresh fruit and meat and fish soon brought their benefits to a company accustomed to salt tack, and in three weeks, scurvy had practically disappeared.

The schoolmaster of the *Centurion*, Pascoe Thomas, in his Journal says:

At this place our Commodore, the rest of the Gentlemen Officers, with several of the Seamen and Marines, continued on shore, having Tents erected for that Purpose. The Commodore's in particular, was situated in a small Square environ'd by a Grove of Myrtle Trees, the Passage to which was mostly natural, and something like to a Labyrinth. Near it ran a fine large Rivulet of Water, to which a Passage was cut through the Woods: the whole together forming a pretty romantick Scene. The rest of the Tents were erected at Several Distances as we could find Convenient, and might be in the whole inhabited by about ninety or a hundred of our Ship's Company.

During this time Anson arranged for the planting of vegetable seeds, and stones of plum, peach, and apricot, for the benefit of those of his countrymen who might call at this delectable island subsequently. He also directed surveys of the coast and harbours, and built a wharf. Juan Fernandez is probably best known as the place where Alexander Selkirk was put ashore in 1704, and where he lived in complete solitude for over four years before being taken off in the privateer *Duke*. He later related his adventures to Daniel Defoe who based his immortal *Robinson Crusoe* on them. This group of islands lies four hundred miles west of Valparaiso in Chile. The vegetation is rich, and the climate mild. Anson lay with his ships in Cumberland Bay, a wide deep anchorage in the south, protected from the prevailing winds, and accessible to the shores. There was no shortage of fresh food here, and fish were plentiful. Young sea-lions abounded, and provided a favourite diet.

Walter relates:

In general there was no difficulty in killing them . . . However, a sailor one day being carelessly employed in skinning a young sea-lion, the female from whence he had taken it came upon him unperceived, and getting his head in her mouth, she with her teeth scored his skull in notches in many places . . . and though all possible care was taken of him, he died in a few days.

On 21st June, a ship was sighted to the northward for a short time, and then disappeared. On 26th June, the same ship was again sighted, and approached so near that she was identified as the *Gloucester*. She was obviously in a very bad way. Anson sent his boat laden with fresh water, fish, and vegetables. It was as well, for she was nearly at the end of her endurance. She had already thrown overboard two-thirds of her complement, water was reduced to a pint a day for each man, and of those who were still alive there were few who could work the ship. Because of contrary winds and currents it was not until 23rd July, four weeks later, that she was able to make the bay and reach an anchorage.

Millechamp in the *Tryal* wrote in his narrative about the arrival of *Gloucester*:

> Nigh a hundred of them Dyed in the time she was drove off which with the mortality she had before met with, reduced their complement to no more than Ninety Men.

The despair and mortification on board *Gloucester* during those weeks can be imagined. A haven of rest and refreshment in sight, at one time but three miles distant, only to be snatched away by foul winds and currents, and periodically to be brought to view again and again, with raised hopes, ending only in further despair as the sick died daily in their loathsome and stench-ridden mess decks: the dead envied by most of the survivors. What a test of resolution. And what a training ground for those who, with Anson, were meeting problems the solution of which were to be Britain's salvation in the Seven Years War. This was the testing time, to be followed by Britain's glorious days of naval victories when names such as Hawke, Howe, Rodney, St. Vincent, Hood, and Nelson, to mention only a few, became synonymous with superiority at sea. Britain should remember also Anson, the architect who paved the way to such glory.

# CHAPTER V

## Events at Juan Fernandez, and the
## End of the *Tryal*

AFTER the arrival of the *Gloucester*, the hope that the remaining ships of the squadron might join Anson at Juan Fernandez dwindled daily, and by the end of July all hope had been given up. The absence of the storeship *Anna* became more particularly felt since she carried most of the squadron's flour for bread-making, and a variety of stores and provisions that could not easily be carried in the warships. Anson had arranged for a copper oven to be set up on shore for the purpose of baking fresh bread for the sick, but at the end of July when the *Anna* had been given up for lost, he was forced to impose a rationing of bread.

Anson had reason to believe Spanish ships had been at the island shortly before his arrival, who might well return, expecting this to be a likely place in which to find him. In his present state he had little doubt that if this were the case he would be forced to leave the island at short notice; he therefore took early action to have his ships cleaned and watered and ready. Mitchel, Captain of the *Gloucester*, had told him that they had been forced by winds, to an island to the westward, which could be confused with Juan Fernandez. Aware of the unreliability of the local charts, Anson felt that some of his ships might possibly have gone there in error. He decided to fit out the *Tryal* and send her on a reconnaissance of bays and creeks in the vicinity. She was ready by 4th August and sailed, but in a calm was rapidly set towards the shore. Saunders her captain fired several guns, and boats were sent to tow her to a safe anchorage. She sailed the next morning with a fair breeze.

On 16th August, at noon, a sail was seen from Juan which at first was thought to be the *Tryal* returning. This soon proved untrue and a warning gun was fired from the *Centurion* to call off the men on shore in preparation to receive an enemy. The ship was now seen to be one of three masts, and there was conjecture that she might be a Spanish ship or even *Severn* or the *Pearl*. About three in the afternoon it became clear that she was no less than the *Anna*. There was tremendous joy, particularly as she was luckier than the *Gloucester* and sailed without delay straight into the bay, anchoring by five o'clock. Bread rationing was immediately abolished.

The appearance of the *Anna* in such good condition after so many months of separation caused some astonishment until her story was heard. She had made a landfall in the parallel of Socoro in the middle of May, but with a split fore-topsail had then been driven towards the shore. Her anchor failed to hold her, and she drove on. Her sheet anchor similarly failed to hold. Rapidly she drove towards the rocks. The coast was steep and rugged. All had been given up for lost, when miraculously a channel opened to view. The two anchors were swiftly cut away, and *Anna* was steered into what proved to be a sheltered harbour. Here she anchored with a three-hundredweight anchor in smooth water. And here she remained for two months while her sick were gradually restored to health. There was much apprehension over the local savages on this coast, and it was therefore with some concern that they watched a boat enter the harbour about a month after their arrival, bearing an Indian family consisting of a man and his wife and a child of three, and a baby still at the breast. The boat appeared to contain all their possessions: a dog, a cat, a fishing net, a hatchet, a knife, a cradle, some bark of trees intended for covering, a reel, some cloth, a flint and steel, and a few yellow roots. The master immediately sent for them and brought them on board *Anna*, determined not to allow any information of the storeship's presence to leak abroad. At night the family were locked in the forecastle; they were, however, allowed to roam the ship during the day, and fed with the men, and were often treated to brandy. Although the woman appeared to like her new existence, the man grew restless. One dark and stormy night, he contrived to break out of the ship together with his wife and children, entered a boat after cutting adrift the others, and made good his escape, pursued only by the shouts of the watch on deck and the cries of those who were roused in the confusion.

*Anna* was the last ship to join Anson at Juan Fernandez. The *Severn* and *Pearl* had both put back to Brazil when they parted company off Cape Horn, though Anson only learnt of this much later, and had assumed that both had been lost. Their losses from scurvy appear to have been even greater than *Centurion*'s and their navigation in the regions of the Horn much worse. This leaves only the *Wager* unaccounted for.

The fate of the *Wager* and her crew is a story combining crime with misfortune, and should be given briefly here, as it was in direct consequence of the mutinous conduct of the *Wager*'s shipwrecked seamen that Anson later, when at the Admiralty in 1748, was responsible for the passing of an act 'extending the discipline of the Navy to the crews of his Majesty's ships, wrecked, lost, or taken, and continuing to them their wages upon certain conditions.'

More successful than either the *Severn* or the *Pearl*, the *Wager*, under Cheap's command, rounded the Horn after being separated from Anson, and proceeded north for the rendezvous off Socoro as ordered. Her condition was no better than those of the other ships of the squadron, and she was little more than a wreck when, on 14th May 1741, she made land in latitude 47° South. She had on board mortars and field guns and considerable equipment suitable for the operations ashore in which Anson's shore forces intended to harry the Spaniards and secure a base. Cheap was resolute therefore that he must join Anson. On sighting land and what proved to be a lee shore, Cheap in his anxiety and exertions to gain sea room, fell down a ladder, and dislocated his shoulder. The ship struck a submerged rock shortly afterwards, and almost immediately settled between two small islands, a cable or so away from the shore. The ship being a wreck, Cheap did his best to get the crew ashore in boats. Many of the crew pillaged the ship, seized arms, broke into the spirit room, and got extremely drunk; some fell into the water, and were drowned. The following day, the ship was in danger of breaking up in stormy weather, and the miscreants, now wishing to be on shore, fired from a four pounder, two shots which passed just over the captain's tent on shore. This was meant to express their dissatisfaction with his delay in sending a boat for them. Authority now seemed to be at an end, many of the men adopting the attitude that it was every man for himself. There were fights and feuds: a hundred men in complete disorder on a barren coast.

Cheap was still determined to join Anson at the rendezvous at Juan Fernandez, and planned to fit up the boats with fire-arms and ammunition saved from the wreck, and then proceed northward. With his hundred men survivors from the wreck, he had little doubt that he could master any Spanish ship they might encounter. Many of the men, however, had had enough, and their plan was to lengthen the long-boat and proceed southward, getting back to Brazil and thence to England via the Straits of Magellan.

This difference of views caused much opposition towards the captain, and fomented a disloyalty which was stimulated by the behaviour of a mutinous midshipman called Couzens. This rather unruly character involved himself in brawls with most of the officers, because of their attempts to maintain the authority of the captain, an authority which to the majority of the crew was distinctly in question since the *Wager* had been lost. The captain and the officers were very much on their guard because of the general insubordination. Matters suddenly came to a head. The purser had, on the captain's orders, stopped the allowance of a man who would not work. While in the process of issuing provisions outside the captain's tent, he was grossly insulted by Couzens, drew his pistol, and fired at him. The shot missed. Cheap rushed from his tent, assumed that it was Couzens who had fired, and shot him through the head. Couzens died a fortnight later. The immediate effect of this action was to restore the captain's authority. The work of lengthening the long-boat proceeded. On nearing completion of the work in mid-October, however, the men were very much aware of the captain's determination to proceed northwards and were equally determined that they should have their own way. Cheap was therefore arrested and kept under guard for the purpose nominally of being taken to England to be tried for murder.

On 13th October, the long-boat, now converted into a schooner, together with the cutter and eighty men, set out for their journey to Brazil. Just before their departure, they set Cheap at liberty, and left him with the yawl and the barge and nineteen men. The long-boat arrived at Rio Grande on 29th January with only thirty of the eighty men who had deserted Cheap.

It was two months before Cheap and his nineteen men were able to embark, on 14th December, in the barge and yawl, and proceed northwards, desperately short of provisions. During these two months, he and his men had lived on shellfish and herbs, and had kept their provisions for the journey. In less than a further two months he was back again at the island where *Wager* had been shipwrecked, having made several unsuccessful attempts to negotiate a headland and having had to ditch most of the provisions in order to avoid destruction. The yawl had been lost, and his men were now reduced in number to eleven. His party was dejected by the series of misfortunes and were weak from hunger and fatigue, but on return to *Wager* island they found several pieces of beef which had been washed from the wreck. This was manna indeed. Moreover they met an Indian who was a native of Chiloe, who promised to take them to the Island of Chiloe not far from Baldivia, Anson's first objective, on condition that the barge and its contents would be given to him.

On 6th March they set off again in the barge, the party now reduced to eleven and one Indian. After a few days, the captain and four officers found themselves marooned ashore, another Indian having taken the barge with the remaining six men, never to return. The original Indian guide was extremely concerned and surprised at this duplicity on the part of his countryman, but promised nevertheless to keep his part of the bargain. There were now left Cheap, Hamilton the lieutenant of marines, Elliott the surgeon, and two midshipmen, Byron (grandfather of the poet) and Campbell. It was mid-March

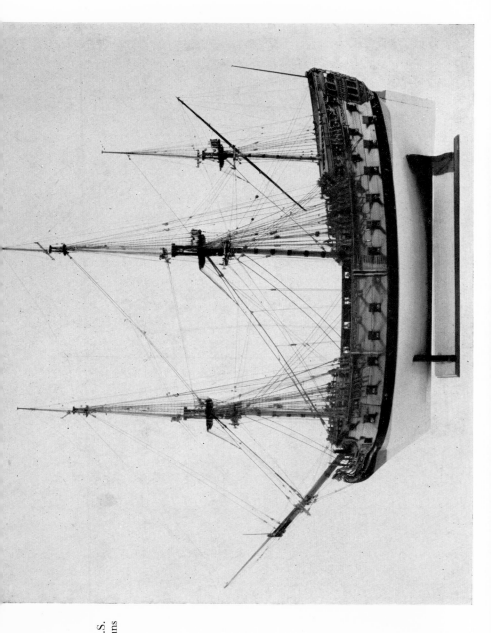

Model of H.M.S.
*Centurion*, 60 guns

Sailors in port
*From a mezzotint by W. Ward after T. Stothard*

before they started again, this time in canoes arranged by the Indian for a passage by land and sea. Elliott the surgeon died soon afterwards, but Cheap and the other three subsequently arrived in Chiloe and were made prisoners. It was all to little purpose from the point of view of support for Anson, but as a story of miraculous survival in the face of a series of misfortunes and disasters, and for sheer tenacity of purpose it is hard to beat. They were treated well by the Spaniards, and in 1745, by an exchange of prisoners, were sent in a French ship back to Europe. Captain Cheap wrote to Anson on his arrival in France, and complained indignantly of the behaviour of his men after shipwreck. It was three years later that Anson was responsible for the passing of the act extending the terms of naval discipline.

But to return to Anson at Juan Fernandez. On 16th August 1741, the remnants of his squadron, the *Centurion*, *Gloucester*, and the sloop *Tryal* had at last been joined by the storeship *Anna*. The latter part of August was spent in unloading the *Anna*. Great quantities of her provisions, particularly rice and oats, had been ruined by the rotting of casks and bags, and *Anna* herself was found to be rotten and decayed. Anson ordered her to be broken up, and her men were sent on board *Centurion* and *Gloucester* to increase their depleted crews. The sorry state of these ships may be realized from a statement by Pascoe Thomas:

> This Island was a happy Haven to us, our Water being near expended, our Men reduced from 518 to about 213, out of whom about 130 were sick and very weak, and the rest, with long Fatigue and the Inclemency of the Weather, almost useless. With the other Ships it was worse, the *Gloucester*'s People being reduced from 460 to about 96, and almost all Sick and helpless.

Walter gives the following figures:

|  | ON LEAVING ENGLAND SEPTEMBER 1740 | REMAINING SEPTEMBER 1741 |
|---|---|---|
| *Centurion* | 506 | 214 |
| *Gloucester* | 374 | 82 |
| *Tryal* | 81 | 39 |
| Total | 961 | 335 |

In the *Centurion* only four pensioners were left of the original fifty; in the *Gloucester* all had perished. The total seamen left in the three ships was insufficient for the proper manning and navigation of the *Centurion* alone. A man less resolute than Anson might well have decided that it was time to return to England, particularly as the feeling among his men must by now have been one of despair. Prospects were hopeless, and there was always the possibility of meeting Pizarro's formidable squadron. Assault and capture of the Spanish settlements were now out of the question, for there were practically no troops. Anson, however, was certain that Pizarro could have suffered no less than his own squadron, and decided to disperse his ships in an attempt to capture a Spanish merchantman or two.

On 8th September, by which time all three ships had practically completed refitting, a sail was sighted to the north-east of the bay, which later disappeared to the eastward. All *Centurion*'s hands were recalled on board by the firing of a gun, and were supplemented by several men from the *Gloucester* and *Tryal*. There was great activity. Rigging was set up, sails were bent, decks were cleared. In the evening, *Centurion* weighed and proceeded in chase of the sail. She had been at anchor in Cumberland Bay three months. There was now considerable excitement on board and great prospects of a capture. The terrors of shipwreck and the ravages of scurvy were now but dim memories. Despair had given way to hope, and Anson's determination had become infectious.

There was no sight of the ship the next morning, but topgallant masts and yards were rigged, all sails set, and with a favourable wind, course was steered for Valparaiso which was believed to be the destination of the Spaniard. Nothing was seen for two days, and Anson decided to return to Juan. At daybreak on 12th September a sail was sighted. As *Centurion* approached her, so she stood away to the southward, beating into a fresh gale from the west-south-west. She appeared to be a large man-of-war, probably one of Pizarro's squadron. Anson had all the decks cleared in *Centurion* and guns ready for action. There followed a rain squall and low cloud which obliterated the Spaniard. There was now great apprehension that she would get away, but the weather suddenly cleared and showed the quarry to be quite near: a merchantman with only three four-pounders. *Centurion* fired four shots at her rigging, and she immediately let fly sheets and halyards to indicate capitulation.

The squadron had at last gained a prize, and had made its first contribution towards 'annoying' the Spaniards.

Anson sent the *Centurion*'s first lieutenant, Philip Saumarez, to take possession of the prize, with directions that the prisoners, who appeared to be terrified, were to be treated with the utmost courtesy and humanity, and were to be sent on board *Centurion*. From them, and from papers found on board the prize, it was learned that Pizarro's squadron had suffered greatly in the heavy seas and tempestuous winds off the Horn, and had had to return to the River Plate with the loss of two of his largest ships, the *Hermiona* and the *Guipuscoa*.

This was comforting news to Anson, but further information was provided which gave considerable encouragement. This was that although a warning of the possible presence of English ships in the Pacific had been broadcast in May 1741 by the Viceroy of Peru, it had recently been withdrawn. The Viceroy had received word overland from Pizarro, after his return to the Plate, about the disaster to his own squadron, and it was assumed that Anson must have suffered similarly, and that no English ships could possibly have rounded the Horn at that time without disaster. It was further learnt that in May 1741, when the Viceroy of Peru had been told that English ships might have got round into the Pacific, he sent out a force of four Spanish men-of-war with the intention of intercepting and destroying the English ships. He rightly assumed that the English ships would be isolated and in a weakened state: they would be an easy prey and would attempt to get to Juan Fernandez. The Spanish warships had cruised on this station and had left Juan Fernandez only a few days before Anson had arrived in *Centurion* on 9th June, his ship practically a wreck and the survivors of his crew almost useless with fatigue and illness. *Centurion*'s faulty navigation must have proved to be her salvation. Although she had lost twelve precious days between first sighting and subsequently reaching the island, during which fifty or more men had died from scurvy, she would have suffered annihilation had she arrived while the Spaniards were still there. This success would doubtless have encouraged the Spaniards to stay on longer, and the *Gloucester*, *Tryal*, and *Anna* must have singly suffered the same fate.

Thomas in his Journal says:

> This was a well-laid Scheme for our Ruin, and in pursuance thereof the Viceroy fitted out three Ships at Callao, one of 50, one of 30 and one of 20 Guns, all double mann'd with the choicest Men they could possibly procure, and sent them to wait for us accordingly . . . they should spare none, but put us all to the Sword without any Distinction. Those Ships arrived at Juan Fernandez sometime I think in May and continued 'till about June the 6th, when imagining that we must be either put back or lost they quitted their Station . . . by which means we happiley miss'd of meeting them there.
>
> Those bloody Orders our Spanish Prisoners themselves were very much ashamed of, and the rather as they were treated by us with all manner of Humanity. Nothing about or belonging to their Persons was taken from them, except by some few rascally Fellows in a clandestine Manner; and those could they have been discovered, would have been severely punish'd. The principal among them din'd daily with the Commodore, and if the least Boy or the meanest Indian or Black among them was any way ill used, he was sure of Redress by a proper Application of the Officers.

The *Centurion*'s prize was the *Nuestra Señora de Monte Carmelo*, a rich merchant ship of 450 tons, having on board her £1,800 sterling in dollars and plate, and a large cargo of sugar and cloth, with a crew of fifty-three, both white and black, and twenty-five passengers.

After most of the prisoners and all the silver had been transferred to the *Centurion*, Anson proceeded for Juan Fernandez with *Carmelo* in company; *Carmelo* sailing under a prize crew of Saumarez, three petty officers, and ten men. Anson had been further informed that the Spanish squadron from Callao, the port of Lima, had been shattered by a storm, and after returning to Callao had been laid up. It would take at least two months to fit them out.

This was encouraging news for Anson, who hitherto must have wondered many times whether in the face of such hopeless prospects and in spite of his terrible losses his decision to continue was the right one. Until the capture of the *Carmelo* he had suffered nothing but misfortune and terrible loss of men, and not a single material advantage to show that the mounting of the expedition had been worth while. With the latest information he decided that he could disperse his ships with safety, and harry the Spaniards until such time as the warships at Callao had fitted out. The Spanish in *Carmelo* had been greatly surprised that the *Centurion* had weathered the passage round the Horn but their surprise was nothing compared with their astonishment on seeing the little *Tryal*, and they could only believe that she had been built after Anson arrived at Juan Fernandez.

*Carmelo* was but one ship of a convoy, and was not the same ship that had been sighted from Juan Fernandez on the 8th September, when Anson had hurriedly sailed *Centurion*, with her depleted crew supplemented by men from *Gloucester* and *Tryal*.

Millechamp in the *Tryal* wrote of this capture:

> *Fourteenth of September. Centurion* with 10 *Gloucester* men and 10 *Tryal* men took a prize. The *Centurion* people will not allow it to be the same we saw for fear the *Gloucester* and *Tryal* should partake of the prize Money though we have no reason to Doubt it. She had on board a Cargo of Bale Goods with the value of £1800 in money.

It may be that there was little expectation generally at that time of finding and taking further prizes, but Anson thought differently and acted swiftly. The morning after his return to Juan Fernandez he sailed the *Tryal*, reinforced by ten men from *Centurion*, to cruise off Valparaiso to look for merchantmen.

The guns from the *Anna*, which had been broken up, were now mounted on board *Carmelo*: they consisted of four six-pounders, four four-pounders, and two swivels. During the next four days the squadron was wooded and watered. Of the prisoners recently taken, six passengers and twenty-three seamen were sent on board *Gloucester*: her captain, Mitchel, was directed by Anson to proceed eighteen hundred miles to the northward as soon as possible to the latitude of 5° South, and thence to cruise off shore just out of sight of the town of Paita. Anson would join him there at an appropriate time later, when he deemed a concentration of force necessary, according to intelligence received.

Anson left Juan Fernandez in *Centurion* on 18th September, with his prize, the *Carmelo*, in company, and proceeded eastward. He met calms and light variable winds, and it was four days before he lost sight of the island. This was then followed by squally weather in which *Centurion* split her topsail. The following day two ships were sighted to the eastward, one small, one large, which proved to be the little *Tryal* in company with a six hundred ton merchantman, the *Santa Maria de Arranzazu*, three times the size of the *Tryal*. The little *Tryal* had taken her after a chase of thirty-six hours. The prize had nearly escaped at night during the chase, but a small chink of light had shown through a shutter which rendered her efforts at darkening ship ineffectual. The *Tryal* had crept up on her in the night. Just when she had begun to feel herself safe, she received a broadside. Capitulation followed soon afterwards. She was bound from Callao for Valparaiso, and had five thousand pounds sterling worth of silver on board, a worthy first prize for Charles Saunders, *Tryal*'s captain. The *Arranzazu* had often been employed as a warship, and was pierced for thirty-two guns.

The little *Tryal*, however, was in a bad way, having sprung her mainmast and lost her main topmast. The following day in a gale she sprung her fore-mast and was unable to carry any sail. Moreover she made more water than could be discharged by the pumps, and was in great danger of being lost. As she was borne away helpless in the gale she fired two guns as a signal of distress. *Centurion* followed her to give support when possible. On 27th September the weather moderated, and Anson sent a boat for Saunders to come on board *Centurion*. Saunders presented a petition, signed by himself and his officers, describing the defective nature of the sloop and the risk of total loss unless she were repaired. Anson considered repair to be out of the question, as it would take up further valuable time. Although reluctant to diminish the appearance of his force, he gave orders for the *Tryal* to be destroyed, and her large prize to be commissioned as a frigate in the King's service and named *Tryal's Prize*. The captain, officers, and men of the *Tryal* were to transfer to the prize, retaining their respective appointments to a King's ship. All stores and guns were also to be transferred. After sinking the *Tryal*, Saunders was to take up station off Valparaiso, together with the *Centurion's* prize, the *Carmelo*, under Saumarez and his small prize crew, being stationed in such a position as to remain out of sight of land yet being able to intercept ships bound for Valparaiso. By this means Anson hoped to prevent news leaking back to Callao of the loss of the two Spanish ships.

He himself that same evening, 27th September, sailed in *Centurion*, to take station to windward of Valparaiso, in a position where incoming ships usually aimed to make a landfall.

Though but two of his original ships were left, prospects were improving, and he was already in possession of two rich prizes.

## CHAPTER VI

# More Prizes, and the Burning of Paita

PROSPECTS of further prizes seemed high, but valuable time had been lost when the *Tryal* was in peril. Anson cruised for days off Valparaiso, but sighted nothing. As each fruitless day followed the preceding, hopes began to dwindle, and morale on board suffered accordingly. The men were not allowed to remain idle. With the twofold object of keeping them occupied and of preparing for boarding or landing parties, Anson gave orders for daily exercises with small arms. Pascoe Thomas remarks:

> 30th September 1741
> The 30th we saw the main land of Chile. This Day we began to exercise our People with small Arms which was the first Time we had done it since we came into those Seas, and which we continued at all proper Opportunities during the Voyage.

A feeling began to grow on board that with little prospect of further prize money to come, it would be nice to know how much had already been won and what each man's share would be. Discontent was growing, but Anson was not one to watch idly. Thomas in his journal gives the following enlightening account of his action:

> On the 5th [October 1741] the Commodore having had Intelligence that there were several Murmurings and Discontents amongst the People by reason the Prize-Money

was not immediately divided, ordered the Articles of War to be read: after which he made a speech, wherein he remarked to them the Danger of Mutiny, and let them know that he had heard of their Murmurings and Discontents, but assured them they were entirely groundless, their Properties being secured by Act of Parliament as firmly as any one's own Inheritance, and the Money, Plate, etc., weigh'd and mark'd in publick; so that any capable Person, if he pleased, might take an Inventory of the whole. He then read an Account of the Particulars, and told them they might (if they pleased) make choice of any Person to take an Inventory for them or buy their Part. This Speech was receiv'd with the Applause, visible Joy, and seeming Content of every one. He then desired they would discover the Author or Authors of such Discontents, assuring them they would receive condign Punishment; but no Discovery of that nature could be made.

Weeks now passed without sighting any Spaniards, and Anson concluded that shipping had been warned of his presence. Moreover he assumed that the news must have reached the Viceroy at Callao, and that the fitting out of the Spanish squadron would be hastened. He therefore determined to join Saunders in the *Tryal's Prize*, and Saumarez in the *Carmelo*, and proceed northwards to the vicinity of Callao, there to join Mitchel in *Gloucester*, and with his combined force, give the Spanish squadron a warm reception if they should emerge. Rendezvous with Saunders and Saumarez was made on 2nd November, and all three ships then proceeded to the northward. On 5th November a sail was sighted and the ships gave chase, *Centurion* soon outsailing her two consorts. As daylight faded, *Centurion* closed her prey, only to lose sight of her in the dusk of the evening. Anson decided to continue on the same course with all sails set, and as luck would have it came up with the ship after about an hour and a half of sailing in the dusk, his second lieutenant, Peircy Brett, spotting her four points on the port bow. Within an hour, after having fourteen shot fired at her, she struck. The third lieutenant, Peter Denis, was sent in the boat with sixteen men to take possession of the prize, and to return with the prisoners. Here are two more officers who owed their early training to Anson. Both attained the rank of Admiral, and commanded fleets; Brett became a Lord of the Admiralty.

The prize, a ship of three hundred tons, was named *Santa Teresa de Jesus*, and was bound from Guayaquil to Callao, with a valuable cargo, but only a little silver to the value of a hundred and seventy pounds sterling. She carried ten passengers; three of these were women, a mother and two grown-up daughters. The daughters were beautiful, the younger one exceedingly so. As soon as Denis boarded the prize, the women, who were terrified of capture, hid themselves. One can imagine the feelings of men who had not seen a woman for a twelve-month. One can equally understand the fears of the women, finding themselves at the mercy of what they believed to be desperate buccaneers whose evil reputation had been broadcast in these seas. Anson, who as reported previously was by no means a woman-hater, was presumably keen to receive the women in his own apartments in *Centurion*, to enjoy the charm of their company and the beauty of their appearance in a little world where neither charm nor beauty were ever present. Here, in the name of courtesy and protection, he could enjoy their society until such time as they could be safely landed. He must have appreciated the devastating effect that their presence would have on his officers and men, and himself as well. However honourable his own intentions, and however discreet his behaviour, the arrival of these beautiful women on board would be a reminder of a lost world. Lust and envy, jealousy and suspicion would be stirred up. There would be many men in *Centurion* who would throw caution to the winds just to touch the women. There would be some who would stop at nothing in order to possess them. Discipline and self control would be grossly endangered, and could not possibly survive such provocation. Anson was well aware of all these points, and made his decision.

He decided that the women should remain in their apartments on board the *Santa Teresa de Jesus*, and should be protected from molestation by a guardian. On being informed of the Commodore's intentions and the honourable treatment which would be accorded them, the women were profoundly gratified, but appeared to find it hard to believe their informants. They were eventually landed with other prisoners at Paita some months later, during which time Anson saw nothing of them: not even to confirm the reputed beauty of the younger women. The women were so sensible of their exceptional and unexpected treatment that they refused to be landed until they had been permitted to call on the Commodore in the *Centurion* to give him their thanks in person.

This story gives us a glimpse of Anson's character and accounts for the veneration of his name in a country where priests in particular had broadcast the brutal behaviour of English buccaneers and cut-throats. Anson's reputation was now firmly established, and with it he carried the reputation of the whole English nation. It is of interest to read what Walter says of this matter at the time:

Nor let it be imagined that the impressions which the Spaniards hence received to our advantage is a matter of small import: for, not to mention several of our country-men who have already felt the good effects of these prepossessions, the Spaniards are a nation whose good opinion of us is doubtless of more consequence than that of all the world besides, not only as the commerce we had formerly carried on with them, and perhaps may again here after, is so extremely valuable, but also as the trans-acting it does so immediately depend on the honour and good faith of those who are entrusted with its management. However, had no national conveniences attended it, the Commodore's equity and good temper would not less have deterred him from all tyranny and cruelty to those whom the fortune of war had put into his hands. I shall only add, that by his constant attachment to these humane and prudent maxims he has acquired a distinguished reputation amongst the Creolian Spaniards, which is not confined merely to the coast of the South Seas, but is extended through all the Spanish Settlements in America: so that his name is frequently to be met with in the mouths of most of the Spanish inhabitants of that prodigious empire.

During her chase of the *Santa Teresa de Jesus* the *Centurion* had outsailed her consorts, and it was not until broad daylight that they came up with her, aided by the firing of guns from *Centurion*.

Anson resumed his passage to the northward, spreading his four ships in the hope of sighting another Spaniard. He must already have had a landing operation in mind, as he now ordered boats to be repaired, and a swivel gun-stock to be erected in the bow of both the barge and the pinnace. The current was in his favour, and the weather fair. The ships were attended by vast numbers of flying fish and bonitos.

On 11th November, at daybreak, a sail was sighted close inshore and to windward, but the wind was so light that it was impossible to close her. Anson ordered his barge and pinnace, together with the *Tryal's* pinnace from the *Tryal's Prize*, to be manned and armed, and to go in chase of the sail.

Lieutenant Brett in the barge was the first to come up with her. Running alongside, he fired a volley of small shot between the masts. Cutlass in hand, he and his men boarded the vessel. There was no resistance.

On his return to *Centurion* with prisoners, Brett informed the Commodore that the ship was the *Nuestra Señora del Carmine* of 260 tons, with a valuable cargo of steel, iron, wax, pepper, cedar, and bale goods worth upwards of four hundred thousand dollars. She was bound for Callao from Paita, which port she had left the day before, after taking in water and provisions.

But the most important information came from one of the prisoners, an Irishman named John Williams, who was in rags, and said that he had just got out of Paita gaol. He was delighted to see his countrymen, and told them that the Governor of Paita had been informed by the master of a ship that he had been chased by a very large English ship, the description of which tallied with that of the *Gloucester*. News had at once been sent to the Viceroy at Lima, and arrangements had begun for the removal of treasure from Paita to Piura, a town some forty or fifty miles away. Information was also received that there was a considerable sum of money in the Customs house at Paita, which was to be shipped any moment to a port in Mexico, in a very fast ship, for the purpose of buying a part of the valuable cargo of the Manila galleon.

Anson had no troops left, and although he was in possession of four prizes besides the *Centurion*, he was desperately short of seamen. Nevertheless he had a large number of prisoners who were consuming large quantities of food and drink, and who would have to be put ashore at an early date. He was in great need of an anchorage where he could refit and replenish his ships. And above all, he had still to carry out his instructions: 'to seize, surprise, or take any of the towns or places belonging to the Spaniards on that coast that you may judge worthy of making such an enterprise upon.' This was the opportunity for which he had waited. This was the sort of operation for which he had trained his officers. Not a moment was to be wasted. He decided to attack that same night.

The *Centurion*'s first and third lieutenants, Saumarez and Denis, were already absent in command of the small prize crews of the *Carmelo* and the *Teresa*, and Anson was reluctant to lose Brett, his second lieutenant; Summers, now one of the two masters' mates in the *Centurion*, who had begun the commission as a midshipman, was therefore sent with a small prize crew to take over the little *Carmine*.

From the prisoners, Anson learnt that the town was defended by a fort with light pieces of cannon surrounded by a brick wall. There was no ditch. The garrison consisted of one weak company, but the town could raise three hundred armed men. Anson decided to keep his ships well out of sight. The eighteen-oared barge and the two pinnaces were again manned: Lieutenants Brett, Denis, and Hughes being in command respectively. The whole party consisted of fifty-eight picked men under the command of Lieutenant Brett. Two of the Spanish pilots were ordered to conduct the boats to the most convenient landing place, and to act as guides after the landing. In case of treachery Anson promised that they would be shot, and the remaining prisoners would be taken back to England. If they co-operated, all the prisoners would be released.

The three boats had a fifteen mile pull to the landing place. Brett had hoped to arrive undiscovered in the darkness, but one of the boats was seen by some people from a vessel which was riding at anchor in the bay: these instantly gave the alarm. Brett pushed on with redoubled vigour. One of the cannons on the fort opened fire. The time was about two in the morning. A shot whistled overhead. The launch ran alongside the jetty, quickly followed by the other two. Brett and his men scrambled ashore, and followed the pilot. In a short time they were in a narrow street. Here they were protected from the cannon. They formed up and marched for the large square at the end of the street, shouting and cheering lustily, and beating drums to give the impression of a large force arriving. They were thrilled to be ashore again after so many weeks at sea, excited at the prospect of loot, and anxious to subdue the populace, and occupy the place as quickly and completely as possible. The inhabitants were terrified by the shouting and beating, and fled in the confusion of a very dark night. Only a few negro women and children remained. As the sailors arrived at the square, where the Governor's house formed one side and the fort another, but with the cannon facing the wrong way, they were greeted by a volley of gunfire from the gallery of the Governor's house. Brett and his men returned the fire, and renewed their terrible din. The enemy withdrew with great speed from the gallery. Brett had been particularly told by Anson to capture the Governor if possible, and now sent half his force to surround the Governor's house while he himself, with the other half, turned his attention to the fort. This he found abandoned, the enemy having clambered over the walls. In the meantime, the Governor, who had been in bed with his wife, a seventeen-year-old girl to whom he had been married only three days, deserted bed and wife and fled with great speed, half-naked, through the window of his bedroom. His wife, wearing even less, was seen to be carried off with great haste by a couple of sentries, just before the house was surrounded. Brett now placed guards and sentries at strategic points. In less than fifteen minutes from the time of landing he had taken Paita. His only casualties were one man killed and two men wounded, one of whom was the Spanish pilot who had been appointed guardian of the girls in the *Teresa*.

The Honourable Augustus Keppel, son of the Earl of Albemarle, had a very narrow escape when a ball shaved past his temple. Keppel was another of Anson's officers who subsequently reached high rank and became First Lord of the Admiralty.

Brett's first task was to remove the treasure from the customs house to the security of the fort. Many of the sailors, overcome with delight at their easy victory, entered the houses and found finery and embroidered clothes which they put on over their own trousers and jackets. This relaxation became infectious, and reached a pitch when some of the sailors, dressed in women's gowns and petticoats, were challenged by Brett to reveal their identity.

At about seven the next morning, *Centurion* arrived in the bay, and the work of transferring the booty, amounting to upwards of thirty thousand pounds and pigs and poultry, began. It was now realized by all how advantageous it would have been had Anson's plan for the capture of the Governor been realized, so that some ransom could have been agreed for the valuable merchandise ashore. Although plate was transferred, it was pointless to put much of the merchandise on board. Anson therefore sent word to the Governor, who was still at large, that he would burn the town and the warehouses if no ransom were arranged.

On the second day, news was received that the Governor would not consider any negotiation, and that a formidable force of those who had fled to the hills where there was a great shortage of water, would return the next night and retake the town. They were to be led by Gordon, a Scots papist, who was a sea captain. He had two hundred horse at his disposal, with trained men; and flourished trumpets, drums, and standards. Anson thereupon doubled his guards, but the force failed to appear; the second night passed without incident.

On the third day, 15th November, the loading of treasure being completed, and the Governor remaining obdurate, Anson ordered the burning of the town; but two churches in an isolated position were to be spared. Into one of these churches Anson sent his prisoners to be kept under close guard until Brett was ready to withdraw. Every quarter received its share of tar and pitch, so that the Spaniards would be unable to avert the fire, and the houses most to windward were then fired. Brett assembled his men and withdrew to the beach, and it was now seen that a squadron of horse descended the hill in a menacing fashion, hoping to hasten Brett's departure. On reaching the beach Brett halted his men, faced the enemy, and the chase came to an abrupt halt. In a few moments the fire began to spread rapidly, the town was thoroughly on fire, and thick black smoke covered the beach. The men now embarked, and the boats had shoved off when a voice of desperation was heard shouting through the smoke. It was known that one of the party was missing, but although the voice could be clearly heard it was impossible to see its owner. Eventually he was found up to his chin in the water, having waded out as far as he could, a non-swimmer, afraid of the water, but much more terrified of the possibility of falling into the hands of the enraged Spaniards. He had had an overdose of brandy that morning and fallen into a sound sleep, from which he awoke to find himself being roasted by the raging fire. Drunkenness had suddenly given way to terror and sobriety, by the help of which he had succeeded in making his way to the beach.

As soon as Brett and his men had returned to the squadron, Anson prepared to leave. Before doing so he gave orders for five enemy vessels which had been at anchor in the bay to be towed out to sea and scuttled after removal of the masts. The sixth, the *Solidad*, he retained. He gave her command to Hughes, the lieutenant of the *Tryal*, with a crew of ten men to sail her. At midnight he weighed, and sailed his squadron of one man-of-war and five prizes out of the bay. These were:

| | | |
|---|---|---|
| *Centurion* | 60 guns | (Anson) |
| *Tryal's Prize* | 600 tons | (Saunders) |
| *Carmelo* | 500 tons | (Saumarez) |
| *Teresa* | 300 tons | (Denis) |
| *Carmine* | 270 tons | (Summers) |
| *Solidad* | — | (Hughes) |

And now an argument between those who had been selected to take active part in the assault on Paita, and those who had patiently remained on board, began to come to a head. Apart from the booty which had been safely stored in the *Centurion*, there was a considerable amount of private plunder which had been appropriated by the sailors on shore, and which they regarded as a bonus for their exertions. Those who had been forced to remain on board, however, pointed out that they also had played an arduous part, not only being denied the thrills of a run ashore, but working short-handed in the ship by day, and guarding prisoners by night. In addition to their unquestioned entitlement to a share of the main treasure, they considered that they had a right to a share of the personal plunder.

Anson addressed the ship's company assembled on the quarter deck of the *Centurion* at evening quarters. He commended and thanked all those who had been detached for duty ashore, and then firmly said that he thought it fair that there should be an equal distribution of plunder in proportion to each man's rank and commission. In order to show that he had no personal interest in the matter, he offered to forego his own share of the plunder, and to divide it among those who had been detached ashore.

Walter, the chaplain, commends such prudence and says that it was to the 'general satisfaction of the ship's company'. Thomas, the schoolmaster, however, was less commendatory at first, and says:

> This action appeared to be very generous; but who were all the fresh Provisions, Sheep, Hogs, Fowls, Pumpkins, Onions, Olives, Sweetmeats, etc. etc. etc. shared among? and to whom did they belong, and who wanted them most?
>
> He [Anson] then commanded that every Man should bring in his share of the Plunder to a common Stock, in order to an equal Division, and that every Man's Chest and Hammock should be search'd to prevent Concealments. This last injunction was . . . executed, and a very strict Search made among those who had nothing to conceal.

It sounds as though Thomas might have been one of those subjected to a very strict search, though with presumably nothing to conceal. At all events he appears to have been resentful and critical of Anson. When the division of plunder was actually made six days later, he had forgotten his reproaches, and had a very different story to relate:

The 22nd a Division was made of the Plunder of Paita, and the Commodore not appearing in that Affair, it was done at the Pleasure and to the entire Satisfaction of five or six (no doubt) very disinterested Officers; and indeed most Things of this Nature during the Course of the Voyage being managed with the same Discretion and Honour, no Room was left for complaining of particular Partialities.

Perhaps he had by then been invited to dine aft, and had fallen under the spell of Anson's company, while partaking of the hogs and fowls, and while imbibing the Commodore's wine.

# CHAPTER VII

# From Paita to Quibo, and the Search
# for the Galleon

ANSON's squadron of six ships, the *Centurion* with five prizes, sailed from Paita about midnight on 16th November, and stood to the westward. The following morning, Anson spread his ships to look for the *Gloucester*, in the rendezvous which he had ordered in the previous September upon leaving Juan Fernandez and prior to parting company with *Gloucester*. Nothing was sighted all day. The following morning at ten, however, a sail was seen. The squadron gave chase. By two in the afternoon they had closed her sufficiently to identify her as the *Gloucester*, with a small vessel in tow; and by three they had come up with her. Anson learnt from Mitchel, the captain, that they had only taken two prizes during the whole cruise, but had nevertheless found on board them plate and money to the value of £1,800 sterling. The *Gloucester*'s barge had come upon one of the prizes close inshore, and had found the occupants, who had pleaded great poverty, dining upon pigeon pie off silver dishes. There appeared to be nothing but jars of cotton on board, but after a careful search, it was revealed that each jar contained a considerable number of double doubloons and dollars concealed in the cotton. This treasure had been on its way to Paita.

But there was something else on board this prize which caught the fancy of Pascoe Thomas, who, like most of the people of those days, liked his victuals. Thomas says:

> On board this Prize of the *Gloucester* were two Horses, which being, I suppose, fat and probably better feeding

65

than their salt Beef or Pork, they killed and eat them; and this, I imagine, gave Ground to that Fiction which one of the spurious Accounts of our Voyage has given of our eagerly hunting and eating wild Horses, whereas in reality we never saw nor heard of a wild Horse during the Voyage.

Anson had at one time after arrival at Juan Fernandez, hoped to receive some reinforcements to his depleted force of men by cruising in the vicinity of the isthmus of Panama, and making contact with Admiral Vernon's fleet which had been sent to harass the Spaniards on the Atlantic side of the isthmus. He had even had ideas of taking Panama itself. Vernon had had a great success in 1739 in the taking of Porto Bello. The attack on Carthagena, however, in March and April 1741, though a brilliant success from the naval point of view, had ended in dismal failure strategically. The capable General Cathcart, having died of dysentery at Domenica, was succeeded by General Wentworth whose indecision and dilatoriness infuriated Vernon. Smollett, serving as a Surgeon's mate in one of Vernon's warships, wrote in his *History of England*:

The Admiral and General contracted a hearty contempt for each other and took all opportunities of expressing their mutual dislike; and each proved more eager for the disgrace of his rival than jealous for the honour of the nation.

Smollett gives a vivid if exaggerated description of the occasion:

... much less surprised that people should die on board than any should recover ... especially as our provision consisted of putrid salt beef, to which the sailors gave the name of Irish horse; salt pork of New England, which though neither fish nor flesh, savoured of both; bread from the same country, every biscuit whereof, like a piece of clockwork, moved by its own internal impulse occasioned by the myriad of insects that dwelt within it ... such was the scurvy in some ships, that, rather than be at the trouble of interring the dead, the Commanders ordered their men to throw their bodies overboard, many without either ballast or winding sheet; so that numbers of human carcasses floated in the harbour until they were devoured by sharks and carrion crows.

On capturing the *Carmelo*, Anson had found papers on board from which he learnt of this military disaster at Cartagena and of the unlikelihood of any further naval assault in that region which could give him any support.

Now that he had sacked Paita and rejoined *Gloucester*, it might be more profitable to take further prizes. He decided to steer northwards in search of the galleon which plied across the Pacific between Manila and Acalpulco in Mexico, carrying the richest prize in the world. This usually arrived in Acalpulco about January. The squadron was now eight strong, but Anson wishing for a less scattered distribution of his men, and finding that the *Santa Teresa* and the *Solidad* were both very slow ships, decided to abandon them. Anchors, cables, hawsers, yards, topmasts, blocks, and certain provisions were got out of them, and the two ships were then burnt. Provisions were also redistributed in the squadron, using the ships' boats, so that no ship would have provisions for less than six months. There still remained a shortage of water, for Paita had had no natural supply. Anson therefore determined to put in at Quibo, an island north of the equator outside the Bay of Panama, noted for its reliable water supply.

On 22nd November, they crossed the equator and experienced for the first time for many months the humid heat of the Doldrums, and missed the cooling breezes of the south-easterly trades. On 27th November, clearance of the *Gloucester*'s prize was completed, and she was scuttled and set on fire. The squadron now consisted of five ships, all good sailers, the *Centurion*, *Gloucester*, *Tryal's Prize*, *Carmelo*, and *Carmine*. They arrived at the island of Quibo, about 7° North latitude, on 4th December, and four of them anchored in thirty-three fathoms in the Canal Bueno (the Good Channel) at the south-east point of the island. The *Gloucester*, however, was forced to tack to the

southward in weathering Point Mariato, and then sprung her
fore-topmast. This prevented her from working to windward,
and delayed her from rejoining the squadron until 12th
December, three days after they had left Quibo and put to
sea in search of her.

While at Quibo the squadron derived benefit from the
turtles which abound there. Walter describes four species, and
dwells on the general value of the food:

> . . . the trunk turtle, the loggerhead, the hawksbill,
> and the green turtle. The two first are rank and unwhole-
> some; the hawksbill (which affords the tortoise-shell) is but
> indifferent food, though better than the other two: but
> the green turtle is generally esteemed, by the greatest part
> of those who are acquainted with its taste, to be the most
> delicious of all eatables.
>
> . . . we usually dispersed several of our men along the
> beach, whose business it was to turn them on their backs
> when they come to land.
>
> . . . When at the island of Quibo, we had already been
> 3 months on board, without otherwise putting our feet on
> shore than in the few days we stayed there (except those
> employed in the attack at Paita), yet in the whole seven
> months from our leaving Juan Fernandez to our anchoring
> in the harbour of Chequetan, we buried no more in the
> whole squadron than two men: a most incontestable proof
> that the turtle, on which we fed for the last four months
> of this term, was at least innocent, if not something more.

Thomas called them tortoises, and in any case was not of the
same mind as Walter. He writes:

> Here are abundance of Tortoises on the shore, of which
> we took on board eighteen or nineteen, with a great
> Quantity of their Eggs, which our People in general
> esteem very much, but which I, for my own Part, could
> never relish nor endure.

A few weeks later Thomas has changed his opinion and says:

We every day caught on the Water great Quantity of Tortoises, or, as the Seamen call them, Turtles, which were at this Time almost the only Food we made use of, being very good, and dress'd several different Ways, as roasted, baked, stew'd, boil'd, and the like. The Broth of them is good and nourishing, and in short without them we must have suffer'd extremely, at this Time our English Provisions of all sorts being very bad, and no fresh Supplies to be had in these Parts.

In comparing Walter's account of the voyage with the journal written by Thomas, one is conscious of more than a disparity of view, which sometimes amounts to an apparent clash of personality; perhaps a jealousy of the chaplain by the school-master. Both were presumably educated men, and both had much the same status as warrant officers on board, though it is probable that Walter, the chaplain, was much closer to Anson in disposition and outlook, and perhaps associated with him to a greater extent. Chaplains had been carried in ships for centuries, whereas the schoolmaster was a relatively recent arrival, having been introduced into the Fleet in the early part of the eighteenth century as a result of a memorandum presented to the Queen, in 1702, by the Earl of Pembroke, Lord High Admiral, stating: 'It being a very great consequence to the Nation that all possible care should be taken to instruct such Young Gentlemen who are, or shall hereafter be, appointed to serve as Volunteers in Her Fleet. . . .'

Anson was a strong supporter of such a doctrine.

Walter goes to great lengths to explain why Anson took the squadron to Quibo for water in preference to Cocos which had been suggested by some, and which seemed to find favour in Thomas' estimation. The different viewpoints are worth comparing. Walter says:

Quibo . . . the Commodore conceived this to be the properest place for watering the squadron. Indeed, there was a small island called Cocos, which was less out of our way than Quibo, where some of the buccaneers have pretended they found water: but none of our prisoners knew anything of it, and it was thought too dangerous to risque the safety of the squadrons, by exposing ourselves to the hazard of our meeting with water when we came there, on the mere authority of these legendary writers, of whose misrepresentations and falsities we had almost daily experience.

Thomas writes of Cocos as if he had proffered advice which was ignored:

This Island is reputed to be very fruitful and pleasant, and to produce limes, Cacao Nuts, and the like in abundance; as also to abound in Hogs, and good Water, as well as to have convenient Landing; from whence I have often wondered that our Rendezvous for watering in our Passage from Peru to Mexico should rather be ordered at the Island of Quibo than at this Place, . . . it would have been more to our Advantage if this last had been pitch'd on.

On 12th December, Anson left Quibo, and on being joined by the *Gloucester* stood to the westward in the hope of picking up the trade wind. Fresh instructions were now given for the immediate and successive rendezvous in case of separation, and courses to steer. The plan was to make for Acapulco in Mexico with all speed to intercept the Manila galleon. Instead of meeting the trades they had hoped for, they experienced dead calms interspersed with violent storms; when the wind did begin to freshen steadily, it came from the west. A month passed in this way. When the wind did choose to be favourable, it blew very hard from the north-east: *Centurion* took *Carmelo* in tow, as did the *Gloucester* the *Carmine*, so that they could reap as much benefit as possible from the wind. This was at least fortunate for one man in the *Centurion*, a sailmaker's mate, who when fishing from the end of the jib boom, lost his hold, and fell over the bows into the sea. The *Centurion*, making six or seven knots, passed right over him. An alarm was immediately sounded. The *Carmelo*, in tow astern of the *Centurion* threw out several heaving lines. As she came up to the man struggling in the water he was able to catch a line and twist it round his arm.

He was hauled on board with no injury other than a wrenched arm.

It was not until the end of January that they neared Acapulco, and there were great fears that the galleon must by now have sailed for Manila. Hope had practically deserted them when at ten o'clock on the night of 29th January, a light was sighted bearing north-north-east. At the same time, the *Tryal's Prize* in advance of the squadron about a mile ahead, reported a sail. There could be little doubt that this was the galleon. Hands were immediately sent to action stations. *Centurion* cast off her tow, as did *Gloucester*, and the ships pressed forward with all canvas. Anson, expecting a short engagement, ordered that the big guns should be loaded with two round shot for the first broadside, and one round shot with grape for the second. Nothing was to be fired until they arrived within pistol shot of the enemy.

There was great expectation of coming up with the light, but the quarry appeared to outsail them. It was not until daylight that the truth was revealed. The light they had been chasing was only a distant heath fire on shore.

After further cruising without success, Anson decided to send the barge inshore to investigate, with Denis, the lieutenant, in charge. Through paucity of accurate navigational information, the barge had to make two trips, and on each occasion was absent many days.

On returning on the second occasion on 19th February, the barge brought back information that the galleon was already at Acapulco, and was preparing for sea, her departure for Manila having been arranged by the Viceroy of Mexico for 3rd March. It was learnt that during her eastbound journey from Manila she was loaded with merchandise of silks and spices to the value of two or three million dollars, leaving Manila about July and arriving in Acapulco in December, January, or February, according to wind and weather. Having disposed of merchandise at Acapulco she generally sailed in March to arrive at Manila in June. The largest of the ships employed on this run was of the size of a first-rate man-of-war, and carried fifty guns.

It was further learned that the squadron's presence had not yet been revealed; a guard at the harbour mouth at Acapulco had recently been withdrawn on the basis that as considerable time had elapsed since Anson had last been heard of, he must have gone elsewhere.

Ships' bottoms were now scrubbed clean as far as possible, and operation orders were prepared and promulgated for the great occasion of intercepting the galleon when she sailed on 3rd March. On 1st March Anson took up station sufficiently far from Acapulco to avoid being seen, but with his ships spread in the arc of a circle, so that nothing could slip through undiscovered. At night, two cutters were sent in to watch at the harbour mouth. On sighting the galleon, one was to follow her and make flares, the other was to return to the squadron to report which way she had sailed, east or west. The *Centurion*'s and *Gloucester*'s complements were reinforced by hands from the three prizes, so that as many guns as possible in the warships could be operated. It had been said that the galleon was heavily armed and manned. Gun drill and small arms practice were carried out every day. As 3rd March came nearer, impatience grew, and everyone was eager for action. As the day dawned, hopes were high. Hour after hour passed, and nothing was sighted. The following day similarly. And then day after day passed, and still no sign of the galleon. At first there was the feeling that there had been a small postponement, but as days grew into weeks, dejection spread, and it began to be thought that the presence of the squadron must have become known.

Anson was already of this opinion, and considered carefully a plan to take Acapulco by surprise. Surprise would have to be complete, otherwise the treasure would be removed from the town before he could lay hands on it. He knew that in addition to the galleon's crew there was a strong garrison, a fort, and a thousand well armed men; but reckoned that two hundred of his men landed at night, and supported by fire from his ships, could quickly take the town and the treasure. On close examination, however, he learnt that inshore winds died away to a calm during the night, and were succeeded before dawn by offshore, and therefore contrary winds. Under the circumstances he was forced to drop the scheme, and decided to continue his vigil for as long as his supplies of wood and water held out. Here he remained until 23rd March, and it is interesting to reflect that it was touch and go whether the galleon would be allowed to leave Acapulco as planned. The Viceroy of Mexico had said no, as soon as Anson's presence had been reported to him, but very strong representations had been made by the merchants whose livelihood depended on the cargo of the galleon, and attention was called by them to the fact that Anson's ships had by now kept the sea too long to offer much of a threat to a well found and well armed galleon whose complement would be more than double Anson's total of three hundred men divided among a few rotten ships.

Anson left the Acapulco station on 23rd March to go to Chequetan, latitude about $17\frac{1}{2}°$ North, for water, and although he had given up hope of the galleon's emerging, he left the cutter behind, manned by Hughes the lieutenant of the *Tryal's Prize*, and six picked men, with orders to cruise for twenty-four days off Acapulco. Anson then worked up to the westward along the coast, but through calms and contrary winds it was not until 7th April that he, in the *Centurion*, together with the *Gloucester*, arrived at the harbour of Chequetan. The *Carmelo* and *Carmine* had fallen off to leeward but were rounded up by the *Tryal's Prize* and joined three days later. It was four months since the squadron had left Quibo their last watering place, and their stock of water had now fallen to an amount which would last but six days more.

During his slow passage to Chequetan, Anson had determined on a new plan, and had decided to sail westward across the Pacific to China, in compliance with his instructions:

> If you shall find no occasion for your staying longer in those seas, and shall judge it best to go to the northward as far as Acapulco, or to look out for the Acapulco ship which sails from that place for Manila at a certain time of the year and generally returns at a certain time also, you may possibly, in that case, think it most advisable to return home by the way of China, which you are authorized to do, or to return home by Cape Horn, as you shall think best for our service, and for the preservation of the ships and the men on board them.

'The men on board them.' How few of them had survived. The total, about three hundred, was scarcely enough to man a fourth-rate, let alone to keep the five ships of the squadron at sea. Anson had already resolved to destroy the *Carmelo* and *Carmine*, and to send their officers and men to supplement the crews of the *Centurion* and *Gloucester*; even before arrival at Chequetan, preparations for the unloading of these two prizes had begun. He now decided that the *Tryal's Prize* must go too, although she was a fine, large ship, a good sailer, and compared with the others, in fair repair. His decision rested mainly on the prospect of difficulties which would face them when they met severe storms or encountered an enemy, and was reputed to be backed up both by Mitchel, captain of the *Gloucester* who sorely needed the men, and by Saunders, captain of the *Tryal's Prize*, who considered his ship unfit for the long passage ahead. Although Walter makes no mention of the fact, there is evidence that this decision caused much heartburning in the *Tryal's Prize*, probably stemming from John Pack, the boatswain of the *Tryal's Prize*, who had great pride of her and who was most reluctant to destroy such a fine ship. Moreover there was a bigger issue in the loss of position and other entitlements of the officers, which is referred to in the narrative of Millechamp the purser, and his description of the appeal made to Anson by the officers of the *Tryal's Prize*.

Pascoe Thomas writes:

*April 1742*
    The 28th we paid the Ships Sides with Pitch and Oil, in order to preserve them from the Heat of the Sun; we likewise fixed a Pair each of new main and fore Shrouds; and the *Tryal's Prize* having been sometime before condemn'd, either from a Representation of Captain Mitchel's that he could not proceed to India with the *Gloucester* without more Hands, or, as others say, from a Representation of Captain Saunders's that the said Ship, the *Tryal's Prize*, was unfit and incapable to perform this Passage: (whatever one, or both, or neither of these by the Truth I can't aver, but this I know, that some of the Warrant Officers in that Ship petition'd against it, tho'

without effect) I say, the *Tryal's Prize* having been condemn'd, some of her Officers and People were disposed of on board of us, and the Remainder on board the *Gloucester*: And being now quite ready for the Sea, we this Evening tow'd on Shore the three Prizes among the Rocks to the Eastward of the Watering-place, scuttled them, and placed proper combustibles for firing them.

It will be remembered that Lieutenant Hughes had on the 23rd March been left behind to cruise off Acapulco in the cutter, a twenty-two foot boat, with six men, to watch for the galleon's departure, which it was thought might be attempted if news leaked ashore that Anson had left Acapulco. Nothing more had been heard or seen of them. They had been instructed to return after twenty-four days, and it was now assumed that they must have been seen and been taken prisoners.

Thomas continues:

> The next Morning we unmoor'd, and having fix'd a small canoe on proper Moorings, and therein a Bottle with a Letter in it for Mr. Hughes, in case he should come there after our Departure, at Four we set the Prizes on Fire, and at Six weigh'd; and the Wind blowing on the Shore, we warp'd out of the Bay or Harbour, till at Two in the Afternoon, having sufficient Searoom, we split and made Sail.

Anson was determined to look for them on his way westward, and prepared a letter to be sent to the Governor of Acapulco, proposing the release of Hughes and his men in exchange for all the Spanish and Indian prisoners that remained in the squadron.

## CHAPTER VIII

# Petition by the Officers of the *Tryal*

IN appointing officers to command the small prize crews which he sent to each prize, Anson had made no promotions. It seems likely that he had in mind all along, the passage he was to undertake across the Pacific, and was aware that he would ultimately need to abandon his prizes, and concentrate all his men in *Centurion* and *Gloucester*. Even with this concentration there would be few enough to work the ships over a long and arduous sea passage, and man the guns when engaging the enemy.

There had been a difference, however, in the case of the *Tryal's Prize* which had been commissioned as a King's ship, with a direct transfer of the captain, Saunders, and the officers and men from the *Tryal*, when she had been destroyed, so that each retained in his new ship, his original status and entitlement.

The destruction first of the *Teresa* and *Solidad*, and later the *Carmelo* and *Carmine*, enabled the officers in charge and the prize crews to return to their ships in their original capacity. The destruction of the *Tryal's Prize*, however, would cause her officers to be out of a job, since there were no vacancies for their particular appointments in the remaining ships the *Centurion* and *Gloucester*. On transfer they would become supernumeraries.

The point is important, and was to lead to a famous High Court action at the end of the voyage, which lasted for years. Walter makes no mention of it, but the opinion of Pascoe Thomas on this subject is given in the extract from his Journal of 28th April 1742. (See previous chapter.)

Lawrence Millechamp, the purser of the *Tryal's Prize*,

describes fully in his narrative, the apprehension of himself and his brother officers concerning the loss of status and emoluments which they anticipated as soon as the *Tryal's Prize* should be destroyed. Saunders, the captain, by this time a great friend of Anson, and confident of his integrity and support, suffered no such apprehensions, but was filled with doubt about the fitness of his ship for the arduous passage that lay ahead. It is also certain that he wished to support Anson in any decision he made. In this he was backed up by his lieutenant Hughes.

The warrant officers of the *Tryal's Prize*, John Pack the Boatswain, James Barcroft the Gunner, John Shepherd the Carpenter, Joseph Allen the Surgeon, John Young, and Lawrence Millechamp the Purser, thereupon prepared a petition and presented it to Anson. Millechamp describes the events:

The officers of *Tryal's Prize* apprehending the Losses they must necessarily sustain and the inconveniences they should meet with on being put on Board any other ship and Captain Saunders having told them that the Commodore had offer'd to commission the *Carmine* for them but that he Captain Saunders had refused her, they resolv'd to present him the following Petition:

'To George Anson Esq. Commodore and Commander-in-Chief of His Majesty's Ships design'd on a particular Expedition.

'The Humble Petition of the Officers of His Majesties Ship *Tryal Prize* Humbly sheweth. That your Petitioners while on Board his Majesty's Sloop *Tryal* met with most unaccountable difficulties and Misfortunes not only by the Extream Violence of the Weather in coming Round Cape Horn, but also by dreadfull Sickness and want of proper Diet, Necessary's and Conveniences; notwithstanding which, in the Terrible Condition they were in your Petitioners did Exert their remains of strength to the utmost of their power, and by their indefatigable Labour and Industry and Toil, together with the joint Assistance of Captain Saunders, Mr. Hughes and about one seaman, did manage and bring the said Sloop safe to an anchor at Juan Fernandez.

'Your Petitioners then Imagined Their Misfortunes at end and thought themselves sure they were so, after their second Danger of Valparaiso you were pleas'd to commission the *Aransaso* Prize and give them Warrants for her, But alas your Petitioners have been lately informed by Captain Saunders that you think it for his Majesty's Service to sink her, which without appointing some other for them, will greatly increase their Misfortunes they being almost all marry'd Men, with Family's and must observe that a small time lost in the first setting out of Mankind is not easily retreiv'd.

'Your Petitioners humbly beg leave to acquaint you that the *Nuestra Señora del Carmin* has been represented to them by Mr. Young, as a good Sound Bottom and capable of making a Voyage to any part of the World.

'Your Petitioners therefore most humbly pray you will be pleas'd to take their Melancholy Circumstances into Consideration, and of your great goodness to appoint the said ship a Ship in his Majesty's pay and continue them in their respective Stations on board her with such number of Men as you shall think meet and your Petitioners as in Duty bound Shall ever pray etc.

Jno Pack, Jas Barcroft, Jno Shepherd,<br/>Jno Young, Jo Allen, La Millechamp

*Tryal Prize*
1 April 1742.'

When this Petition was delivered the Commodore replied that he could not help destroying the *Tryal Prize* as hands were needed for the *Gloucester*: The officers need not worry for there was no doubt that they would be continued on the pay list and would be used to fill various vacancies as they arose. He would recommend them as soon as they arrived in England and he would send them an answer in writing.

It is important to notice that there is no reference to prize money, and there is no guarantee of any employment by Anson for the officers and their servants: they are to be supernumeraries.

The men, however, were to become part complement. Anson's letter to Captain Mitchel of the *Gloucester* says:

Jno Pack—Boatswain
Jno Barcroft—Gunner
L. Millechamp—Purser
etc. . . .

'You are hereby required and directed to receive on Board his Majesty's Ship *Gloucester* under your Command the twenty-five Men named within Margin being Officers & Servants, Petty Officers Seamen & Marines late belonging to his Majesty's Ship *Tryal Prize* bearing the Warrant Officers and Servants as Supernumerarys with their proper Qualifications, the Petty Officers, Seamen & Marines of Colonel Robinson's Detachment as part of your Complement, Victualling all of them as you do the Ships Company during their continuance on board you, for which this shall be your Warrant. Given under my Hand this twenty ninth day of April 1742 at Chequetan.

To Capt. Mathew Mitchel          G. ANSON
    Commander of His Majesty's
    Ship *Gloucester*.'

Millechamp sums it up:

Can any reasonable being whatsoever imagine from these Orders that the Officers of the *Tryal Prize* were not intitled to their Pay and any Prize Money that should be taken while they continued on Board either of these Ships? does it not here plainly appear even under the hand of the Commanding Officer that the *Tryal Prize* was Destroy'd for the Preservation of the two other Ships, & does it not also plainly appear that all the Men belonging to these Ships were not so many as the Complement of one of the fourth Rates; and God knows we at that time had a thousand Difficulties to encounter & the least of them full as terrible as the Engaging the Galleon.

Anson's letter left little doubt that pay would be continued to the supernumeraries, 'with their proper Qualification,' but the question of entitlement to prize money was not mentioned. Temporarily at any rate, it looks as though Millechamp and his brother officers were satisfied with Anson's assurance, though a little doubtful about the official interpretation which might be placed on it. This was not the end of the story. This small party transferred to their new ship the *Gloucester* as ordered by Anson. But this was not to be their last transfer, and we shall hear of further developments first hand from Millechamp, and his opinion of Anson, at a later stage in the voyage.

# CHAPTER IX

# The End of the *Gloucester*

It was at the end of April that Anson, having watered and wooded the *Centurion* and *Gloucester* at Chequetan and made repairs, and transferred everything possible from the three prizes before destroying them, sailed westward to look for Hughes off Acapulco prior to setting course for China.

While at Chequetan he had been particularly careful about stragglers ashore, as he was apprehensive that news of his intention to cross the Pacific in search of the galleon might leak out and frustrate his plans. It was already becoming apparent that the Viceroy had delayed the sailing of the galleon; perhaps had cancelled the sailing altogether for this reason.

Nevertheless in spite of his precautions and strict orders, and the provision of a guard near the watering place ashore at Chequetan, not only for the purpose of repelling attacks but to prevent the curious wandering further afield, one of his men, Louis Leger, had been reported missing. This man was the Commodore's cook, a Frenchman, and a Papist, and at first it was suspected that he had deserted. In fact he had been carried off by Indians while attempting to get some limes for his master's store, had been stripped naked, and ill used. He was subsequently taken as a prisoner to Acapulco, then to Mexico, then to Vera Cruz, and then was shipped on board a vessel bound for Spain. By an accident the ship put into Lisbon where Leger escaped and reported to the British Consul who sent him to England. The importance of this escape was that Leger was the first to reach England to report the safe rounding of the Horn by Anson and his subsequent actions up to the time of arrival at

81

Chequetan. It is ironical that this man survived the hazards of the passage round the Cape, had missed death by scurvy, and after ill use by the Indians and tortuous journeys, had escaped at Lisbon, only to arrive in England to meet eventual disaster; he was killed in a brawl at night in London.

Pascoe Thomas' description is of interest:

> About the 13th or 14th, if I mistake not, LEJERE a FRENCHMAN, the Commodore's Master-Cook, having been on Shore, was missing at Night. This, together with the Fellow's being a Roman Catholick and of a mutinous Temper, made us imagine he had deserted to the Enemy, in order to give them an Account of our Strength and Designs as far as he knew; but the Man himself arriving in England gave this account of it, to wit, that rambling about a Mile or two without our Centinels in order to pick some Lemons for the Commodore, he was surprised in the Woods by a Party of Indians, who made him Prisoner, and at first used him very ill and threatened to kill him, but on his humble submission caused him to be convey'd to Mexico, from whence after Some Time he was carried to La Vera Cruz, on the North Seas, and thence by some Means or other made shift to get to England. This is his own Account of the Matter; and I think, considering that he used his best Endeavours and Expedition to return to England, we ought in Charity to believe him. Since our Arrival I am sorry to hear that this poor Fellow was barbarously murder'd at London, by some Ruffians in a Night Rencounter; the Particulars of which are not come to my Knowledge.

By Sunday 2nd May, Anson was once again off Acapulco, and the following day sent in a Spanish officer together with six other prisoners in one of the captured launches to take to the Governor his offer of an exchange of prisoners. For two days he cruised at a great distance, having been driven off by off-shore winds. At eleven on the morning of 5th May, a cry from the masthead reported a sail at a considerable distance to the south-eastward. Anson now closed the sail which was believed to provide the Governor's reply, and to the great joy of all on board it was found to be their own cutter with Hughes and his six men on board, all alive, but wan and meagre in appearance, with long beards. They had been cruising for six weeks, during which time they had been swept two hundred and fifty miles to the eastward and back again. They had at one time run out of water, were unable to put into any watering place because of dangerous surf, but had had a miraculous relief by the arrival of a heavy rain storm when they had been on the point of death from thirst. They were certainly brave, determined men following the pattern set by Anson himself.

Walter says:

> . . . the crew of the cutter, consisting of six men and the lieutenant, were the very flower of our people, purposely picked out for this service, and known to be everyone of them of tried and approved resolution, and as skilful seamen as ever trod a deck.

Pascoe Thomas, however, implied that their valour may have been at the expense of discretion:

> They told us that if they had miss'd us, they design'd to have run down into the Bay of Panama, and taken a Bark, in order to transport them to Asia, for they were resolv'd to have died to the last Man rather than have fallen into the Hands of the Spaniards. They were certainly seven brave stout Men, yet I think their heroick Scheme had more Madness than Reason in it, as might easily be shewn, were it worth while to detain the reader . . .

Having recovered the cutter with Hughes and his six men, Anson, who was anxious not to lose any more time in his departure for China, immediately sent ashore the remaining Spanish and Indian prisoners. Two captured launches were equipped with masts, sails, and oars, and a stock of water and provisions for fourteen days, and embarked thirty-nine prisoners from the *Centurion* and eighteen from the *Gloucester*. They eventually arrived safely, and were full of praise for the treatment they had received from Anson while in captivity. The

Governor had already replied with courtesy to Anson's letter, and had moreover sent out two boats laden with choice refreshments and provisions which he intended as a present for Anson. His boats were unable to find Anson's ships, and returned to port after being forced to throw their gifts overboard in a storm which threatened their destruction.

By 6th May, the squadron had lost sight of the land astern, and was at last making for the south-westward with the object of picking up the north-east trades and then sailing westward along the parallel of $13\frac{1}{2}°$ North which was the track normally taken by the galleon on her westerly leg to Manila. If the galleon had by any chance slipped out unseen, Anson hoped to catch her, for she was unlikely to be as fast a sailer as either *Centurion* or *Gloucester*. There had been great hopes of a fast passage which would take no more than two months. Nevertheless it was seven weeks before the squadron at length entered the trade wind belt, having in the meantime made little progress. Moreover the ships were now becoming crazy and frail, and easily suffered damage. *Centurion* sprung her foremast. No sooner had this been repaired than *Gloucester* sprung her mainmast, which on examination was found to be so rotten and decayed that it had to be cut down by twenty-six feet to a short stump on which to step the topmast. This slowed down the progress of both ships. But the worst event was the return of scurvy. With expectation of a fast passage, the maintenance of clean and airy conditions between decks, and the provision of abundant rain water and fresh fish, it had been hoped to keep the squadron free of this devastating complaint. Discovery of these first and growing symptoms, together with the unexpected slowness of the voyage, now produced a melancholy outlook which was itself a condition that accelerated the disease. The surgeon of the *Centurion* had attributed the heavy mortality suffered during the passage around the Horn to the severity of the climate and the exclusion of fresh air due to the necessity to batten down the ship in the tempestuous weather. This no longer applied. Nevertheless, Walter ascribes the trouble to the pollution of the air on board, and his theory is of interest when one bears in mind tales that one hears in the present day from people who have suffered strange complaints, causing among other things discoloration of the flesh, due to living in old houses reputed to be full of dry rot. These same people have got well, on moving from the vicinity of the dry rot.

It is almost certain that the benefit of limes and lemons were known or believed in by some, but little mention is made of this, though it is of interest to recollect that the Commodore's cook was ashore in search of limes when he was captured.

Walter says:

> . . . as a continued supply of fresh air is necessary to all animal life, and as this air is so particular a fluid that, without losing its elasticity, or any of its obvious properties, it may be rendered unfit for this purpose by the mixing with it some very subtle and otherwise imperceptible effluvia; it may easily be conceived, I say, that the steams arising from the ocean may have a tendency to render the air they are spread through less properly adapted to the support of the life of terrestrial animals, unless these steams are corrected by effluvia of another kind, which perhaps the land alone can afford.

This remark reminds one of the story of a man far gone with scurvy, not expected to recover, who was carried ashore, and asked to be buried up to his neck in the earth. He recovered.

Thomas wrote in his journal:

> 11th June 1742
>
> And much about this Time abundance of scorbutick Symptoms, such as Blackness in the Skin, hard Nodes in the Flesh, Shortness of Breath, and a general Lassitude and Weakness of all the Parts, began to prevail, almost universally, among our People. This with the great Mortality we experienced from this Distemper in our Cape Horn Passage, and the Time we might still expect to be at sea; and no Trade Wind being yet settled: These Considerations, I say, gave us dreadful Apprehensions of what this Passage might terminate in, and the Event shewed that we had but too much Reason for them.

Thomas himself became afflicted with the disease a few weeks later. He describes his symptoms, which began with a pain in the toe, slowly spreading to the whole body, the flesh gradually turning black. He has little use for Henry Ettrick the surgeon, who although a good practical surgeon was full of words and theories that had no meaning or were inconsistent.

Anson had a quantity of Ward's Pills and Drops which were experimental. After first trying them on himself he gave them to the surgeon for issue to those who wanted them. According to both Walter and Thomas they generally caused violent 'Vomit and Stool' producing a temporary alleviation followed by a relapse at a later stage.

During this passage, Thomas writes a complaint in his journal, about the price of fish, which may again be a criticism of Anson.

> . . . the *Gloucester*, when they could find Opportunity to fish, had always much greater Success than we; whether their Fishermen had more Art than ours, or whatever else occasion'd it, the Fact is true: They had also a better Way of disposing of them, when taken, if I may be allow'd to judge, than we; for Captain Mitchel constantly ordered several Boys, who were very dexterous at it, to catch Fish for the Ship's Company, especially the Sick: and these were very justly and regularly divided among them; Whereas our Fisherman were left alone to make their Advantage of what they took, and prey on their Fellow Sufferers; and they took care not to overslip the Opportunity, for the least Fish you could purchase of them would cost you a Bottle of Brandy; which at this Time was worth four, or perhaps six, nay sometimes eight shillings, or Half a Guinea; and you must be very thankful, and acknowledge yourself to be highly obliged into the Bargain, or else expect None next Time, and very often fail of it notwithstanding.

This has a familiar ring. But we must be lenient to poor Mr. Thomas, for his pay at that time was only that of a Midshipman Ordinary: twenty-four shillings a month. And he was already a sick man in dire need of fresh food.

*Gloucester* and *Centurion* had both suffered serious defects. Further were now to follow. The trade wind favoured them from the end of June for most of July, and then gave way to a westerly. This in itself was dispiriting, but was attended by a further misfortune when the *Gloucester*, rolling badly, carried away her fore-topmast and smashed her fore yard. For ten days repairs were carried out with the assistance of twenty men from the *Centurion*, the *Gloucester* being taken in tow. Scarcely had these repairs been completed when a storm arose and *Gloucester* sprung a leak. The next day her fore-topmast again went by the board. This was quickly followed by the jury mainmast. The terror that slowly spread through the ship can be realized from an extract of Millechamp's narrative:

> The *Gloucester* having sett her Jury Mast we sail'd slowly on and were in the most terrible apprehension of all Dying before the ships could reach any Port.

By this time she had seven feet of water in the hold in spite of the pump being kept working continuously. Her crew had by now been reduced through scurvy to seventy-seven men, eighteen boys, and two prisoners; and three-quarters of the crew were sick.

*Centurion* had also sprung a leak and this was so severe that every available man and officer had to man the pumps. It was obvious that the two ships could not continue with their depleted complements. Both were in a very bad way, neither wishing to admit defeat, but each needing more hands if they were to survive. Mitchel of the *Gloucester* applied in writing to Anson for help. Anson sent his carpenter on board *Gloucester* to examine and report. This man confirmed that the stern post had worked loose and that the ship herself was extremely decayed in every part. It was also obvious that her crew were so sick and fatigued that the work of pumping could not continue. She had no spare masts, and the vital repairs could not in any case take place at sea.

The decision was now taken to destroy the *Gloucester*. Millechamp writes on 13th August 1742:

Mr. Anson plainly seeing it was impossible to save either of the ships without destroying the other prudently resolv'd to destroy the *Gloucester* as being the smallest and most Disabled ship of the two.

Anson's order for the destruction of the *Gloucester* made it clear, however, that it was done in order to save the men of the *Gloucester*, as it was evident from his carpenter's survey that the ship could not be saved. This is slightly different from Millechamp's implication that one or other ship had to go because each needed more hands. It also fails to acknowledge the fact that *Centurion* could not have survived without the additional hands.

At the first favourable opportunity Anson ordered Mitchel and his crew to transfer to *Centurion*. These included Millechamp and the warrant officers of the *Tryal's Prize*, who had previously petitioned against transfer to *Gloucester*, where they had become supernumeraries. Those stores that were still above water, and some of the prize money, were put on board *Centurion*, but this took two whole days, for the work was difficult due to the excessive slow rolling of the waterlogged ship, and the paucity and feebleness of the men available to carry out the work. Four of the sick died while being hoisted into their new vessel.

It was decided to blow up the *Gloucester* to avoid any chance of her falling into the hands of the Spaniards who were in possession of the island of Guam. There were many difficulties of navigation in those days, not only through the absence of a reliable chronometer, but also due to the uncertainty of the longitude attributed to certain places on various charts. At this time Anson was uncertain of his longitude but believed himself to be not far to the eastward of the Marian Islands or Ladrones, for which he was steering along the parallel of latitude of $13\frac{1}{2}°$ North. Guam was one of these and could not now be far away. It must be avoided at all costs.

On 15th August, at eight in the evening, the *Gloucester* was set on fire, her hold now almost full of water. At four the next morning her magazine blew up and she sank from view. From the *Centurion*, now twelve miles distant, all that could be seen was a vast pillar of black smoke reaching to a considerable distance into the sky. This must have been a sad moment for Mitchel who had lost his command, and for Anson who was now left with but one ship of that gallant squadron that had left St. Helen's almost two years ago.

It is interesting to read the final passages in the *Gloucester's* journal for the period 3rd November 1740 to 16th August 1742, which can be seen at the Public Record Office. Mitchel's comments are important, as they establish beyond doubt that the ship could not be saved, and that the transfer to *Centurion* was essential. This point will be referred to in a later chapter. Of all his crew only nineteen were 'tolerably well', . . . 'and some of these incapable of any Duty soon after they went out of the Ship.'

Remarkable Observations and Accidents H.M.S. *Gloucester*
Mathew Mitchel

Saturday Aug 14 1742.

I called a consultation of all my officers, and it was their opinion that it was impossible for us to save the ship for the following reasons (viz)

She has sprung a leak and gains on us tho' constantly pumping.

She has no mast except in the foremast region and mizon topmast nor any spare mast fit to be got up, her knees and clamps are work'd quite loose.

She has but 77 men, 18 boys and 2 prisoners, including officers, of which 16 men and 11 small boys keep the deck tho' very infirm, all the rest violently afflicted with the Scurvey. Both officers and men and boys have work'd 24 hours at the Pump without intermission and are so fatigued that they cannot stand to it any longer.

That there was 7 foot of water in the well, that we could not come at any fresh water to drink.

This was what I sent to the Commodore and early in the morning he sent me an order to send all Sick men on board the *Centurion* and what stores I could get out and to transport officers & what few men I had on board the *Centurion* as soon as possible.

Mon 16 Aug.

I left the Ship on fire and went on board the *Centurion* according to the orders I rec'd from Commodore Anson. I found the *Centurion* very leaky and hardly men to work.

The following are the only people that went out of the Ship tolerably well, Mr. Baird 1st lieut., John Pack Boatswain, Robert Lesly Boats Mate, James Hall, Alex Nesmith, Surgeons Mate, John Ashley Corporal, James Walker Ships Steward, Alex Jamieson Captain's Man, John Bell Swabber of Steerage, Robt. Orme, Wm. Curtis, Jos. Smart, 3 Lads and 4 Small boys, and some of these incapable of any Duty soon after they went out of the Ship.

Swabber of Steerage must have been a relatively healthy job. Millechamp wrote a stirring account of the *Gloucester*'s end.

She burnt all Night making a most Grand Horrid Appearance, her Guns which were all Loaded, Fired so regularly at about the Distance of a Minute between each, as the Fire came to them, that they sounded like Manning Guns, such as are fired at the Funeral of some great Officer: at Six a Clock the next Morning the Fire having reach'd her Powder Room, where was upwards of 200 Barrels of Gun Powder, she Blew up: we soon after heard the Report which sounded like a great Clap of distant Thunder. Thus ended the *Gloucester*, a Ship justly esteem'd the Beauty of the English Navy.

It might be expected that there would be reason for satisfaction now that *Centurion* was unencumbered by a defective ship. In fact conditions were appalling, for not only was sickness increasing, but the wind had dropped completely since the last storm, and it was found that the ship had been driven four degrees of latitude to the northward of her track. Six, eight, sometimes twelve men died every day.

Thomas writes in his Journal:

We were at this Time in a miserable Condition, the ship Considerably lumber'd with Prize Goods, and the

Small Room we had left throng'd with the Sick, whose Numbers were now very much increas'd with those from the *Gloucester*; the Dirt, Nauseousness, and Stench almost every where intolerable, more People daily disabled with the Disease, no Sign of Land, but very little Wind, and that fair but variable, very bad Provisions and Water, and the Ship very leaky.

If they missed the Ladrones, the next land was fifteen hundred miles away, and in their present condition there would be little hope of surviving that journey. Calms continued during which the carpenters did their best to shore up the leak in *Centurion's* bows. The leak was reduced, but water nevertheless continued to enter under the breast hook on each side of the stem. Then a gale sprang up from the south-west.

But on 22nd August, a week after the sinking of the *Gloucester*, they encountered a favourable current setting them to the southward. Hopes were now raised. The next day two islands were sighted and there was tremendous joy. A boat was sent to examine one and returned with the devastating news that it was barren. Sixty coconuts were brought off, but it was reported that there was no water and no good anchoring place. They had landed only with considerable difficulty because of a heavy swell. Melancholy now spread throughout the ship and was not completely dispelled the next morning when three further islands were discovered. The sick and the disconsolate were now of the opinion that most of the islands would be barren, and those that were not barren would, like Guam, be occupied by the Spaniards. Death faced them whichever way they looked. Either by scurvy or destitution, if left on board; or by hanging or the sword, if taken by the Spaniards.

*Centurion* steered for the middlemost of these islands which they believed to be Tinian. The current was still favourable, but the wind remained light. Progress was very slow. Anson was determined that no information of his presence and sad condition should reach the Spaniards at Guam, if it could be avoided. He attempted to disguise *Centurion* as the Manila galleon, hoisted a red flag at the fore-topmast head and Spanish colours aft, and took the precaution of mustering all hands who were well enough to use small arms. Upper and quarter deck guns were loaded with grape shot. The cutter was now sent in shore to find a good anchorage. At the same time a proa was seen to leave shore and make for the cutter, its occupants certain in their minds that this was the Manila galleon. In a short while the cutter returned with the proa in tow. A Spaniard and four Indians were the occupants, and upon examination it seemed that the island and its facilities exceeded the voyagers' wildest hopes. It had good water, an abundance of fruit, and an incredible amount of cattle, pigs, and poultry. This Spaniard was the only one in the island, and was in charge of the provisions which the Spanish Garrison at Guam stored here. There were twenty-two Indians and a small barque of fifteen tons.

There was inexpressible joy throughout the ship. Anson immediately had the pinnace sent in to secure the barque and prevent any escape of the inhabitants. Here was a paradise, and everybody summoned as much energy and spirit as was possible. No more than seventy-one hands could be mustered, and they were so feeble that it took five hours to furl the sails after *Centurion* had anchored in twenty-two fathoms. Such was the state of the residue of Anson's squadron on 27th August 1742, a squadron which had sailed less than two years before, 1,510 strong.

# CHAPTER X

# Marooned Ashore at Tinian

On the morning following the arrival at Tinian, a party of twenty men under the second lieutenant was sent ashore to occupy the landing place and ascertain what sort of opposition might be expected. The intention was to set up as soon as possible tents for the sick. The party was well armed and included Walter the chaplain. They met no opposition, for the Indians had withdrawn to the woods in fear. To their delight they found huts ready for immediate occupation, and one large store-house which was adapted as a hospital.

For two days the work of carrying the sick ashore went on. First they had to be got up out of the ship and carried in their hammocks into a boat, then rowed ashore, and finally carried up the beach in their hammocks on the men's shoulders, and into the huts ashore. Anson himself assisted in this work, and every one of his officers. With many it was a race against time. Walter relates how incredible were the immediate benefits of being landed. On these two days during which a hundred and twenty-eight sick men were landed, twenty-one died. And yet in the remaining two months of their stay on this island they lost no more than ten altogether. One of those landed on the first day was Pascoe Thomas; 'extremely ill and helpless,' he writes in his Journal. The scene can be imagined, with the few fit fully occupied not only with the transport of the sick, but with all sorts of tasks including defence from surprise attacks: the desperate demands from the sick who outnumbered the fit: the anxieties of Anson concerning the next move.

Thomas writes:

On our being brought on Shore, it rain'd very hard. So that we were in a manner half drown'd before we could be carry'd up to the Tent: our Bedding was soak'd through, and abundance of it, for want of Help, left washing in the Break of the Sea: nor could those who carry'd us up to the Tent assist us any farther, but left us there half naked on the cold Ground, or a hard Hide, to help ourselves of which we were utterly uncapable; nor had we for the greatest Part any Person to get us a sour Orange, or a lime, or one Drop of Water; tho' all These Things abounded within our View, and almost our Reach.

However, such of us as the Distemper had not mortally seiz'd began in 2 or 3 Days time, by the Help of Staffs to support ourselves, to get out to procure a little Water, and a few acid Fruits; by the Assistance of which we recovered apace.

This wonderful haven Tinian that miraculously appeared when all seemed lost, beneficially stocked with nearly everything that the men desired, and yet practically deserted in spite of being so near Guam, the large island of the Marian group at that time occupied by the Spaniards, is described by both Walter and Thomas in glowing terms. It was no more than twelve miles in length by six miles in breadth, had a sandy soil that produced woods and meadows rather than the normal tropical forest growth, and hills and valleys of moderate undulation. The cattle consisted of heads of some thousands, milk white in appearance with brown or black ears. Poultry of varied description ranged the woods in great numbers and greatly contributed to the 'cheerfulness and beauty of the place'. There was an abundance of wild hogs which made excellent food. But most important was the presence of the acid fruits to which reference is occasionally made by both Walter and Thomas, and it becomes apparent that it was about this time that the anti-scorbutic value of these fruits was definitely realized.

In the woods were coconuts, guavas, limes, sweet and sour oranges, and breadfruit. The latter served in place of bread throughout their stay.

Walter writes of the breadfruit:

Admiral Sir Charles Saunders
*From an oil painting by Sir Joshua Reynolds*

The sack of Paita, 1741
*From an oil painting by S. Scott*

Cumberland Bay, Juan Fernandez

This fruit is fittest to be used when it is full grown but still green, in which state, after it is properly prepared by being roasted in the embers, its taste has some resemblance to that of an artichoke. As it ripens it becomes softer and of a yellow colour, when it contracts a luscious taste and an agreeable smell, not unlike a ripe peach.

Fish was available but 'surfeited those who eat of them' and was therefore forbidden. This could have been no hardship under the circumstances.

Considerable fresh water was near at hand, and the climate was healthy. Why then should such a paradise be almost deserted? It was learnt from the Indians that fifty years earlier there had been thirty thousand people in the island; then a plague had destroyed great numbers in all the islands, and the Spaniards in Guam had ordered an evacuation and transfer to recruit their numbers.

As soon as the sick had been settled on shore, great efforts were made to carry out repairs on board and to stop the leak. Guns were transferred aft to bring the ship up by the bows. Sheathing was ripped off at the water line and seams were caulked.

By 12th September, many of the sick ashore had recovered sufficiently to return to duty on board. But now Anson himself was sick of the scurvy and had a tent erected ashore, convinced that the only cure was to live on shore for a spell.

On 22nd September, a typhoon suddenly hit the island. At five in the afternoon *Centurion*'s small-bower cable parted, and the ship swung off on the best-bower: a strong tidal current set in and forced the ship to the southward.

The sea rose quickly to a tumultuous height, smashing the long-boat moored astern. The boat-keeper, savagely bruised, was thrown on board the ship by a miracle. At eleven, the best-bower parted, and *Centurion* began to drive out to sea. The night was dark. There was heavy rain and lightning. A mighty roar of the wind and the high seas thrashed and crashed on to the shore. Anson and the majority of his officers and crew, including Saunders and Mitchel, were ashore. The situation was alarming

95

in the extreme. To those few on board it was almost catastrophic. Saumarez, the first lieutenant, was on board and took command. Walter also was on board, and so was Brett. Guns were fired, and lights shown to indicate their distress. In the tumultuous seas every man on board thought this was the end. Shrouds were loose. Topmasts remained unrigged. Fore and main yards had been struck down. No sail could be set except on the mizzen. Leaks began to open up in the heavy seas. In this desperate situation, with barely enough hands to man the pumps, *Centurion* drove towards the neighbouring island of Aguiguan, only six miles distant.

At daybreak the next morning nothing could be seen of *Centurion* from Tinian, and there was utmost consternation at the prospect of being marooned on the island: marooned until they should be taken as pirates by the Spaniards of Guam, and infamously deprived of their lives.

Anson attempted to rally his men, pointing out that the ship was not yet lost and might well return; but if she did not, it would be because she had been driven to leeward, in which circumstances she was bound to make for the original rendezvous, Macao in China, not more than two thousand miles away. He stated his intention to enlarge the Spanish barque and to join *Centurion* at Macao.

Two days later, the storm having abated and there being no sign of the ship from any quarter, work began on the great project. Trees were cut down, and a dock was dug out of the soil to take the barque. Anson impressed on all the need for speed and determination in this new project, and set an example by taking a hand in the work. He stated that he would expect no more from any man than he himself was prepared to give, and tackled the job with great resolution. In his own mind he was almost convinced that *Centurion* had perished, yet secretly hoped for the miraculous.

A few days later two small sails were sighted. Anson scrutinized them through his telescope. Suddenly he withdrew from the assembly, and retired to his tent. He was certain that these were survivors from *Centurion*. He passed some bitter moments, absolutely overwhelmed at the realization that the last of his high hopes had vanished. His expedition had fizzled out. There was absolutely nothing now to show of his successes. His treasure and all were lost. He alone and the residue of his gallant followers now remained to make a perilous and ignominious return to England.

A few moments later it was reported that there were two Indian proas making for the shore, whereupon the Commodore immediately ordered a concentration of force with everybody concealed and ready to secure the occupants of the boats on arrival. They came near to the shore, but after a long wait withdrew to seaward.

The lengthening of the barque proceeded, and preparations for departure advanced rapidly. By luck, carpenters and a smith were on shore, together with tools and a forge. Nevertheless much ingenuity was required, and it was necessary to devote considerable thought concerning rigging and provisioning.

Pascoe Thomas says:

> Our daily Allowance was to be four Ounces of jerk'd Beef, one Cacao-Nut, two Oranges, and three Pints of Water; a small Allowance, but sufficient for Life.

Thomas also writes of some discontent and subversion among the 'Common People' who 'resolved to desert us in four or five Days more, and run the risk of staying on the Island, rather than venture themselves to China in that Bark.'

It speaks well of the Commodore's influence and personality that the work proceeded smoothly and quickly. The question of navigation became a great problem when Anson discovered that there was neither compass nor quadrant available. He had brought a pocket compass ashore with him but had lent it to Lieutenant Brett who had been driven to sea in the *Centurion*. By extraordinary good fortune however a small compass was found in a chest stowed away in the barque, and a quadrant with missing vanes was found on the beach. By an incredible piece of further luck some vanes were found in the drawer of an old table that had been driven on shore, and these fitted the quadrant well enough to enable it to measure a rough altitude.

Pascoe Thomas relates:

*October 1742*
Wednesday the 6th, we got the Bark into the Dock in order to lengthen her.
Friday the 8th, we sawed the Bark asunder, and got her two parts to a proper Distance for being lengthened. This Night terrible Thunder, Lightning and Rain, but very little Wind.

By 9th October, more than two weeks after the loss of the *Centurion*, the enlargement and fitting out of the barque were so advanced that plans were made to leave the island on 5th November. But two days later in the afternoon, one of the *Gloucester*'s men, on a hill in the middle of the island, sighted *Centurion* at a distance. He ran as fast as possible to the landing place to spread the news, yelling with great glee, 'The Ship, the Ship!' Anson who was at work on the barque, threw down his axe, and for the first time allowed his emotions to break through his customary reserve and imperturbability. In a kind of frenzy everyone ran to the beach to feast his eyes on the ship.

Walter, who had acted as a seaman in the *Centurion*, writes of their return after a nineteen days' absence:

By five in the evening the *Centurion* was visible in the offing to them all; and, a boat being sent off with 18 men to reinforce her, and with fresh meat and fruits for the refreshment of her crew, she, the next afternoon, happily cast anchor in the road, when the Commodore immediately came on board her, and was received by us with the sincerest and heartiest acclamations.

Thomas, who had remained on shore throughout all, has a more laconic statement:

At Five in the Evening, we saw our Ship in the Offing endeavouring to get in, and the next Day in the Afternoon she anchor'd in the Road. We now left off our former Employ, and prepared to leave the Island in a better Ship.

It was five days after *Centurion* had been driven from Tinian before those on board were able to secure the sheet anchor that had failed to hold them, and get up their main-yard and set their courses. There were but a hundred and eight hands on board, all fully employed to the maximum, and it speaks well of Saumarez that he was able to save the ship and bring her safely back. Her arrival ended the severe labours of both those on board and those on shore, and the reunification of the two parties spread great joy and a renewed expectation of successes ahead.

The jubilation on the return of the *Centurion* to Tinian proved fatal for two men, John Cross and Thomas Stevens, who, according to Millechamp, 'made too free with the Commodore's Bounty grew Pott Valliant, Quarelled and Fought on the Brink of a Well they were filling Water at, where lay a longe Range of Casks on a kind of Diclivity supported only by that which lay nighest the Well, in their struggling they happen'd to move that Cask, which with the weight of above 20 others that were behind it, forced them both into the Well and Rowled in after them, by which means they both were Drowned.'

Anson was now determined to leave at the earliest opportunity. After completing with water (fifty tuns), and taking in a large supply of fresh fruit and coconuts, he ordered the barque to be set on fire, hoisted all boats, and weighed and proceeded for Macao in China, setting course for the southern end of the island of Formosa.

Little of incident now followed. Morale was high and health was excellent. It was necessary to replace the bower anchors which had been lost at Tinian, since the sheet anchor was too heavy and unworkable for ordinary manoeuvring. For this purpose, the small anchors which Anson had had removed from prizes were lashed by their shanks to four pounder guns, and served admirably as extempore anchors.

On 13th November they anchored in Macao road, nine miles from Macao, and received news that there were eleven European ships lying in the Canton river, of which four were English.

The feelings of those on board at being once more in friendly waters are best understood by referring to Walter's account of the voyage:

99

Thus after a fatiguing cruise of above two years' continuance, we once more arrived at an amicable port and a civilised country, where the conveniences of life were in great plenty; where the naval stores, which we now extremely wanted, could be in some degree procured; where we expected the inexpressible satisfaction of receiving letters from our relations and friends: and where our countrymen, who were lately arrived from England, would be capable of answering the numerous enquiries we were prepared to make, both about public and private occurrences, and to relate to us many particulars which, whether of importance or not, would be listened to by us with the utmost attention, after the long suspension of our correspondence with our country, to which the nature of our undertaking had hitherto subjected us.

To many it must have appeared as though the expedition was virtually over. They had survived extremes of tempest, danger, and misery, and in spite of widespread sickness and perpetual defects and disaster had 'annoyed' the Spaniards as instructed, and gained valuable treasure. An easy journey home through friendly waters to complete the circumnavigation of the world, and they would live to enjoy the fruits of their labours.

But Anson had other ideas. He was determined to look once more for the galleon and to take her. In the meantime he would have *Centurion* refitted.

Two captains were still with him, now without commands, and these he sent home. Saunders, who had been promoted from the *Centurion* and given command of the sloop *Tryal* when Cheap died in 1741, took passage to England in a Swedish ship and carried dispatches from Anson. Anson had formed a very high opinion of this officer and gave him his early promotion. He was to be instrumental at a later date in his selection for a most responsible appointment in the Seven Years War. Mitchel, who had been the gallant captain of the *Gloucester* until she had practically rotted under his feet, returned in a ship of the East India Company. Walter, the chaplain, obtained leave from the Commodore, and travelled with Mitchel.

It is obvious that Anson revealed little of his intentions at this stage, but led everybody to think that *Centurion* would sail for England as soon as she had completed her refit.

Walter's account is no longer first hand after this event. But it is pertinent to refer to Millechamp's narrative at this juncture as he has something to say about the departure of various people to England. He himself remained in *Centurion*. Anson was reluctant to allow any of his ship's company to depart, as he knew it would be impossible to replace them, and he had no intention of returning to England yet.

Millechamp says, soon after arrival at Macao:

> The officers of the *Gloucester* and *Tryal's Prize* now used their endeavours to go to England, and notwithstanding they secured themselves passages, Mr. Anson would by no manner of means suffer them to leave him. . . . However he took great care to send home Captain Saunders and Mitchel and Coll. Cracherode who he well knew had they stay'd must have shared with him in any future Prize Money he should take.

It is obvious that Millechamp is of the opinion, and presumed Anson to be so too, that prize money would be payable in accordance with rank rather than appointment. It is evident, however, from Anson's depositions given in the Law Courts in 1745, that he regarded all officers transferred to *Centurion* from *Gloucester* and *Tryal* as supernumeraries not serving in any active appointment. They had all been transferred to save their lives. Saunders and Mitchel would have had no claim to prize money as captains, as they were merely passengers.

# CHAPTER XI

# Further Search for the Galleon

THE reason that prompted Anson to go to the Portuguese island of Macao rather than to the Chinese port of Canton was to get advice on local arrangements for storing and refitting. The Chinese at Canton were great traders, and handled a considerable number of European trading ships, the bulk of which were English East Indiamen. They had probably never seen a man-of-war, and would not understand the European custom which waived the payment of dues in the case of warships. Neither would they see any reason for treating His Majesty's Ship any differently from the trading ships. Anson, however, was determined to maintain the prestige and status of the Royal Navy, and was under the impression that these would be respected in a Portuguese settlement. He was soon to learn that the Portuguese Governor of Macao was no more than a puppet in the hands of the Chinese, and was powerless to grant or do anything that had not first been approved by the Chinese Viceroy of Canton, or his subordinates, through an intricate network of commercial graft and intrigue that proved impenetrable.

It was difficult at first to understand the deception he met, when promises were made which were never fulfilled and excuses given that had no reason. The real reason was that as the Chinese lived by trade and regarded Anson as a pirate, they were reluctant to replenish and refit a ship which would destroy commerce. There was ample justice in their attitude, particularly as they were neutrals who could see no sense in one country making war on another, and no difference between unwarranted piracy and the strategy of war. Add to this the refusal of this pirate to pay what to them were customary harbour dues, and one can understand that obstruction would persist.

Anson had been anxious not to prejudice the ordinary arrangements which existed for the English East Indiamen, and this had been another reason for anchoring at Macao, rather than in the great river of Canton where the traders would lie.

After a month of delay without getting any repairs done, and with no success in his approach to the Viceroy of Canton through the various subordinates and merchants, Anson became anxious about the fruitless passage of time and resolved to apply direct to the great and lofty pinnacle. On the 17th December, he wrote to the Viceroy, informing him that he was Commander-in-Chief of a squadron of his Britannic Majesty's ships of war which had for two years been cruising in the South Seas to fight the Spaniards with whom his country was at war, and that he was on his way back to England, but had put in at Macao with grave defects and in great want of provisions. He hoped that repairs and provisions would be made available without delay.

There was great reluctance at first on the part of the Chief Customs officer at Macao to accept this letter for delivery, until Anson threatened to send it in his own boat with an officer. This produced an answer. Two days later, in the morning, a mandarin of first rank arrived, together with two lesser mandarins and a considerable retinue of officers and servants in eighteen boats, with coloured banners and gay music. They anchored ahead of *Centurion*. They requested a boat, saying that the mandarin had been ordered by the Viceroy to examine the condition of the ship. A boat was immediately despatched. On board *Centurion* Anson had ordered a guard of a hundred men dressed up in the regimental uniform of the marines and formed up on the main deck. There were also drums. He would soon show this official whether he were a pirate or not. The mandarin arrived on board and was received on the main deck in great state by the colourful guard and a salute of drums. He was then conducted to the quarter deck where Anson met him and took him aft to his spacious cabin in the stern of the ship to state his requirements. There followed an inspection of the ship, and in particular Chinese carpenters were instructed to examine the state of the leak. Anson now took great pleasure in showing the main armament to the mandarin who expressed great surprise at the size of the lower deck guns and the weight of the shot. The Commodore took this opportunity of pointing out that in spite of this tremendous weapon which lay at his disposal for complying with the instructions given to him by the King, and which could if necessary be used for the enforcement of ship maintenance and provisioning in the manner of a pirate, he had suffered nothing but rebuffs and delays in his orderly requests. These guns could, of course, destroy the whole of the navigation of Canton without the slightest risk to the ship, but the mandarin must observe that hitherto he had behaved with courtesy and restraint.

The mandarin stated that he was fully aware of Anson's needs, and promised that they would be speedily and fully granted. The mandarin and his two attendant mandarins then dined with Anson in his dining cabin, finding some embarrassment in the use of knives and forks, but showing no difficulty in consuming several bottles of the Commodore's best wine.

It is of interest to read what Pascoe Thomas writes in his Journal concerning the visit:

> The Commodore received him on the Quarter-Deck, and introduced him into his Cabin, where having entertained him for some time, and satisfied most of his Demands, he then Carry'd him and many of his Attendants, to view the Ship between Decks; at this, to them a novel Sight, they sufficiently express'd their Astonishment. The Mandarin, after this, desired to see for himself where the Ship was defective, and particularly the Hole in the Bottom, where the Water came in. On this Mr. Saumarez, our first Lieutenant, and some other Officers, were ordered to conduct him and some of his Retinue, down forward, to see as much of the damag'd Plank about the Leak, as they could; but the Mandarin was so frightened at going down such a Depth, that he could not proceed, but return'd without seeing it; however some of his Retinue

proceeded. Having seen what they could, and been satisfy'd as to their Enquiry, after about 2 or 3 Hours Stay, they took their leaves; and at their Departure we saluted the Mandarin with 15 Guns, which doubtless very well pleased his Vanity. However, some of this polite Company, as I afterwards heard, made bold with a Gold Snuff-Box of the Commodore's, and I think one or two of the Silver Spoons; but not to give these our generous Benefactors any Offence, I believe it was never enquired into.

It was about this time that Anson first received news of the fate of the *Severn* and the *Pearl*, both of which he had until now assumed to have been lost off the Horn. One of the officers of an Indiaman informed him that they had returned to Brazil. The *Severn* had suffered more sickness than any other ship of the squadron, but nevertheless had had under Captain Legge a high reputation for excellent station keeping when in company. Towards the end, before she had parted finally from the squadron, she had shown increasing difficulty in keeping correct position as her death roll mounted. The Commodore received the news of the survival of these two ships with great joy.

In spite of the mandarin's promises, little happened until nearly three weeks later when a warrant was received from the Viceroy for the refit to take place. A thousand pounds sterling was to be the price of repairs to ship, boats, and masts. This was considered to be an unreasonable sum but it was found impossible to arrange for much reduction in this charge. Caulking of decks and upper works now began, and arrangements were made to careen the ship. For this purpose she was emptied of guns, casks, stores, powder, and ammunition. Two junks were obtained from Canton, by which *Centurion* was to be hove down for repairs to the sheathing on her bottom. Progress was so slow that it was not until the 22nd February that heaving down began. This was completed by the 3rd March by which time she had a new sheathing throughout. Everything was now replaced in the ship, and repairs to masts began. Provisioning, watering, and wooding continued at the same time.

There had been much apprehension of attack during the careening, so this operation was carried out with as much dispatch as possible. A rumour had been received that the Governor of Manila, hearing that *Centurion* was to careen at Macao, had arranged for a ship to burn her. The captain of this ship was to receieve forty thousand dollars for his pains, but when it came to advancing the money, the Governor had decided that it would be more appropriate for the merchants to raise the money and pay the captain, since they would be the beneficiaries, rather than that the money should be paid from his own coffers. The plan then fizzled out.

It was the beginning of April before *Centurion* was fully rigged and ready for sea. The ship was desperately short of men, not only from the point of view of navigation, but particularly so for an action. In his report to the Admiralty at this time Anson says:

> The number of men I have now borne is 201, amongst which are included all the officers and boys which I had out of the *Gloucester*, *Tryal Prize*, and *Anna* pink, so that I have not before the mast more than 45 able seamen.

Before sailing, however, he augmented his crew by the addition of twenty-three men; Dutch, Lascars, and Indians. Having left the impression that he was bound for England via Batavia, he received on board mails for Batavia, and many of his officers were given introductions to friends there.

On the 5th of April, the Commodore went on shore to Macao to take leave of the Portuguese Governor, who, though limited in his powers, had treated Anson civilly from the outset. He was saluted with fifteen guns as he left the shore. The following afternoon *Centurion* weighed and warped to the southward to find a better anchorage. The monsoon season had begun, accompanied by squalls and rainstorms. Further watering and provisioning took place until the 19th April, when *Centurion* weighed and proceeded to sea. To those who understood navigation, there seemed to be some question whether the Commodore would really attempt a passage to Batavia at this season when head winds might be expected for most of the journey. They were not long to remain in doubt, and the event is best described in Pascoe Thomas' own words. His description

is of particular interest as it is apparent that his opinion of
Anson seems to have changed about this time from a somewhat
critical one to one of enthusiastic commendation. It is all the
more of value since Walter's story after leaving the ship at
Macao is no longer a first-hand account.

Thomas says:

Being now at Sea, I have very little room to enlarge,
there being nothing entertaining in a Sea-Journal, where
no uncommon Accidents intervene. We were in a Sort of
Uncertainty for some time as to where the Commodore
intended for, and what were his real Designs: Indeed, we
who knew after what Manner the Winds generally blew in
those Seas were very well satisfied that it was morally
impossible at this Season to proceed to the Southward; on
the other hand, we were uncertain what Intelligence the
Commodore might have had, or what probable Hopes he
Conceived, of meeting with the Acapulca Ship. However as
we knew him to be a Person of consummate Prudence and
Policy, we did not much doubt but he proceeded on the
very best Grounds and Informations that could possibly be
got, and would not rashly and unadvisedly undertake a
wild Goose Chace. And indeed the very Courses we steer'd
as well as the Winds would permit, gave us good Intimation
where and on what we were bound; nor were we long
without a Certainty, for the Commodore being now at Sea
had no longer any Occasion to conceal his real Intent. He
ordered all the Ship's Company on the Quarter-Deck, and
there in a short Speech acquainted them with his Design;
adding that he understood, that some Reports tending to
intimidate the People had been industriously spread among
them, as that the Manila Ship was so very strong, and her
sides so thick, that no Shot would penetrate them; but that
those Reports were vain and groundless, and that he
resolv'd to be so near her, that his Shot should go through
both Sides at once. This Speech much reviv'd the Spirits of
the People, who were really weary of this fatiguing and
tedious Voyage, and began to long after their Homes; but
this filled them with the Hope of Riches, and made them

eager to encounter new Difficulties and Dangers; and is another Proof of the Commodore's great Capacity, who very well knew that some such Method was absolutely necessary to make himself be followed with Alacrity and Pleasure, and to inspire them with that Confidence and Assurance of Success, which scarce ever fails under Such Conduct.

What a testimonial for one's Commanding Officer. What a wonderful report from a schoolmaster. What a splendid insight into those great qualities of leadership which Anson had developed during his years in the Navy, but more particularly during these last two years.

Anson's speech was received by the men with acclamation, and they spontaneously gave him three hearty cheers. He now steered for the Island of Formosa, and then steered to the southward to take up his intended station, where he arrived at the end of May. This was off the Cape Espiritu Santo which was known to be the landfall for the westbound galleon. Here Anson cruised sufficiently far out to be out of sight from the land.

During this time hands were busily employed in exercising the heavy guns and firing small arms. Not an opportunity was missed to see that every man on board knew his action station and was fully acquainted with what was required of him. Targets were hung up at the yard-arm, and accuracy of fire and speed of loading were encouraged by the award of prizes.

As June advanced so the impatience of the men increased and disappointment developed.

An officer's journal records:

> May 31. Exercising our men at their quarters, in great expectation of meeting with the galeons very soon, this being the eleventh of June, their stile.

Anson had stated that he expected two galleons since one had been prevented from sailing in the previous year because of his presence off Acapulco. He thought they could take them both.

108

June 3. Keeping in our stations, and looking out for the galeons.

June 11. Begin to grow impatient at not seeing the galeons.

June 13. The wind having blown fresh easterly for the forty-eight hours past, gives us great expectations of seeing the galeons soon.

June 15. Cruising on and off, and looking out strictly.

June 19. This being the last day of June, their stile, the galeons, if they arrive at all, must appear soon.

The following morning was squally and rainy. At five there was a shout from the masthead, and a sail was reported bearing south-east, dead to windward, about eighteen miles. *Centurion* luffed up close to the wind, and stood towards her. There was now immense joy on board. To the Commodore's surprise, the ship instead of bearing away as he had expected continued to close him, obviously intending to fight.

At half past seven the galeon was close enough to be seen from the *Centurion*'s deck. At this time she fired a gun and took in her top-gallant sails, as if slowing down for her consort. *Centurion*, now cleared for action, continued to bear down on the galeon. About thirty marksmen lay waiting in the tops. There were not enough hands to man all the guns with the normal complement, so Anson had devised a scheme whereby certain men would stand by their guns to load, while teams of ten or twelve men would proceed along the battery to run out and fire those guns that were loaded. Firing was not to begin until they were within pistol shot range, and then instead of broadsides with intervals in between, keeping pace with the slowest, all guns would be kept firing at maximum possible frequency. In this way the Spaniards would be unable to carry out their well-known practice of falling down on deck to take cover until a broadside was fired, and then to work their own guns until the next broadside could be seen to be ready for firing.

At half past ten the galeon, now only three miles away, hoisted Spanish colours at the ensign staff and the Royal Standard of Spain at the main-top-gallant masthead. At the same time she fired a gun to leeward. Under topsails she brought to, her head to northward. The ships were now closing at a relative speed of something less than two knots. *Centurion* rigged her sprit-sail yard fore and aft. This was to enable her to lie alongside if necessary with the intention of boarding. The galleon, with a show of audacity in keeping with her enormous crew of five hundred odd men, did the same. *Centurion* answered by opening the lower deck ports and running out the guns.

A little after noon, there were several rain squalls which obscured the view. On each occasion of clearance, however, the range was seen to be closing, with the galleon resolutely lying to.

A little after half past twelve, at a distance of half a mile, *Centurion* hoisted the Commodore's broad pennant and the battle ensign. Anson noticed that the galleon's crew were still clearing the decks, and were throwing cattle and lumber overboard. He therefore gave the order to open fire with the port chase to cause as much confusion as possible. She answered immediately. Soon afterwards *Centurion* overreached the galleon and lay on her bow to leeward. The fight now began in earnest. Anson could traverse nearly all his guns on the starboard side on to the galleon. The galleon could bring only those in the forward part of the ship to bear. *Centurion* kept up a brisk and regular fire. Round after round left each gun as the trained teams moved rapidly along the batteries.

From the tops of the *Centurion* the marksmen with their first volley had driven the Spaniards from their tops. Now they raked the galleon's decks. Every Spanish officer but one fell. This caused tremendous confusion. There were many bodies lying about the deck, and gangs of men would appear for the purpose of sweeping them away, only to meet the same fate.

Slowly the *Centurion* lost her advantageous position across the bows, and after half an hour she was close alongside. The galleon now gave as good as she received. On the galleon's deck, however, men were tumbling down in heaps. Their commander, known as the general, together with some of the officers, was showing great determination and exhorting the men to continue the action.

About this time the galleon's ensign staff was shot down and the ensign caught fire. The galleon's fire was slackening. A Spanish officer rushed to seize the ensign to stifle the flames. Anson saw this from his quarter deck. He also saw some of his

The taking of the *Cobadonga*, 1743
*From an oil painting by S. Scott*

The First Battle of Finisterre, May 1747

marksmen aim. He yelled at them to cease fire. The general was still rushing from place to place. Suddenly he fell with a musket ball in his chest. The Royal Standard was immediately lowered from the masthead. The galleon had struck. Anson was now in possession of the rich prize which had been the object of his hopes for the last eighteen months. Her name was the *Nuestra Señora de Cobadonga*, and her commander was a Portuguese of great skill and courage named General Don Jeronimo de Mentero. She was much larger than *Centurion*, had five hundred and fifty men, thirty-six mounted guns, and twenty-eight four pounders. She was well furnished with small arms, and provided against boarding by a strong network of two inch rope, laced over her waist.

The fight had lasted an hour and twenty minutes, during which the Spaniards lost sixty-seven men killed in action and eighty-four wounded. Her commander, though badly wounded, survived. *Centurion* lost two men killed. Lieutenant Brett and sixteen men were wounded.

Scarcely had the action ceased when a fire broke out in *Centurion* in some oakum near the after powder-room. Great clouds of smoke belched from this as the fire spread, but the conflagration was soon got under control with a few buckets of water.

Thomas writes:

> During the Fight the Commodore behaved in the most gallant Manner; he gave his Orders with Coolness and Calmness, and, though his piercing Eyes were every where, he seemed as perfectly unconcerned, and present to himself, as if he had nothing to mind. This Calmness of Behaviour caused the whole Engagement to be carried on in the same Manner: every Man knew his Duty and performed it without the least Confusion, Noise or Disorder; and exclusive of the continual Thunder of our Cannon, I have seen and heard six Times more Confusion, Noise, and Hurry in hoisting out one Cutter than we had during this whole Engagement.

Anson's modest official report is also worth reading. He says:

On the 20th June I got sight of her and gave chase, She bearing down upon me before the wind; when she came within two miles she brought to, to fight us. After engaging her an hour and a half within less than pistol-shot, the admiral struck his flag at the main-top-mast head. Her masts and rigging were shot to pieces, and 150 shot passed through her hull, many of which were between wind and water, which occasioned her to be very leaky. The greatest damage I received was by my foremast, mainmast, and bowsprit being wounded, and my rigging shot to pieces, having received only 15 shot through my hull. I was under great difficulty in navigating 2 such large ships, in a dangerous and unknown sea, and to guard 492 prisoners.

Anson commissioned the *Cobadonga* as a ship in His Majesty's service, and gave the command to Philip Saumarez, his first lieutenant. Saumarez's appointment to the *Centurion's Prize* caused a number of promotions in *Centurion* of which one was that of the Honourable Augustus Van Keppel, son of the Earl of Albermarle, who now became third lieutenant in place of Denis who became second lieutenant in place of Brett. Brett succeeded Saumarez as first lieutenant of the *Centurion*. A party of fifty officers and men from *Centurion*, of whom Pascoe Thomas was one, boarded the prize to secure her. Two surgeons were also sent to take care of the general and the other wounded. One of these was Allen who had been surgeon of the *Tryal*. Half the *Cobadonga*'s complement were kept on board to clear up the mess and to work ship under guard: the other half were sent on board *Centurion* as prisoners, and many expressed great indignation when they saw and realized the slenderness of the crew to whom they had surrendered. The officer prisoners, numbering eighteen, were accommodated in the first lieutenant's cabin under guard, and the men were put into the hold with two hatchways left open for air, and four swivel guns manned for security. The general was given the Commodore's cabin, and a sentry was posted to look after him. Pascoe Thomas had much to say about this gentleman, describing him not only as a courageous soldier but also as a 'deceitful scandalous Villain!' In view of his position he was accorded treatment appropriate to his station, so that his chests, which he claimed carried only his personal effects, escaped search. He also claimed that his sword belt, set with valuable pearls and diamonds, had been left in his cabin in the *Cobadonga*. These could not be found, and this caused Anson to suspect looting by the boarding party, of which Thomas had been one. Suspicion fell on all and sundry, and after wide and frequent searches had failed to produce the lost property, restrictions were placed on movements to ensure that the stolen property would not be taken ashore. Thomas was afterwards informed by an Irish priest that the jewels were all the time in the possession of the general himself, who subsequently landed them at Canton and sold them there after his release.

Thomas writes:

> What did this rascally General deserve at our Hands, who had suffered so severely on his Account? And was not the Commodore's lenity in suffering him to carry off his Effects without a Search, and Credulity in believing his Report of the Loss of those Things, and wrongfully suspecting his own People, justly blameable?

Thomas is back in his critical mood again, and it seems difficult not to blame Anson for his credulity and lenity under the circumstances. But Anson was a good judge of men, and it is unlikely that he was taken in by the general. It is far more likely that he guessed the truth, but felt himself bound by a code of ethics towards his prisoner guest to an extent which compelled him to appear to accept the word of this gentleman. It was typical of all his behaviour towards prisoners. He also knew his own men well enough to understand that many of them would miss no opportunity of appropriating personal loot if they knew that they could get away with it.

As soon as the prisoners were secured, Anson arranged for the treasure to be brought on board *Centurion*, and then sailed for Macao where he arrived with the *Cobadonga* in company on 11th July. The treasure consisted of 1,313,843 pieces of eight and 35,682 ounces of virgin silver. This brought the total value up to about four hundred thousand pounds. In addition he had burnt or destroyed merchandise to the value of six hundred thousand pounds and been the cause of the dispatch of Pizarro's squadron which had ended in great disaster for the Spanish ships. He had sufficiently 'annoyed' the Spaniards, and it was now time to think about returning to England. The second galleon which he had hoped to find in company with *Cobadonga* had completed her voyage to Manila before he left Macao, when delayed in his efforts to speed up refitting and provisioning. This he learnt from one of the prisoners taken from the *Cobadonga*.

On 15th July, Anson sailed up the Canton River with the assistance of two Chinese pilots, both somewhat under duress, and with his prize, anchored 'in five Fathom Water, close alongside of a very pleasant Spot of Rice Land, very low and even with the Water's Edge, and the Rice being green and flourishing it look'd very pretty and delightful.'

The next day the Commodore sent his second lieutenant to Canton, with a letter for the Viceroy informing him that he proposed to call. In the meantime, the news of the capture of the galleon by a smaller ship with a slender crew spread rapidly, and Anson's prestige rose when the Chinese understood that England was at war with Spain and that the galleon would have reversed the tables and taken the *Centurion*, had she been able, as apparently had been the fond hope of the general in command.

On 20th July, three mandarins, accompanied by a vast retinue and twelve junks, arrived on board the *Centurion*, and gave Anson the Viceroy of Canton's authorization for the daily purchase of provisions and his apologies for being unable to receive Anson until September when the weather would be cooler for the assembling of mandarins and troops. They raised the question of harbour dues, to which Anson replied that he had no intention of paying them as they were meant for trading vessels and not for men-of-war. On being asked if he would consider the release of the prisoners taken on board the *Cobadonga*, since they were friendly to and carried on great commerce with China, Anson, who was delighted at the prospect of ridding himself of this burden, agreed though with the appearance of some reluctance, provided the Chinese would fetch them. This they did on 28th July, sending two large junks which bore away the general and 396 prisoners. Prior to this, ninety prisoners had departed, and now ninety-five were retained on board mainly at their own wish.

Although daily provisions were made available for purchase, Anson discovered that the stocks he required for his long passage to England were not forthcoming, in spite of daily promises that action had been taken and that the stores would soon be in readiness for delivery. Towards the end of September, having still received no further word from the Viceroy, and being tired of the deceit and graft that attended every transaction, Anson sent word to the Viceroy that he intended to proceed up the river to Canton on 1st October, and would desire an audience of the Viceroy. Even now he was subjected to false reports stating that the Viceroy would prefer him to postpone his visit for a few days. Then came further reports which conflicted with the earlier, and to add to the confusion the captains of the English, Danish, and Swedish traders wrote to him in a joint letter begging him not to offend the Viceroy. He replied that he was now fully determined to visit the Viceroy and that he was convinced that he had hitherto received nothing but forgeries and fraudulent messages.

In expectation of trouble and possible detention during his absence from the *Centurion*, Anson appointed his first lieutenant, Brett, to be Captain of the *Centurion* in his absence, and directed him to take certain action if he failed to return. This was that he should destroy the prize, and then proceed down river in *Centurion* to await orders.

Anson insisted on being accompanied and pulled up river by a boat's crew of eighteen and a coxswain, and these he had clothed in a uniform dress similar to that of the Thames watermen of the time. They were to wear scarlet jackets, and blue silk waistcoats with silver buttons, and caps with silver badges. This was before the Navy had regulation uniform which Anson himself later introduced for officers. He was a great believer in ceremony and formal dress.

On 13th October, the captains and pursers of the English, Danish, and Swedish ships came down the river from Canton in their respective barges to wait on the Commodore. Thomas, still in the *Cobadonga*, describes the event:

> At Four in the Afternoon the Commodore, attended by Captain Saumarez of the Prize, in his eighteen oar'd Barge, his own Pinnace and Cutter, and the aforesaid Commanders, put off the *Centurion* accordingly; on which the ship being mann'd, he was saluted with 19 Guns. As he passed by us in the Prize, we likewise mann'd Ship and saluted him with 15: and as he passed by the European Ships at Wampo, most of them there paid him the same Compliment.

The French abstained. The Commodore arrived safely in Canton that same evening.

There now followed a repetition of the previous events. Promises were followed by evasions and excuses. Each time Anson proposed drastic action, he was met by apprehension and concern on the part of the European traders who were scared of the effects that such action would have on their relations and commerce with the Chinese. Arrangements, however, were made for the preparation and setting aside of the stores and provisions which he required, and for which payment was demanded in advance.

By 24th November, Anson's patience was exhausted, and as the north-east monsoon had set in, he was anxious to be away before other ships could leave with the news of his capture of the galleon and his intended return to England. The stores were ready and awaited only the magic word from above for their delivery on board. He therefore sent one of his officers to the mandarin who guarded the principal gate of the City of Canton, with a letter addressed to the Viceroy.

Two days later a fire broke out in the suburbs of the city and spread rapidly. Anson arrived quickly on the scene with officers and a boat's crew. To prevent the fire from spreading further he ordered them to pull down some wooden sheds. These attempts at assistance were at once frustrated and obstructed by the Chinese, and he was informed that he would be held accountable for whatever he pulled down. He therefore withdrew with his men to the English factory to secure the Company's treasure and effects.

The fire now began to assume alarming proportions. A mandarin came out of the city with four or five hundred firemen, who thereupon made feeble and fruitless efforts to pull down the very buildings that Anson's men had tackled. Others contented themselves with holding small idols near the fire, hoping that good joss would save them. The next on the scene was the Viceroy himself who realizing at once that the whole city would soon be in jeopardy, sent an urgent message to Anson, imploring him to return to render assistance and to take any measure that he thought fit. Anson immediately returned with about forty of his men. Watched by the whole populace they set to with great determination and agility. They leapt with great daring on to the roofs of the low buildings, and tumbled them to the ground, delighted to show the spectators how effective such resolute action could be. In a short time they had isolated the region of the fire and got it under control to the amazement and relief of the terrified spectators. Meanwhile Anson had also been asked by various rich merchants to provide guards for their warehouses to prevent looting. Anson complied with these requests, to the intense relief of the merchants. From public enemy number one he had suddenly been transformed into the local hero.

The following morning he received numerous calls from the principal citizens. They thanked him for his efforts, and frankly admitted that without him the city of Canton would have been totally demolished. Soon afterwards came also a message from the Viceroy, fixing an audience for 30th November. Anson now realized that all his local difficulties were at an end.

At ten on the appointed morning, a mandarin called on Anson to say that all was ready. The Commodore, together with Saumarez and Keppel and his retinue, now set out on this historic and much delayed mission. He was met at the outer gate of the city, by a guard of two hundred soldiers, and escorted to the Emperor's palace where the Viceroy lived. Here was a parade of ten thousand armed soldiers in colourful dress to greet him, and through the ranks of which he was conducted to the great hall of audience, where he found the Viceroy seated under a richly embroidered canopy in the Emperor's Chair of State, attended by all his council of mandarins. The Commodore was given a seat, and then addressed himself to the Viceroy through his own interpreter. He gave an account of all the delays and frustrations he had suffered in his attempt to secure an audience, and then explained his position as an officer of the Royal Navy of Great Britain, and his duty to lay before the Viceroy an account of the grievances of the British subjects and officers of the East India Company trading with China, and the impositions to which they had been subjected by merchants and officials of the lower order. He followed by saying that he wanted a licence to embark all the provisions and stores which he had purchased, and that as soon as these were on board he intended to leave the Canton River and return to England.

The Viceroy replied that the licence should be issued immediately, and then thanked Anson for his services in saving the city from destruction by fire, and wished him a prosperous voyage. The Commodore then took his leave after thanking the Viceroy for his assistance, and left with the same ceremony that had greeted his arrival, this time augmented by a salute of three guns.

The provisions began to be sent on board the very next morning, and four days later Anson left Canton for the *Centurion* down river. By 7th December all preparations were completed, and Anson sailed to Macao with *Centurion* and the prize. A few days later, however, he received a petition from Saumarez and his officers describing the state of the prize, and asking for a survey:

Sir,

It is with the utmost regret we find ourselves obliged to represent to you the condition of His Majesty's Ship the *Centurion's Prize*, the defects of which appear to us too urgent to be neglected, having from our own observations and experiences, since our being on board her, great reasons to apprehend her unfit for the sea, equally proceeding from the consequences of the engagement as from the neglects and want of timely reparations during her being in the enemies hands.

Leaks . . . shot holes . . . pumps decayed and unservice-able . . . cutwater loose . . . mast, yards, disabled . . . shrouds shot thro' . . . and rotten.

These circumstances joined to the ill condition we observe the ship to be in, equally in several of her timbers as in her whale and upper works, gives us reasons to suspect her weakness, and as her working and labouring in a sea may add to the above mentioned defects, puts us under an indispensable necessity of representing these several articles to you. Begging you would be pleased to order the ship to be examined and surveyed by such officers as you will judge proper.

Permit us the officers undermentioned to subscribe ourselves.

Your most obedient humble servants

| | | |
|---|---|---|
| Centurion's Prize | Philip Saumarez | Captain |
| Dec. 13th 1743 | Thomas Summers | 1st Lieut. |
| in Macao Road | George Carpenter | 2nd |
| | William Langdon | 3rd |
| | William Cherry | Boats$^{\text{n}}$ |
| | Rob. Man | Gunner |
| | John Knight | Carpenter |
| | J. Farmer | Purser |

To Commodore Geo. Anson Esq.

C in C of H.M. Ships designed on a particular expedition.

Anson thereupon sold the prize for six thousand dollars, and Saumarez and the crew were re-embarked in *Centurion*. On 15th December all transactions being now completed, he sailed for England, returning via the Cape of Good Hope, and in anticipation daily of hearing that they were now at war with France.

After an uneventful voyage they arrived at Spithead on 15th June 1744, having, in a fog in the Channel, sailed right through a French fleet of considerable force. England was now at war with France. They had thus narrowly averted yet one more disaster, a disaster which would have meant the loss of all their treasure, now safely arrived in *Centurion* after her epic voyage.

Walter concludes his account of the voyage in words that cannot be bettered:

> Thus was this expedition finished, when it had lasted 3 years and 9 months, after having, by its event, strongly evinced this important truth, that though prudence, intrepidity and perseverance united are not exempted from the blows of adverse fortune, yet in a long series of transactions they usually rise superior to its power, and in the end rarely fail of proving successful.

# CHAPTER XII

# War with France

ALTHOUGH news of Anson's expedition had been brought to England by Captain Saunders who had left Canton towards the end of 1742, the events related had taken place prior to the capture of the Manila galleon. It was not until Anson himself arrived at Spithead in June 1744 that the news of the Manila prize reached England.

One of the first to whom Anson wrote was Lord Hardwicke who had become Lord Chancellor ('the great and good Chancellor') in 1737, and who was one of the signatories of the letter sent by the Lords Justices to Anson with the orders for the voyage on 28th June 1740. This was the beginning of a great friendship which was to be backed by mutual trust and respect for the other's integrity and ability. One detects, however, in this letter, striking in its modesty and conciseness, an apprehension concerning public reaction and also some anxiety about continued patronage. The public of the day were seldom indifferent to naval exploits. They were either effusive with recognition and flattery if they thought a job had been well done, or loudly demanding for penance if there were any hint of failure. Anson's letter to Lord Hardwicke may be seen in the British Museum (MS 35,359). It reads:

*Centurion* at Spithead
June 14th 1744

My Lord,

I ought to have written to your Lordship on arrival at Canton, when in all probability my expedition was at an

121

end, as to any service I could undertake against the enemy; but I was so ill satisfied with any success on being abandoned by one part of my squadron, and the remainder being either wrecked or reduced to such a condition, by the bad treatment we met in passing Cape Horn that it was not possible for me to keep above water. These misfortunes gave me an uneasiness I could not express to your Lordship; which was not a little aggravated by the reflections of what I could have undertaken for His Majesty's service if the squadron had got into the South Seas in tolerable plight—for I have good reason to believe that with one fourth part less strength than I carried from Spithead I should have left the Spaniards a very uneasy remembrance of my having been in this part of the world. After my ship was fitted in China, I determined to attempt the galleon from Acapulcho, though I had not half my Complement of men. Here fortune favoured me; for I met her at the entrance of her port, with nearly three times my number of men to defend her. After an hour and a half's engagement within pistol shot, the admiral struck his flag and became my prize. Though the expedition has not had all the success the nation expected from it, which is a great misfortune to me, I am persuaded no misconduct can be justly laid to my charge as Commander-in-Chief; and I should have great pain in returning to my country, after all the fatigue and hazard I have undergone in endeavouring to serve it, if I thought I had forfeited either your Lordship's favour and protection or the esteem of the public.

Mr. Keppel is my 3rd lieutenant. I have recommended the bearer, Mr. Dennis, my 1st lieutenant, to the Secretary of State, and hope they will prefer him, for he well deserves it.

ANSON

The completion of Anson's circumnavigation of the world after an absence of nearly four years took England by storm. The knowledge of his great losses in ships and men, together with the stories of privations and sufferings only added to the romance of the *Centurion*'s voyage and her taking of the Manila galleon. England was in great need of some spur after years of Walpole's dismal administration which had ended with the Carthagena fiasco.

The news of Anson's return provided it. Not only had he survived a journey full of terrible vicissitudes, but he had succeeded in crippling Spanish power in the Pacific and had caused the Spaniards great anxiety over their South American possessions. He was also responsible for their losing millions of pounds' worth of treasure or merchandise. All this had required resource, determination, great skill, and unflagging qualities of leadership in the face of great and tragic misfortunes.

On arrival at St. Helen's, Anson had sent his first lieutenant, Denis, ashore, with a report for the Duke of Newcastle, Secretary of State, as it was through the Secretary of State that he had received his instructions from the King. The Duke of Newcastle at once acknowledged his report in an appreciative letter:

Whitehall, June 15, 1744

Captain Anson—Sir,

I received this morning by Lieutenant Dennis the favour of your letter of yesterday's date, with the agreeable news of your success in capturing the great Acapulcho ship and of your safe arrival at Spithead, after the many fatigues and dangers that you have gone through in the course of your expedition. I laid it immediately before the King, and have the satisfaction to acquaint you that His Majesty was pleased to express his great approbation of your conduct and to give you leave to come immediately to town as you desire. As I hope very soon to have the pleasure of seeing you, I shall only add the assurances of my being with the greatest truth and regard,

HOLLES NEWCASTLE

P.S. I am extremely obliged to you for your goodness to Mr. Keppel and Mr. Carpenter. I will not fail to mention to His Majesty your recommendation for your lieutenant, Mr. Dennis, whom I will also recommend to the Lords Commissioners of the Admiralty. Give me leave very particularly to assure you that I take a great part in the good fortune and in the honour you have acquired for yourself and the service you have done to your Country.

The name of Anson was now on every tongue, and yet his return was greeted with some coolness at the Admiralty. In reply to his modest report announcing his arrival at Spithead and giving an account of his transactions at Canton and the taking of the galleon, the Secretary of the Admiralty stated that he had communicated the report to their Lordships, and took this opportunity of 'wishing you joy on your arrival in England.'

Anson reported in another letter to Their Lordships that he had promoted his former first lieutenant, Brett, to acting captain during his absence from *Centurion* while at Canton, and requested confirmation of the promotion.

This request somewhat incensed Their Lordships, because Anson's own appointment as Commodore had included his captaincy of the *Centurion*, and had expressly barred him from having a captain under him in that ship. Technically Their Lordships were obviously right, but it would have been an act of grace and realism in view of the special circumstances of Anson's absence from *Centurion* while at Canton, and the fact that they were disposed to promote Brett anyway, had they upheld Anson's request.

Instead they replied that Anson had no power to make such an appointment, and that it could not be confirmed.

On 19th June, Anson's own promotion to flag rank was announced, and he received a letter stating that the King had been pleased to raise him to the rank of Rear-Admiral of the Blue.

Anson pondered for some time over this. He decided that he could not accept promotion if the Board were to ignore his recommendations given in the greatest sincerity and understanding.

He replied as follows:

June 24, 1744

I am extremely concerned to find myself under the necessity of resigning a commission I have lately been honoured with, and which I return enclosed to your lordships. It has ever been my opinion that a person trusted with command may and ought to exceed his orders, and dispense with the common rules of proceeding, when extraordinary occasions require it. In what I have acted I have had no other view than the honour and advantage of H.M. Service. Since upon application to your lordships you have not been pleased to confirm it, it is with great mortification I am obliged in the matter to decline a service which has been, and ever will be, the great pleasure and pride of my life.

I am, my lords,

You most obedient humble servant<br>ANSON

Anson returned his commission with this letter and it was thereupon cancelled by Lord Winchelsea, the First Lord of the Admiralty, who was not an admirer of Anson. This transaction is recorded in the minute book of the Admiralty:

Saturday 30 June 1744
The Right Honourable the Earl of Winchelsea, Mr. Cockburn, Dr. Lee, Sir Charles Hardy, Mr. Phillipson. A letter from Admiral Anson was read, enclosing his commission of rear-admiral of the blue, and representing his concern to find himself under the necessity of resigning the same, because a commission he had given to Captain Brett, to command the *Centurion* under him was not confirmed. Resolved, that the said commission be cancelled.

Prior to this transaction, Corbett, the Secretary of the Admiralty had written to Anson on 25th June 1744, immediately on receipt of Anson's letter declining his promotion. It was a long, pompous, and somewhat inconsequential letter, intended to be a friendly appeal to Anson to reconsider his decision. It is worth recording, although it failed to move Anson.

Admiralty Office, 25th June 1744

Dear Sir,
Though the giving advice is the most hazardous office of friendship, it is (in proper season) the sincerest proof of it.

It is from that motive I address this letter to you on the first occasion you have ever given me for it in a course of more than 20 years' happiness of your acquaintance. The conduct you have shown in the late perilous expedition, the happy completion of it with so much judgment and resolution, has distinguished your character in an uncommon manner, and made you to be regarded as one of the ablest to serve and support your country.

Is it possible for one of such excellent endowments to justify so tenaciously an act, irregular, unnecessary, unprecedented, as to make the confirmation of it a condition of your continuance in the Service or of the acceptance of the late mark of His Majesty's regard for you?

The reason you urge for insisting on the commission you gave constituting a captain under you in the *Centurion*, is, that it has ever been your opinion 'a person entrusted with command may and ought to exceed his orders, and dispense with the common rule of proceedings, when extraordinary occasions require it'.

Your opinion is very just. When a commander finds his orders or instructions insufficient, and he can do his country better service by violating or exceeding them, it indicates a great mind to judge and make a successful use of such occasions.

But the application of this rule does not avail here. You are named to go with a squadron upon a distant expedition, without any captain under you in your own ship. You accept the command, and serve all the time, according to these terms. But after the whole expedition is at an end, and not one ship is left with you but your own, nor any other service to perform but to return home, you appoint a captain under you. Do any of these extraordinary occasions appear here wherever common rules of proceedings should be dispensed with? Does a journey of a few hours to an audience of the Vice-King at Canton come up to it? The precaution you took before setting out, to secure the King's Ship and the treasure in case any accident happened to your person, was a prudent and necessary measure, but the trust was conditional and to take place upon an inability to act yourself, which did not happen.

If what I have been saying, dear Sir, has any tone of conviction, you will no longer insist on an act your good sense must condemn, when you consider that the Lords of the Admiralty have a true regard for you, are much concerned for the temper you are in with them, and would gratify you in anything that consisted with reason and the rules of their office. They have given you proof of it. You took the galleon into the King's service, and they have confirmed the officers you appointed to her, and yet there seemed as much reason to commission any merchant ship, for she never was to serve as a man-of-war against the enemy, which is the only reason of putting prizes into commission. I am well assured that the captain you contest for would be provided for to his satisfaction, as well as others who have served with you in the voyage, and are under your protection.

In the present case the Lords of the Admiralty had no precedent; and would you make one? It cannot be defended. The moment it is admitted, the Admiralty is no longer master of any rule or order; but every commander who goes abroad without a captain may appoint one as soon as he is clear of the land of England, and insist on it from the precedent.

An admiral of great rank, in the Mediterranean, wanted a second captain. His reasons were specious: he had a very large fleet under his command, and the assistance of only one flag officer, who was infirm; himself was next in post to the only admiral who is allowed two captains. But as the establishment did not allow it, they could not act generously because there was no precedent; it was not granted, and not being granted, was not assumed.

The late Lord Torrington, under whom we both served, and now revere his memory, in his expedition to Sicily gave a commission to a person to be a lieutenant contrary to rule. Lord Berkeley, being then at the head of the Admiralty, would not confirm it. In ten years after, Lord Torrington coming to the Admiralty and being solicited to continue the Commission refused it, saying he would never ratify any act of his own which he was convinced to be wrong. This is one of the many things I have admired in him: moderation, and obedience to laws and rules of Government are truer characteristics of a great man than defending singular opinions.

I will trouble you no more, but leave it to your consideration which is most praiseworthy—to give up a hasty resolution, which (as far as I can hear) all your brother officers condemn, as all must who deal sincerely with you; or in a sullen fit to fly in His Majesty's face, give matters for pleasure to his enemies, and throw yourself out of a service you have been bred to, and in which you have so well succeeded?

I am, with most sincere regard and esteem,
> Dear Sir,
Your most obedient and most humble servant,
> > THOMAS CORBETT

On the day that Anson received this letter Brett was promoted captain, but the date was not antedated to the occasion when he had been appointed to command the *Centurion* in the Commodore's absence at Canton.

Anson now remained unemployed as a captain on half pay, his commission to flag rank cancelled. And this might well have been the end of the story, but for the fact that in December 1744, Winchelsea and the Board of Admiralty were turned out.

Winchelsea's successor as First Lord was the Duke of Bedford who at once selected Anson to be a member of the Board of Admiralty, not only in order to make amends for the Admiralty's curt treatment of Anson, but because he knew that this was the man who would be able to select the right officers for the Navy and who would be able to take action to improve the corrupt and decadent administration of the dockyards. Anson was promoted Rear-Admiral of the Blue, his promotion being back-dated to June 1744. He was to be a junior member of the Board, but Bedford's second member to himself was the Earl of Sandwich. There were two other naval officers on the Board, Rear-Admiral Lord Vere Beauclerc and Rear-Admiral Lord

Archibald Hamilton, but neither had had much active service. There were also two civilians, Legge and Grenville. Anson was therefore the only man on the Board who was familiar with most of the problems and difficulties, and who also knew a considerable number of the naval officers. His prestige both in the Navy and in the country generally was very high, his experience unprecedented, and he had the full support, confidence, and friendship of both Bedford and Sandwich. Here was the beginning of an Administration that was to pave the way to a flourishing Navy.

The wonderful successes of the Seven Years War and the formation of the British Empire were soon to follow. Without Anson's transformation of the Royal Navy and his determination to command the seas, such successes would not have been possible. Around the nucleus of the British Empire thus formed, there later developed spontaneously the Commonwealth of freedom loving Nations, headed by a descendant of Britain's reigning monarch, George II. In no way differently does the maintenance of freedom continue to depend on command of the seas, a truth which many will probably ignore, as in those precarious days of two hundred years ago and many times since.

France, though not openly at war, had been assisting Spain in an underhand manner for three years before declaring war on Britain on 20th March 1744.

She had formed an alliance with Spain, and supported the Elector of Bavaria in his claims to succeed the Emperor Charles VI of Austria whose possessions included Bohemia, Silesia, Hungary, the Netherlands, and the Duchy of Milan. Charles had wished to leave his possessions to his daughter Maria Theresa. By supporting the Elector of Bavaria, Spain hoped to recover Milan; France hoped to be rewarded with the Netherlands.

On the death of the Emperor in 1740 an unexpected claimant suddenly appeared in the shape of the new monarch on the throne of Prussia, Frederick II, who had a magnificent army and was anxious to use it. At about the time that Anson arrived at Juan Fernandez with his sadly depleted crew, and when Vernon was about to attack Carthagena, Frederick occupied the rich province of Silesia with thirty thousand troops and subdued the feeble opposition of the Austrian army of Maria Theresa who dared to oppose his occupation.

When France took the side of Bavaria in this dispute, George II of England, Elector of Hanover, opposed her, and in the last battle in which a sovereign took the field, won a resounding victory at Dettingen. It was now necessary, however, to secure greater control in the Mediterranean. Spain had never forgiven the British seizure of Gibraltar by Rooke in 1704 and Minorca by Leake in 1708, but now, more than ever before, it was important for Britain as an ally of Austria to safeguard Austrian possessions in Italy, and to prevent any large concentration of the Spanish and French fleets.

France had formed an alliance with Spain with the declared intent, among others, of concluding no peace with Britain until Gibraltar should be returned to the crown of Spain. She aimed at complete domination in the Mediterranean. Another object in view was to put the Stuarts back on the throne of Great Britain.

Britain's first efforts in this war were deplorable, for early in 1744, some months before Anson had returned from his voyage, a combined Spanish and French fleet was allowed to get away after an irresolute action off Toulon. A naval victory at this time would have been a great spur. This, however, was not to be, until Anson himself showed the way three years later. The combined French and Spanish fleet that put out from Toulon numbered twenty-eight, and it was their intention to join with the Brest fleet that had eluded the British blockade and was making for the Straits. The British fleet in the Mediterranean under the command of Admiral Mathews, the Commander-in-Chief, numbered also twenty-eight, but their bottoms were foul, and the Franco-Spanish fleet thereby hoped to elude them. Mathews had the weather gage, and determined to fight. He elected to use the Battle Instructions, which had fallen into obsolescence since there had been no major naval battles since the beginning of the century. He was a courageous but tactless officer, and was at loggerheads with his second in command who behaved so stupidly and woodenly that he never brought his squadron anywhere near the enemy; moreover it became obvious that the Battle Instructions were so rigid that a slavish regard for them would prevent the exercise of any initiative. The escape of the allied fleet was a first class disaster for Britain, and British naval prestige sank to a very low level. Only one success was recorded in this futile action and that was the taking of a French prize, the *Poder*, by the *Berwick* whose young captain, Edward Hawke, was later to become famous for his victories.

The nation clamoured for redress. In the House of Commons a member moved for an immediate inquiry without giving the Admiralty time to instigate a court martial. A motion was made for certain officers involved in the battle to appear at the bar of the House of Commons for examination, and this led to a resolution to petition the King for a court martial. This struck directly at the authority of the Board of Admiralty in whom alone the power was vested to order a court martial. Anson who had just joined the Board was determined that some remonstration was necessary. He was virtually alone, as the Duke of Bedford was laid up with gout, and the Earl of Sandwich was ill of a fever.

'I am extremely concerned,' wrote Anson to his brother, 'both in public and private respects, that the Board is so indisposed at such a juncture. Heaven restore and preserve it.'

Anson presented the matter to the Duke of Newcastle and asked him to explain to the King how injurious to the jurisdiction of the Admiralty the affair had become, since the King was assuming powers which were clearly vested in the Board of Admiralty, and a dangerous precedent might be established. His point was taken and no case of similar interference has occurred since.

At the court martial Mathews was dismissed the service, but Lestock, the second in command, because he was a prominent Whig, it is said, was acquitted. Of the eleven captains who were tried, two were acquitted, four cashiered, three dismissed, one died on passage home, and one deserted into Spain.

The rigidity of the Fighting Instructions, which had been produced by Torrington in 1703, contributed greatly to the misunderstanding which had led to such a fiasco at the Battle of Toulon. The rigidity had been imposed with a purpose, but it was Vernon who first realized that such rigidity would obstruct the development of initiative, as it did at Toulon, and that some Additional Instructions were necessary to give some very necessary flexibility. Vernon, though a brilliant seaman and an able tactician, was a difficult man and made many enemies. He issued his Additional Instructions to his squadron, but never fought a sufficiently large scale action to put them to the test. Anson, however, was quick to realize the value of these Additional Instructions which would lead to a closer understanding between the commander and his subordinates in a variety of situations. He not only adopted Vernon's Instructions and arranged for them to become official but added several excellent ones of his own, and it is probable that these included for the first time the idea of ships sailing on a general line of bearing: the line ahead and line abreast were the only two that had hitherto been recognized. Anson also saw the importance of exercising in tactics in order to become familiar with the instructions and to face commander and subordinates with the sort of situation in which quick decisions would have to be made.

Anson's arrival at the Admiralty had come at a time when morale in the Navy was low, and the Administration generally corrupt and decadent. He was determined to instil a new spirit and to encourage initiative among officers. He was also set on an improvement in the neglected administration of the dock-yards. Considerable fleets of the French navy were fitting out at Brest and Rochefort at this time with the intention of wresting from Britain her failing sovereignty of the seas, and to land a French army in England. The exiled Stuarts were then to be re-established on the throne of Great Britain. A vast French army concentrated at Dunkirk, and all England waited daily in expectation of invasion.

The British fleet was active in the Mediterranean and on the West Indies Station. France and Spain hoped to keep them busy there and leave the way clear for invasion. It was now, however, that Anson instituted a Western Squadron of about twenty ships, under Sir John Norris, to cruise off Brest and to keep watch in the Channel. The suggestion is thought to have been made by Vernon, but it was Anson who put it into effect. Norris withdrew to the Downs to entice the French fleet up the Channel. Dunkirk was full of transports with men, stores, and ammunition, and as the French fleets from Brest and Rochefort stood up channel invasion seemed imminent. At this moment a storm developed, reaching such severity that the French ships of war were shattered and dispersed, and the transports foundered in harbour with tremendous loss of life. The danger of invasion was momentarily over.

On the 23rd April 1745, on his 48th birthday, Anson was promoted to Rear-Admiral of the White. The significance of the white will be explained later when dealing with Anson's reforms in promotion.

# CHAPTER XIII

# Anson at Admiralty

ALTHOUGH the danger of a full-scale invasion of England was now over, Prince Charles, the Young Pretender to the throne, was determined to try his luck, convinced that he would find overwhelming support once he got to Britain. He embarked in a sloop, the *Doutelle*, on 4th July 1745, and was joined by the *Elizabeth*, sixty-four guns, a French man-of-war which was to escort him to the Western Isles of Scotland. On passage they encountered the *Lion*, fifty-four guns, an English man-of-war, commanded by no less a person than Peircy Brett, now a captain of seniority back-dated to the occasion when Anson had left him in command of *Centurion* in the Canton River.

Brett immediately ran his ship alongside the *Elizabeth*, and a tremendous duel began. The *Lion* pounded the *Elizabeth*'s hull. The *Elizabeth* aimed to destroy *Lion*'s rigging. For five hours the battle raged, tremendous slaughter being effected in both ships. The *Lion* was now reduced to a floating hull, masts and rigging shot away. The *Elizabeth* though with a battered hull, was able to set sail and crawled away to reach Brest. The *Doutelle*, after attempting to rake the *Lion*, made off with all sail and landed Prince Charles at Moidart on the west coast of Scotland. Brett and all his lieutenants were wounded: sixty-two of his men were killed or died of wounds. The *Elizabeth* had fared slightly worse in casualties and had also lost her captain.

Prince Charles was disappointed in the lack of general enthusiasm which greeted his arrival. He received little encouragement at first, but nevertheless hoisted his standard on the 12th August 1745, and rallied the disaffected clans. At the same time vigorous measures were taken in England, and these increased after Charles' success at the battle of Prestonpans. Anson extended these measures to the Channel Squadron so that a watchful eye could be kept on any French attempts to send reinforcements to the rebellious clans. Admiral Vernon, the victor at Porto Bello in 1739, was appointed to the command, and hoisted his flag on 2nd August 1745. Great activity followed, particularly by frigates and small, fast vessels, and resulted in the capture or destruction of French transports. Howe first came to notice at this time while in command of the sloop *Baltimore*, for a gallant action against the French during which he was badly wounded in the head. Howe had been a midshipman in the *Severn* in Anson's expedition, and was later to become First Lord of the Admiralty and defeat the French at the battle of the Glorious First of June 1794.

The unexpected initial success of the '45 rebellion and the crossing of the border caused great consternation in England. When the rebels reached the Midlands, George II ordered his yacht to await him at the Tower stairs. The concern is very well brought out in extracts of letters written to Anson by his brother Thomas, from Shugborough, the family seat in Staffordshire. These may be seen in the British Museum.

December 4th '45, Wednesday.

Thomas Anson to the Admiral.

Dear Brother,

You will share my disappointment when I relate ye sequel after your alarm of your midnight march and most positive assurances that ye Rebels were at Newcastle: I went to Stone in ye morning full of ye Battle I was to see and met Crowds of People coming back in great Consternation who cry'd out, 'it was begun'. I heard no firing, when I came I found all the Troops in and about the Town upon heaps. I forc'd my way to ye Duke's Quarters where I learn'd that ye Rebels were at Leek. Having been long tir'd to Death I got home as fast as I could, and find ye Rascals left Leek at one this morning and tis suppos'd will be at Derby tonight.

Shugborough, 7 December 1745

. . . ye rebels yesterday morning marched out of Derby and lay at Ashburn and ye adjacent villages. A person I sent to reconnoitre saw ye whole body pass along a valley at the other side of Weaver Hills, the road to Newcastle or Leek.

Ye rebels exceed 7,000: 3,000 or 4,000 good troops, the rest rabble and boys. Ye Pretender's Son marched at the head. He is something under 6 feet high, wears a plaid, walks well, speaks little, and was never seen to smile. My situation is still the same—between two fires.

It looks as though Charles was already beginning to realize the hopelessness of his cause, and would soon be in retreat from the Duke of Cumberland's troops. We have heard much of the 'Butcher' and his cruelty, but the following extract from another letter to Anson indicates that cruelty was also much in evidence among the rebels.

Shugborough 9 December 1745

They marched out of Leek yesterday, and are probably returning by ye same route they came.

Ye rebels are greatly exasperated at their reception in Derby: their leader was observ'd to be much more gloomy than usual; their ladies wept; and their whole body marched out with visible dejection and despair. They have plundered and ravaged, murdered two or three people, and wounded others, so that their name is in horror and detestation. Their cruelty will probably increase, if they have time to exert it, which I fancy ye Duke will not give them.

The Duke was certainly giving them no time at all now. Not only were the rebels in retreat but they were being overtaken by the Duke's cavalry. In a final letter on the subject from his brother, Anson read:

Shugborough 14th December 1745

Ye rebels marched out of Preston yesterday, our horse marched in that afternoon, and it was thought would be up with them by noon today.

The rebels were by now in the utmost distress, without shoes or stockings in many cases, and with no hope of getting away. Before the end of the year they had surrendered at Carlisle and withdrawn to Scotland. The rebellion was virtually over.

Admiral Vernon had been in command at the Downs during this period and had been indefatigable in his efforts to ensure that no French reinforcements should reach Britain. There followed, however, at this time a most unhappy harsh event which needs examination since Anson must be held largely responsible, and for which there is a great measure of justification. It must be remembered, however, that there had also been much justification for the Board's attitude in accepting Anson's virtual resignation when he had been unable to obtain confirmation of Brett's promotion, though opinion generally would have favoured clemency.

Vernon came from a good family, and had been educated at Westminster under the famous Dr. Busby, who kept his hat on his head in the presence of monarchs lest his pupils should be led to believe that there lived a greater man than he. Vernon's father had been a well known Member of Parliament and had reached high rank. It was inevitable therefore that Vernon himself should enter politics and become a veritable firebrand. It was mainly through his efforts in the House of Commons that Walpole agreed to allow him to attempt the capture of Porto Bello in 1739. This had been a resounding victory in spite of Walpole's opposition. Even in victory Walpole had been pessimistic. 'They may ring their bells now,' he muttered gloomily; 'before long they'll be wringing their hands.' His prophecy almost came true in the 1745 rebellion. Vernon had by then become extremely critical and dissatisfied. He later developed a system of pamphleteering, calling to light the abuses of the age and the neglect of the Navy, and circulated pamphlets such as 'Some Seasonable Advice from an Honest Sailor' and 'A Specimen of Naked Truth from a British Sailor'. These could not fail to offend the administration, particularly as they came from the famous victor of Porto Bello, whose success had stirred the whole nation at a time when they were tired of insults and pillage heaped on them by Spaniards.

While in command of the Channel Squadron, having been

promoted Admiral of the White just prior to hoisting his flag in the Downs, Vernon corresponded with the Board of Admiralty frequently, and hinted that he was so dissatisfied that he would resign. It is certain that he was unwell, and at length, without giving any reason at all, he wrote to the First Lord and asked to be relieved of his command. At this time Anson was forty-eight, and a Rear-Admiral. Vernon was sixty-one, and a full Admiral.

The Board without hesitation replied giving their consent. Anson it is true was extremely busy, already struggling to put various matters right. Nobody more than he knew how bad things were in the Navy. It must have been with relief to the Board that they appointed a successor to the Channel Command and instructed Vernon to come ashore, for his numerous letters had used intemperate and abusive language.

26 December 1745

. . . we require you to deliver up the Command of all his Majesty's ships, and also of all other ships and vessels employed in His Majesty's service, and that are under your orders, to Vice-Admiral Martin; . . . and having so done, you are to strike your flag, and come ashore.

This was not the end, for Vernon continued his abuse and produced his two pamphlets. In April 1746 he was summoned before the Board and asked if it was he who was responsible for the pamphlets. There were present His Grace the Duke of Bedford, the Earl of Sandwich, Rear-Admiral Anson, Mr. Grenville, Mr. Legge, and Lord Barrington. Vernon refused to answer. The following day, 11th April 1746, the Board 'signified his Majesty's pleasure' that Admiral Vernon should be struck off the list of flag officers. It is impossible to condone Vernon's behaviour, but strict justice would have required a court martial in which the sentence could well have been severe censure or reprimand, or a resolution that he should no longer be employed. To be dismissed without a trial from the Service in which he had shown courage, initiative, and great resolution in action was a harsh blow. He retired to his seat at Nacton in Suffolk and died eleven years later. The British will always remember him for his great victory at Porto Bello.

An important event in 1745 concerned Anson's old friend Peter Warren whom he had first met in the West Indies. The Peace of Utrecht had confirmed Britain's possessions bordering the Gulf of St. Lawrence; Acadia (rechristened Nova Scotia) on one side, and Newfoundland on the other. In order to neutralize this strategical threat to their colonies, the French had built a powerful fortress at Louisburg on the island of Cape Breton which virtually guarded and controlled the entrance to the St. Lawrence. Commodore Warren commanded a naval expedition which, in conjunction with detachments of troops from the British Colonies, made an assault on Louisburg and enforced its capitulation by the French on 27th June 1745.

For some time after the occupation of the harbour and fortress at Louisburg by the British, valuable French prizes were enticed into the harbour, whose cargoes amounted in value to more than a million sterling. Warren was promoted Rear-Admiral of the Blue. This timely success by Warren, who was a man universally liked, was applauded by the public, but had not the same appeal that a victory at sea would have had. Anson received a personal account of the assault, and must have been doubly gratified that the Navy had scored a success and that it was his old friend who had commanded the operation.

The gateway of the St. Lawrence was now open to the British, and all French America exposed to attack. Owing to preoccupation elsewhere this success was not followed up, and the assault and capture had to be done all over again by Boscawen, Wolfe, and Amherst, in 1758. (See map, page 233).

There was no opportunity for a big fleet action in 1746, but British naval prestige began to be restored in a series of small actions in which individual British ships showed superiority in gunnery and seamanship in spite of the enemy's greater numbers in guns and men. The resolution and constant practice which Anson had fostered so much during his expedition were bearing fruit, and the slaughter in the French ships was great. His old lieutenant, Philip Saumarez, now captain of the *Nottingham*, sixty guns and four hundred men, successfully engaged the *Mars*, sixty-four guns and five hundred men, and lost only three men killed. The French lost twenty-three killed. The *Portland*, Captain Stevens, captured *L'Auguste* after a close action of two

hours in which the Frenchmen had five hundred killed to the
*Portland*'s five men. The *Defiance* lost one man in capturing the
*Ambuscade* in which the slaughter was ten times or worse that of
the British ship.

Privateers were also involved as well as the King's ships.
A Mr. Brown, master of the *Shoreham*, a privateer with but
two guns and twelve swivels, engaged a privateer of ten guns,
eighteen swivels and seventy-eight men from Bilbao for five
hours. Having killed forty-six men, he found all his ammunition
spent and took the privateer by boarding. He was given a
commission in the King's service for his determined action, and
appointed to command a sloop of war. Two privateer actions
are mentioned in a private letter to Anson from Mr. Legge, a
member of the Board of Admiralty. The first was that of
Phillips who boarded and recaptured the *Solebay* against great
odds. At the recommendation of Anson and the Duke of
Bedford, the King granted him a purse of five hundred guineas
and a gold medal of the value of two hundred guineas. The
second was that of Molineux Shuldham who showed great
gallantry in action against two privateers, though losing almost
half his men and himself wounded three times. He was given
a captain's commission. It is clear that Anson missed no
opportunity at this juncture of inspiring boldness and leadership and of advocating just reward for services rendered. He was
determined to reinstate the Navy as the symbol of Britain's
power.

It was in 1746 that Anson turned his attention seriously to
the ships themselves. He was concerned with two main points.
The first was to ensure that ships were soundly built, so as to
be able to take much punishment if necessary, and continue
fighting in all weathers. The second was to produce a classification that would truly indicate a ship's role. The existing
classification of rates had little uniformity, and for years ships
had been built to meet particular schemes rather than to
conform to some standard requirement.

The first requirement was that ships of the same rate would
have the same dimensions and could thus be provided with
standard equipment that would fit them all equally. The ships
were required to be stiff, so that they would not heel over

easily with the wind. This could be achieved by a design which lowered the centre of gravity without lowering the centre of buoyancy. The result would be that ships would remain upright in a breeze and could more easily keep their lee ports open, and fight the guns in heavy weather.

The existing rating before Anson brought in a change was as follows:

| Rate | Guns | Tons |
|------|------|------|
| 1st | 100 | Over 1,500 |
| 2nd | 90 | 1,000–1,500 |
| 3rd | 80, 90 | 750–1,000 |
| 4th | 60, 50 | 350–750 |
| 5th | 40 | 200–350 |
| 6th | 20 | 200 and under |

Any of the first four rates could fight in the line of battle, which meant that the line would vary from powerful three-deckers with a hundred guns to two-deckers with only fifty guns. The weak link in the chain would be the obvious target for attack.

Anson decided to divide ships into two groups: battleships that would be 'fit to stand in the line', and cruisers that would be too weak for the line but fast and able to perform a number of other duties such as shadowing the enemy fleet and fighting their own kind. This classification was eventually adopted by all navies and lasted for two hundred years. Anson subdivided his main groups as shown in the table on page 142.

One of the famous ships to follow from Anson's efforts was the *Victory*, a great favourite with flag officers as she was not only formidable in fighting power but fast and manœuvrable. The 5th and 6th rates of his classification became the fast frigates which Nelson found so much an essential part of his naval strategy.

A further very important reform was to be initiated by Anson about this time. This concerned the system of promotion to admiral. Until 1743 there were only nine flag officers. They

| Class | Rate | Guns | Tons | Decks |
|-------|------|------|------|-------|
| BATTLESHIPS | 1st | 100 and over | 2,500 | Three |
| | 2nd | 90 | 1,800 | |
| | 3rd | 74, 64 | 1,500–1,800 | Two |
| | 4th | (60), 50 | 1,000 | |
| CRUISERS | 5th | 36, 32 | 750 | Single |
| | 6th | 28, 24 | 500 and under | |

were promoted by selection from the captains' list and served until they died, which meant not only that some senior active service admirals were very old but that there was a very considerable bottleneck for promotion from the enormous captains' list to the very small flag list. Sir John Norris in command of the Western Squadron in 1744 was eight-four. He was the one and only Admiral of the Fleet and remained so, though without a command for the last five years of his life, until he died.

The allocation of nine flag officers had developed from the large single fleets of the Dutch wars. The fleet was divided into Red, White, and Blue squadrons which occupied positions in the Centre, Van, and Rear respectively. Each squadron had an admiral. The centre was the senior post and it was here with the Red squadron that the senior admiral, the Admiral of the Fleet, was stationed. Admiral of the Red was therefore synonymous with Admiral of the Fleet. The squadron in the van would have the next senior, the Admiral of the White, and the squadron in the rear would have the Admiral of the Blue. Squadrons were, however, themselves large and unwieldy and were therefore divided into Centre, Van, and Rear divisions, each with a flag officer, the Admiral being in the Centre, a Vice-Admiral in the Van, and a Rear-Admiral in the Rear. The junior flag officer would thus be the Rear-Admiral of the Blue in command of the Rear Division of the Rear Squadron.

Edward, Lord Hawke
*From an oil painting by Francis Cotes*

Elizabeth, Lady Anson
*From an oil painting by T. Hudson*

By 1743, Britain's wars were conducted on a widespread scale. One fleet was no longer sufficient, and the number of flag officers had been increased to twenty-one, composed as follows:

1 Admiral of the Fleet
3 Admirals of the White
3 Admirals of the Blue
2 Vice-Admirals of the Red
2 Vice-Admirals of the White
1 Vice-Admiral of the Blue
3 Rear-Admirals of the Red
3 Rear-Admirals of the White
3 Rear-Admirals of the Blue

This eased the bottleneck for promotion only very slightly. But the chief disadvantage of the prevailing scheme was that nobody ever retired. The result was that there were very many captains who had been passed over, but who were kept on the Active List, receiving half pay, but never knowing when they might next be employed. Three captains had been nominated for promotion to rear-admiral in 1744, being selected from the captains' list as follows: Isaac Townsend, 51st; Henry Medley, 52nd; George Anson, 56th. There were no further promotion lists until 1747: but Warren was promoted Rear-Admiral of the Blue after his capture of Fort Louisburg on 27th June 1745.

A memorandum was prepared, and in due course an Order in Council effected a change, though as with so many reforms there was a provision which excluded many of the captains from reaping the benefit through no fault of their own.

His Majesty is pleased to order that, at the next promotion of flag officers, such captains of the navy, who, notwithstanding their seniority, shall happen to be set aside by such promotion, as well as those who have been already set aside by any former promotions, shall be appointed, by commission, rear-admirals in general terms, provided that all such captains shall have served at sea since the commencement of the present war with Spain.

It looks as though it was Mr. Legge who was responsible for the sting in the tail, as he writes to Anson as follows:

> I have, with much difficulty, so far got the better of our noble friend's implicit tenderness to length of service, or in other words, to seniority of inexperience, as to limit the retrospect of that plan to those who have served since the commencement of the war with Spain.

That there could exist such an attitude of contempt for 'service' by those who could influence or affect rewards for it, is a grim realization of the possible misuse of power. Nevertheless the inference that service was tantamount to 'seniority of inexperience' indicates the significance of officers' part-time employment, and emphasizes the fact that many officers could soldier on for years without an active appointment.

There now followed nine promotions to active flags, and nineteen to rear-admiral 'in general terms'. This was the first retirement scheme. Promotion on retirement then lasted for nearly two hundred years, by which time retirement schemes had become general and an officer was compelled to retire in his existing substantive rank instead of being promoted on retirement.

Among the nine promoted to active rank were Hawke and Boscawen. Hawke who was forty-two, and a very senior captain, was made a Rear-Admiral of the White. Boscawen was dipped down for, a captain of only ten years' standing and not quite thirty-six in age.

The nineteen whose services were no longer required were said by the public to have been promoted to the 'Yellow Squadron', or more briefly to have been 'Yellowed'. They were not strictly entitled to be called Rear-Admiral as ranks were at that time only associated with posts. The usage of rank as title was, however, growing and it presumably became easier to refer to Mr. Smith, Rear-Admiral of the Yellow Squadron, as Rear-Admiral Smith.

# CHAPTER XIV

## The Engagement in the Law Courts

AFTER *Centurion*'s triumphant arrival at Spithead in 1744, Millechamp, the purser of the little *Tryal* and the *Tryal's Prize*, had written in his Narrative:

> . . . but the affair is not yet over, for now as we had nothing else to encounter or make us unhappy we must fall out one among another concerning the Distribution of the Money we had taken by which means we had more Terrible Engagements in the Courts of Law, than ever we had in the South Seas, or even in taking the Galleon, the Gentlemen who were the immediate officers of the *Centurion* pretending that the others who were of the *Gloucester* and *Tryal Prize* had no right to share because a Mann of Warr cannot bear more than her Established Compliment of officers, they would therefore exclude them from their Shares as officers: but this matter is too Dry and Tedious to insert here.

The matter was, however, to be the subject of discussion for many years, and can be read in detail in the Hartwell Collection ('39 MS 9416) at the National Maritime Museum.

In the beginning, the lieutenants and other officers of the *Gloucester* and *Tryal's Prize* who had been transferred to *Centurion* alleged their right to a share of prize money which accorded with their status as officers. This was admitted by the Judge of the High Court of Admiralty.

In a proclamation of the Lords Justices issued on 19th June 1740, it had been stated that:

Bounty money should be divided in 8 parts

Captain should have 3 parts (if actually on board: to give Flag Officer 1 part of this, if borne.)

| | |
|---|---|
| Lieuts, Boatswain, Gunner, Purser, Carpenter, Master's Mate, Chirurgeons and Chaplain | 1 part equally divided |
| Midshipmen, Carpenter's Mates etc. Chirurgeon's Mates, Coxswain, Quartermaster, Master at Arms, Corporals | 1 part equally divided |
| Trumpeters, Steward, Cook, Armourer, Gunsmith, Cooper, Swabber, Barber, Able Seamen, Ord. Seamen, Soldiers | 2 parts divided equally between them |

Whether the officers were to be regarded as in their 'proper qualification' or merely as supernumeraries therefore made a considerable difference in the share which would be allocated to them. The higher their share the less to go round those officers who had been appointed in a vacancy to fill permanent appointments in the complement of the *Centurion*. The latter therefore appealed against the allegations made by the *Gloucester* and *Tryal* officers which had been admitted by Admiralty.

An extract of the original allegation is worth reading and is given here with the main points 'alledged, pleaded, and propounded' by those who had been transferred as supernumeraries after their ship had been destroyed.

### Allegation

A Copy of the Allegation given in by the Lieutenants, and other Commission and Warrant Officers, of His Majesty's Ships the *Gloucester* and the *Tryal Prize* and admitted by the Judge of the High Court of Admiralty: from the Admission whereof, the Lieutenants and other Commission and Warrant Officers of His Majesty's ship

*Centurion* have appealed to the Lords Commissions for Appeals in Prize Cauzes.

## THE NUESTRA SENORA DEL COBADONGA

Proxy and Proctor for Patrick Baird 1st Lieut., Samuel Scott 2nd Lt., Thomas Foley 3rd Lt., Robt. Lambert, Master, John Pack, Bosn, James Barcroft, Gunner, Nehemiah Winter, Carpenter, and Lawrence Millechamp, Purser of H.M.S. *Gloucester*,

and John Hughes, Lt., Joseph Allin, Surgeon, and John Sheppherd, Carpenter, of H.M.S. *Tryal Prize* alledged pleaded and propounded

that before *Tryal Prize* was destroyed the officers petitioned the Commodore to commission the *Carmin* which was quite sound: Commodore refused to comply.

that at the time *Gloucester* was destroyed, *Centurion* was in as great distress: could not have proceeded to China or any other port without assistance of officers and crew of *Gloucester* and *Tryal Prize*.

. . .

13. That after *Centurion* arrived at Tinian 27 August the officers of *Gloucester* and *Tryal Prize* did duty on board as Officers: and some particularly, on the 22nd Day of September 42, the *Centurion* being drove to Sea, from Tinian, Patrick Baird, 1st Lieut. of the *Gloucester*, by the orders of Lieut. Philip Saumarez, the Commanding Officer then on Board the *Centurion* did take his watch and charge of the *Centurion* as Lieut.

14. That, 12 November 1742, arrived at Macao they applied to Commodore Anson, for leave to return to England, but were refused, as the *Centurion* was weakly manned.

15. 16. 17. Were ordered to perform various duties in *Centurion*.

18. John Hughes, quartered to aid Lieut. Peircy Brett, the Officer of the Upper Deck, (which officer was wounded, carried off, in the Beginning of the Engagement) did, then *command* on that Deck, until the Spanish ship struck.

19. John Hughes Lieut, Joseph Allin Surgeon, and John

Shepherd, Carpenter, of the *Tryal Prize*, Sam Scott and Thomas Foley Lieuts, John Pack, Boatswain, and James Barcroft, Gunner of the *Gloucester*, were ordered on board the Prize to do Duty as Officers.

21. That, all and singular the Premises were and are true . . . the Party Proponent prays that it may be pronounced that his said Partys, were aiding and assisting, in the Capture of the said Prize and for their Right to a Share in the said Prize, *as officers*, by you be given in this Behalf.

So much for the Allegation which was admitted by the Judge of the High Court of the Admiralty.

There then followed a case made by the officers who had filled complement billets in the *Centurion* at the time of the *Cobadonga* action. This was known as the appellants' case in which they desired that the Admiralty admission of the allegation should be reversed, and that the respondents' allegation should be rejected.

### The Appellants Case

| | | |
|---|---|---|
| *Appellants* | Philip Saumarez | 1st Lieut. |
| | Peircy Brett | 2nd |
| | Peter Dennis | 3rd |
| | Justinian Nutt | Master |
| | Thomas Adams | Boatswain |
| | Adam Hayes | Carpenter |
| | John Nuttale | Gunner |
| | John Rule | Purser |
| | Thomas Summers ⎱ | Master's |
| | John Campbell ⎰ | Mates |

Commission and Warrant Officers of H.M. Ship the *Centurion*

| | | |
|---|---|---|
| *Respondents* | Patrick Baird | 1st Lieut. |
| | Samuel Scott | 2nd |
| | Thomas Foley | 3rd |
| | Robert Lambert | Master |

| | | |
|---|---|---|
| | John Pack | Boatswain |
| | James Barcroft | Gunner |
| | Nehemiah Winter | Carpenter |
| | Lawrence Millechamp | Purser |

late belonging to H.M.S. *Gloucester*

| | | |
|---|---|---|
| and | John Hughes | Lieut |
| | Joseph Allin | Surgeon |
| | John Shephard | Carpenter |

late belonging to H.M. late Ship the *Tryal Prize*

The Appellants opposed the receiving of the Allegation as not by Law admissible since the Respondents neither being officers or in Pay as officers of the *Centurion* at the time of the said Capture.

The Appellants humbly hope, the said decree of the Judge of the Admiralty, of the 7th day of September 1744 for admitting the said Allegation, shall be reversed, and set aside; and that the Respondents said Allegations shall be rejected.

This was in the autumn of 1744, a few weeks after the return of the *Centurion*. The case was to go on for nearly three years, but is briefly summarized by revealing comments in longhand on the original printed sheets:

Anson gave evidence as a witness:

| | |
|---|---|
| 1st deposition | 30 March '45 |
| 2nd deposition | 22 October '45 |

Extracts from Sir George Lee's manuscript:

25. The officers of the *Gloucester* and *Tryal Prize* were not acting and assisting as officers commanding on board the *Centurion* at the time of taking the *Cobadonga*.
Respondent [Anson] on the representation of the Captain and Officers of the *Gloucester* on 13 Aug 1742 order'd the officers and Ship's Company belonging to the

*Gloucester* on board the *Centurion* to save them from perishing and not to reinforce the *Centurion*.

Much was made of the assistance given by *Centurion* to both *Gloucester* and *Tryal Prize* at Fernandez which was greatly superior to that given in return.

Written in longhand on the document:

May 19th 1747. After 4 nights hearing, the Lords reversed the sentence of the Judge of the Admiralty and were of opinion that the officers of the *Gloucester* and *Tryal* not being proper officers of the *Centurion*, could not within the meaning and intention of the Act of Parliament and Proclamation share in the prize with the proper officers of the *Centurion*: but did not give costs.

Lords present Dukes of Dorset, Richmond, Bedford and Argyll. Earls Pembroke, Winchelsea, Chesterfield and Cholmondely, Fitzwater, Gower, and Bath, Lord Sandys, Lord Chief Justice Willes and Mr. Doddington.

Argyle Bedford Cholmondely Bath and Willes were strongly for reversing: Pembroke and Winchelsea strongly for affirming: Sandys was doubtful.

Anson's share of the prize money was by right very considerable and would be little affected by the outcome of this tedious case. One cannot help inquiring, however, about his attitude to the case. It can be assumed that he at first supported the 1744 decision of the Judge of the High Court of the Admiralty to admit the allegation made by the officers of the *Gloucester* and the *Tryal's Prize*, although the wording of his reply to the petition made by the officers of the *Tryal's Prize*, prior to their transfer to the *Gloucester*, appears to be carefully worded to avoid any mention of entitlement to prize money.

When the Appellants made their case, Anson appeared as a respondent, but nevertheless seemed to make no attempt to refute the objection made by the Appellants.

One's sympathies are naturally with the Respondents, who had to be content with a seaman's share, and it appears strongly as if they got a raw deal in being treated as 'not proper officers' in spite of the evidence produced to show that many of them played a responsible part as proper officers. In the cold light of justice, however, dependent upon clearly defined rules, it must reluctantly be admitted that the ultimate answer was correct, if unfortunate. Had the admission of the allegation not been reversed, a precedent would have been established which would make nonsense of the rule that an officer of a ship could only be such by appointment into a complement billet. As the years of trial proceeded, Anson was assuming greater responsibility for proper administration at top level, and obviously realized that there could only be one outcome from the legal point of view.

But before we drop this 'long and tedious affair' it is worth looking at Anson's letter of 7th December 1742, written at Canton, and sent to England in the care of Saunders, who travelled home in a Swedish ship and arrived there on 29th May 1743. This was the first report of the voyage to reach England and can be seen in full at the Public Record office. The extract concerning the destruction of the *Tryal's Prize* will suffice here:

Dec 7th 1742
Canton in China.

Captain Michell by his letter of the 29th of March having made great complaint to me for want of Men and therein Signified to me, that it was impossible for him to Sail the Ship out of these Seas without more strength: and his Majesties Ship *Centurion* being also very indifferently mann'd thought it for his Majesties Service to Destroy the *Tryal Prize* (although she was in repair) to reinforce the Said Ships with her men; therefore ordered all his Majesties Stores on board the *Tryal Prize* late belonging to the *Tryal* Sloop to be delivered into the charge of the officers of his Majesties Ships *Centurion* and *Gloucester*, and ordered Seventeen of her Men on board the *Centurion* and forty-five on board the *Gloucester* including Negroes.

On the 29th of April I ordered his Majesty's Ship *Tryal Prize* to be run ashore and Burnt I also ordered the *Carmila* and *Carmin* Prizes to be Destroyed.

Here is evidence that Anson ordered the destruction of the *Tryal's Prize* ('although she was in repair'), because he needed the men. There may have been some truth therefore in the point made by Millechamp, and some justification in the case made by the *Tryal's* officers for a 'proper officers' share of prize money. In the case of the original *Gloucester* officers who were transferred to *Centurion* when their ship was in dire peril of sinking, it is clear that it could be argued that it was at their own request and in order to save their lives. The *Tryal* officers, however, who had been transferred to *Gloucester*, and were subsequently transferred to *Centurion* just before the *Gloucester's* end, could argue that although the later transfer was necessary for their survival, the occasion might never have arisen had they been permitted to remain in their original ship which was at the time 'in repair'.

The allegation, however, was made as one by the *Tryal* officers and the *Gloucester* officers together. And had been rejected.

Poor old Lawrence Millechamp. One feels sorry for him, denied his 'proper officer's' share of the prize money, although he had twice lost his ship. We can only hope that his narrative became a best seller in part compensation. As for John Pack and the others, perhaps they had better luck next time, for there were ample opportunities for valuable prize money in the years ahead.

# CHAPTER XV

# Anson's Victory off Finisterre

THE dismissal of Vernon in April 1746 created a vacancy for promotion to Admiral, and it is likely that Anson's promotion to Vice-Admiral of the Blue, two steps in promotion, dated 14th July 1746, followed as a result.

The Western Squadron, which he had instituted, had performed useful work in gallant individual ship actions, but there had been no fleet action since the fiasco off Toulon. Anson felt that a successful full scale action was necessary, so that British naval prestige, which had suffered severely in Admiral Mathews' ineffectual action, could be restored. Not only had prestige fallen, but morale was low, and the British public was losing confidence in the security from invasion which they traditionally expected from the Navy. In two recent cases, commodores of convoys had actually run away from the French. Anson himself must very much have felt the call of the sea at this time. His whole character was such that if there should be a job to be done, he felt that he was just the man to do it. With judgment, resolution, foresight, and preparation, and supported by trained officers and men and good ships, he was confident that he could perform all that was required. A decisive naval victory was becoming increasingly necessary.

The First Lord, the Duke of Bedford, supported his views and wrote on 18th July 1746, saying that he agreed with what Anson had said to the King on the subject of uniting all ships 'cruising to the westward, whether in the Bay, off the Isle of Bas and St. Malo's, or off Cape Clear, into one Squadron.' Anson therefore had himself appointed to the command of the

Western Squadron in the vacancy left by Vernon, and hoisted his flag in the *Yarmouth* on 9th August 1746, retaining his seat on the Board of Admiralty meanwhile. This was to be a wonderful opportunity of seeing at first hand how the Navy at sea was faring, and how the support and maintenance from the dockyards was working.

His first action on joining *Yarmouth* was to ask Admiralty for Peircy Brett to be appointed as his flag captain in *Yarmouth*, a sixty-four-gun ship carrying four hundred and eighty men.

Anson's reports and letters at this time describe the poor state of the fleet. He writes of bad food and bad beer, delays in supplies, sickness of the men, arrears of pay, slowness of rigging ships by the dockyard, provision of wrong size guns, difficulties of getting ships cleaned and scraped. He criticizes the administration of the dockyards and describes the difficulties of obtaining local action because of rigid rules requiring reference to Admiralty.

All through the following winter Anson exercised and operated his squadron. Fair weather and foul he kept watch at the approaches to the Channel in the hope of intercepting French convoys from the West Indies or India, or of finding the French fleet breaking out of Brest. He complains bitterly of a shortage of frigates and sloops which were essential for speedy reporting and communication of messages.

The size of the active part of the squadron was always reduced by the necessity for ships to refit and clean. As soon as bottoms had been scraped of barnacles and slime they were daubed with tallow, and the ship was ordered to sail at the earliest opportunity for the station where she was most likely to fall in with enemy privateers. She would then be in her fastest condition and have the best chance of coming up with her foe.

Anson's main reason for his strenuous activity during the winter was that he believed the winter to be the favourite time for arrival of French and Spanish convoys, because of the long dark nights free from surveillance, and because they expected the British ships to be in port. It is obvious from correspondence that Anson had a great realization of the need for secrecy and the security of information. He would never forget the loss of surprise which had been occasioned by the long delay and lack of secrecy over the preparation of his South Seas expedition. In his letters to Cleveland, the Secretary of the Admiralty at this time, he asks him not to allow the letters to fall into the hands of his clerks.

With recollections of the loss of masts suffered by the ships of his squadron, he makes a suggestion in a letter of 31st October 1746, which will speed up repairs.

It frequently happens in winter time that Channel cruisers spring or carry away their masts, and are sometimes obliged to wait several days till new ones are made, to the great hindrance of H.M. Service. I therefore desire their lordships will give directions to the Navy Board to have always a set of masts ready finished at all His Majesty's yards, for ships of the 3rd rate and downwards.

The last phrase is typical of Anson's attention to detail. His ships suffered much damage in the winter gales, and the crews underwent hardship and privation. He was, however, getting nearer to his objective: but a friendly word from a Dutchman to the French once again frustrated his efforts. In a letter to the Duke of Bedford he says:

How cordially I have cursed the Dutch who I find prevented General de Jonquiere's whole fleet falling into my hands the last winter, where he came from Chibatou— by one of their vessels informing him he was within 20 leagues of me, and must see me the next morning: upon which he altered course, and steered for Rochefort.

There is an interesting reference to Keppel and Boscawen: two of his best captains obviously sent off on a responsible job.

Feb 6 1747

Returned on Feb 1 with a hard gale and thick fog. Brought to 5 leagues off Portland, then to back of the Wight, and anchored: but at 4.0 a.m. the cable parted. The *Yarmouth* drove up the Downs, and asked permission

to go to Woolwich, as the weather was so extremely bad—
but Keppel was sent to cruise off the Channel, to intercept
privateers, and Boscawen off Cadiz.

So far Anson had failed in his main objective, which was to
destroy the enemy fleet. But he had by now achieved a semblance
of order and understanding and instilled an aggressive spirit
into his squadron. He continued to complain of delays in the
dockyards:

April 17 1747

I found on my arrival at Plymouth that none of the
frigates were clean. This as you will easily perceive, was
no small disappointment to me, as I had sent previous
orders to their captains to clean and hold themselves
constantly in readiness to sail at a moment's warning. I
feel the want of them very much in disciplining my ships;
and shall be still more sensible of it if I meet with an enemy's
fleet having nothing with me to repeat my signals.

News had recently been received of two French expeditions
fitting out, one to recapture Louisburg in Cape Breton Island,
which Warren had taken in 1745, and the other to go to the
East Indies. Anson had at once transferred his flag from the
*Yarmouth* to a ninety-gun ship, the *Prince George* commanded by
Captain Bentley, and sailed from Plymouth on 9th April 1747
with his squadron. His old friend Rear-Admiral Warren,
second in command, flying his flag in the *Devonshire*, was with
him and no less a company than Brett, Saumarez, and Denis,
the latter in command of the *Centurion* herself. Here was a team
of old shipmates and band of brothers that would brook no
opposition: they were resolved on success.

The squadron consisted of:

| Ship | Guns | Men | Captain |
|---|---|---|---|
| *Prince George* | 90 | 770 | Bentley |
| (Wearing the flag of Vice-Admiral Anson) | | | |
| *Devonshire* | 66 | 535 | West |
| (Wearing the flag of Rear-Admiral Warren) | | | |

| Ship | Guns | Men | Captain |
|------|------|-----|---------|
| *Namur* | 74 | 650 | Boscawen |
| *Princess Louisa* | 60 | 400 | Watson |
| *Monmouth* | 64 | 480 | Harrison |
| *Prince Frederick* | 64 | 480 | Norris |
| *Defiance* | 60 | 400 | Grenville |
| *Nottingham* | 60 | 400 | Saumarez |
| *Yarmouth* | 64 | 480 | Brett |
| *Windsor* | 60 | 480 | Hanway |
| *Falkland* | 50 | 300 | Barradel |
| *Centurion* | 50 | 375 | Denis |
| *Bristol* | 50 | 300 | W. Montague |
| *Pembroke* | 60 | 400 | Fincher |
| *Ambuscade* | 40 | 250 | J. Montague |
| *Falcon* Sloop | | | Gwyn |
| *Vulcan* fireship | | | — |

A private intrigue aimed at detaching the *Defiance* and the *Bristol* from Anson's squadron, and went so far as to order this in a letter which it was hoped the First Lord would sign without reading. Grenville of the *Defiance* was related to George Grenville, one of the Lords of the Admiralty, to whom is attributed this intrigue. Montague of the *Bristol* was a brother of the Earl of Sandwich who repudiated his kinsman on hearing of the case. The intrigue was exposed. The Duke of Bedford then lost no time in removing George Grenville from the Board. He was replaced by Wellbore Ellis. The reason for the intrigue was the quest of prize money which was more readily obtainable by private ships cruising alone on distant hunting grounds. There was no question of cowardice, for both captains fought well in the subsequent action; Grenville died in action.

Anson's force was now formidable, consisting of six battle-ships and nine cruisers according to his new rating; but only one sloop. He was still not satisfied, and continued to press the Admiralty for better arrangements at the dockyards. Ships could now be cleaned as required, but would then suffer delay because stores were not available. On the eve of his action with the French he writes:

*Prince George* at Sea 2 May 1747

to Admiralty:

Thos Corbett Esq.

It is great pain to me, that I am obliged to repeat in almost every letter, the frequent delays the ships of my Squadron meet with in fitting out for the Sea, and the Complaints I receive of there not being Stores enough at Plymouth to answer the demands, even when the Tallow is upon their Bottoms. I submit it to their Lordships whether it would not tend greatly towards the good of the Service, that the Navy Board should have Directions to keep an Extraordinary Magazine of all Kind of Stores at that Port, during the War.

On 3rd May 1747, at daybreak Anson was off Cape Finisterre with his ships spread out in a single line abreast, a distance of one mile between ships. He was then able to cover a wide search area. At seven o'clock, the sloop *Falcon* which had been cruising off Rochefort, joined the flagship and informed him that they had sighted the French fleet the day before at four p.m. The fleet consisted of thirty-eight sail, of which nine appeared to be men-of-war, the rest merchantmen under convoy, all steering to the westward. Anson's great chance had arrived.

He immediately steered for the south-west. At nine thirty Boscawen in *Namur* reported sighting the French fleet to the south-west. This report was followed shortly after by one from the flagship's masthead lookout. Anson made the signal for general chase, and by noon observed that nine of the enemy were shortening sail and forming a line of battle ahead, while the convoy continued to the westward with all the sail they could set.

At one o'clock, Anson re-formed his ships in line abreast, to bring the slow sailers up with the fast, and half an hour later formed into line ahead, preparatory to engaging. By then he was of the opinion that the French intended to escape him, and ordered his ships in the van to 'lead more large' in order to get to grips quickly. This order was shortly followed by the signal for general chase, the position being reminiscent of that at the Battle of Cape Passaro, in which Anson had fought twenty-nine

The liberty of the subject
*From a coloured etching by J. Gilray*

The *Royal George* off Deptford

years earlier as a lieutenant in the *Montague*, and had taken part in the capture of the *Volante*. His decision was timely.

Now it was a free for all, and there was no need to pay regard to the line of battle. The first ship to get up with the rear of the enemy line was the *Centurion* herself, with Denis in command. She had always been a fast sailer. She immediately engaged the rear ship. Two of the largest enemy ships now bore down to assist the rear ship. By this time *Namur* (Boscawen), *Defiance* (Grenville), and *Windsor* (Hanway) had entered the action, and having disabled the rearmost ships, sailed ahead to cut off the ships in the van of the enemy line.

*Yarmouth* (Brett), and *Devonshire* (West) with Admiral Warren on board, followed close on their heels and were soon engaged in the rear. The *Prince George* passed them and made for the enemy flagship, the *Invincible*.

By seven o'clock, all the ships in the enemy's rear had struck; the others followed suit soon afterwards.

The action had been furious and sustained. Boscawen was wounded in the shoulder. Grenville was killed. The casualties were great, five hundred and twenty killed and wounded on the British side, seven hundred on the French. Anson had had a tremendous superiority, but he had seized his opportunity and had captured the whole of the opposing force. He brought to at seven o'clock that evening, and despatched *Monmouth*, *Yarmouth*, and *Nottingham* to pursue the convoy.

Anson's prizes in the battle were: Men-of-war bound for Quebec: *Le Serieux* (66), *Le Diamant* (66), *Le Rubis* (52), *La Gloire* (54); men-of-war bound for East Indies: *L'Invincible* (74), *Le Jason* (54); Indiamen bound for East Indies: *Le Philibert* (30), *L'Apollon* (30), *La Thetis* (30).

The sloop *Falcon* which had been despatched to shadow the escaping convoy returned the following day with the Indiaman *Dartmouth* (18), and Brett and Saumarez brought back the *Vigilante* (22) and *Modeste* (22), and the greater part of the convoy.

The Commander of the *L'Invincible* having struck to Anson repaired on board the *Prince George* to deliver up his sword, and endeared himself to Anson and his officers by his gracious manner and turn of wit.

'*Monsieur*' he said, '*vous avez vaincu* L'Invincible *et* La Gloire *vous suit*.'

This epigrammatic prophecy came true, for in the following month his Majesty was pleased to create Anson a peer of Great Britain, with the title Baron Anson of Soberton in the County of Hants.

Finisterre was a crushing defeat for the French. Anson had had great superiority, nevertheless he had achieved a very necessary victory, a victory which was a culmination of persistence, training, and preparation. The battle itself could easily have fizzled out but for Anson's quick decision to order a general chase, and for the organization whereby each British ship attacked the first enemy it could reach with the intention of crippling her and leaving her to be dealt with by slower ships coming up in support.

Besides the capture of six men-of-war and several armed Indiamen, privateers, and merchant ships, ten thousand troops were taken and all their money, stores, and guns which had been destined for Canada. The money was taken to Portsmouth and put into twenty waggons to be carried to London, where a grand military procession took place to the Bank of England. Thousands cheered and there were illuminations and bonfires in every street. Anson had once again captured the admiration of the people. His victory came as the first for many years and the first substantial one in the war. It not only inspired the Navy but fired the imagination of the people. Strategically it was also of great importance not only in causing a serious reverse to the French, but in ending two separate expeditions which were aimed at crippling British naval and colonial power in two different parts of the world.

Anson gave Denis, the Captain of *Centurion*, the honour of hurrying to the Admiralty with the news of the victory.

The First Lord wrote to Anson:

> You will easily believe no one in this town did with greater joy receive the news of your great success against the French than myself: and universal I may say it is, as I am just come home through illuminated streets and bonfires. The King told me this morning at his levee that

I had given him the best breakfast he had had this long time, and I think I never saw him more pleased in my life. He has ordered Captain Denis a reward of £500 for bringing this welcome news.

Rear-Admiral Warren received the military Order of the Bath and the accolade of Knighthood. Boscawen received a special mention, and was promoted Rear-Admiral of the Blue in July 1747.

Anson returned to the Admiralty after his victory, leaving the command of the Western Squadron in the hands of Sir Peter Warren. He was now even more fitted for his post on the Board of Admiralty: his prestige was tremendous, his concern for the welfare of the Navy greater then ever, and his experience unparalleled. He was moreover now a very rich man. He appears to have been unaffected by his successes except perhaps to be even more resolute to carry out reforms where necessary. He remained modest, undemonstrative, and imperturbable, and as ever reluctant to commit himself to any unnecessary speech or writing.

A letter to the First Lord from the admirable Warren, and therefore to be considered sincere and unaffected and worthy of recording, says of Anson:

May 18, 1747

I well know his modesty will not suffer him to acquaint you that it was owing (under God) to his own good conduct as an officer. In my life I never served with more pleasure, nor saw half such pains taken to discipline a fleet.

It must have been about this time that he saw a good deal of Lord Hardwicke the great and virtuous Lord Chancellor (1737–1755), who was a great admirer of Anson and who had been one of the signatories in 1740 of the 'Additional Instructions' issued by the Lords Justices for 'George Anson, Esq. Commander-in-Chief of His Majesty's Ships to be sent into the South Seas in America.' Lord Hardwicke had been one of the first to receive a personal account of the South Seas expedition from Anson when he returned to Spithead in 1744.

The Lord Chancellor had an attractive daughter, and it is probable that an attachment, possibly an understanding, began to develop at this time. A family friendship had existed for years, since Anson's aunt had married Thomas Parker, afterwards Lord Parker, who became Lord Chancellor in 1718.

Anson had always a desire for uniformity and precision. This is apparent in a number of circumstances, an important one being the standardization of ship ratings, equipment, and stores. He also attached importance to appearance and ceremony as contributory factors towards good discipline and prestige. This was evident when he dressed and armed a detachment of seamen to accompany him to Canton to visit the viceroy.

The nearest approach to uniform in the Navy had hitherto been the wearing of soldiers' old coats by lieutenants serving in ships of the Mediterranean Station based at Gibraltar and Mahón in Minorca. These were red coats trimmed with black and were probably quite serviceable.

In 1748, a design for a standard uniform was introduced by Anson to be worn by flag officers and captains. It is not clear exactly what this uniform consisted of. It probably began as a full dress uniform of the resplendent pattern which we see Anson wearing in his portrait by Reynolds, and modifications for every day wear and mess wear must have developed from this.

In the portrait we see a waistcoat of white cashmere with vast pockets trimmed with blue. The outer coat is of thick blue cloth with sleeves cut short to show the lace waistcoat sleeves, and with lavish gold lace decoration on pockets, cuffs, and lapels.

The wearing of such a uniform was without doubt a very expensive privilege, and it is probably for that reason that its use was confined to flag and senior officers, combined with the overriding factor that a visible indication of position was considered necessary for the sake of prestige and discipline. The army had worn uniform for centuries. One account says that the new naval uniform was selected by the King, and was a copy of a blue riding habit with white collars, cuffs, and facings which he had admired when worn by Diana, Duchess of Bedford, granddaughter of the great John Churchill, Duke of Marlborough, and wife of the First Lord. She had ordered a new habit in the Saumarez fashion, and when riding in the Mall entered into conversation with George II who commended her taste. It is evident from a letter written by Keppel to Philip Saumarez that some experimenting had been going on while Anson was commanding the Western Squadron. The following is an extract:

London
25 Aug 1747

Tim Brett tells me you have made a uniform coat, &c, after your own fancy; my Lord Anson is desirous that many of us should make coats after our own tastes, and then that a choice should be made of one to be general, and if you will appear in it here, he says he will be answerable your taste will not be amongst the worst.

Poor Philip Saumarez had not long in which to take up this challenge, for he was to die gallantly in action, two months later, at the second Battle of Finisterre.

The introduction of a naval uniform supplied a long felt need. Another long delayed requirement was the revision of the Articles of War. These were articles which had been given the force of law by Acts passed in 1652 and 1661 following recommendations made by Robert Blake after his defeat by Tromp at the battle of Dungeness in 1652. Blake complained that several masters of armed merchant ships had run away and left him in the lurch, and that he had no redress except to report them. A disciplinary code of laws applicable to ships was drawn up by the Judges of the Admiralty Court and passed by the House of Commons. There were thirty-nine articles, and of these one third carried the death penalty. They sounded quite fierce, but in practice had not been applied with any harshness, and in some ways applied a more lenient justice than had been applicable under the old code based upon rules and customs of the sea. In recent failures, such as the escape of the French navy at the Battle of Toulon in 1744, it was considered that there had been too much leniency, and there was a general feeling that the Articles of War required tightening up.

A Bill was passed at the end of the war, entitled 'A Bill for amending, explaining, and reducing into one Act of Parliament, the Laws relating to the Navy'. It is necessary to look at one of the amended articles in particular, as this later had a special application to the sentence which ended the Court martial of Admiral Byng.

Article 12, before the amendment, read as follows:

> Every person in the fleet, who through cowardice, negligence, or disaffection, shall in time of action, withdraw or not come into fight, or engagement, or shall not do his utmost to take or destroy every ship which it shall be his duty to engage; and to assist all and every of His Majesty's ships, or those of his allies, which it shall be his duty to assist and relieve; every such person, so offending, and being convicted thereof by the sentence of a court martial, shall suffer death, or such other punishment as the circumstances of the offence shall deserve, and the Court martial shall judge fit.

After the amendment the sentence was left as death, without alternative, the words 'or such other punishment as the circumstances of the offence shall deserve, and the court martial shall judge fit' being deleted. The alteration was intended to reserve the prerogative of mercy for the Crown.

Another act of 21 Geo. II, arranged 'for extending the discipline of the navy to the crews of his Majesty's Ships, wrecked, lost, or taken, and continuing to them their wages upon certain conditions.' This measure was a consequence of the mutinous conduct of some of the men of the *Wager* of Anson's squadron, who defied the captain after she had been shipwrecked. There is no doubt that this was a necessary measure. The wisdom of amendment to Article 12, however, was later to come very much into question, and the amendment led to one of the most distasteful events in British naval history.

# CHAPTER XVI

# The Navy Once More Paramount

AFTER his victory at Finisterre Anson returned to the Admiralty, and the command of the Western Squadron then devolved on Admiral Warren. Soon afterwards, in July 1747, Anson was promoted two steps to Vice-Admiral of the Red. The vigil at the Western approaches to the Channel continued. On 20th June, Fox, the Captain of the *Kent*, 74 guns, had sighted a homebound French convoy of about a hundred and twenty ships escorted by four warships. His own force, though superior, was slower, but a freshening breeze proved favourable, and as he approached the convoy the escort made off, leaving the convoy to scatter as best they could. In the fading light, Fox was able to round up and capture forty-five merchant ships laden with very rich cargoes of sugar, indigo, cotton, coffee, and hides, besides 1,197 French seamen. The four French warships arrived safely in Brest.

A few weeks later news reached Anson at Admiralty that a large convoy was fitting out with the intention of sailing from Basque Roads for the West Indies, with a strong escort commanded by Monsieur de l'Etenduère. Orders were immediately issued from the Admiralty that fourteen ships were to be brought to instant readiness. Hawke, who, as Captain of the *Berwick* in the Mathews fiasco of 1744, had been the only officer to show outstanding initiative, had hitherto received little recognition. In July 1747, however, when Anson was promoted Vice-Admiral of the Red, Hawke received his promotion to the flag list, and hoisted his flag in the *Gloucester*, a new ship of fifty guns, as second in command to Warren.

Warren was ailing in health, and on the 5th September, found himself compelled to resign his command. Hawke then shifted his flag to *Devonshire* and took over the command, for the squadron was now in station in a strategic position waiting for the French convoy. Anson was a little uneasy at leaving the squadron under the command of so young and junior a flag officer, but had not forgotten Hawke's initiative at Toulon and decided to retain him in command. This occasioned much surprise and criticism.

It is interesting to see among Hawke's ships the *Yarmouth*, this time with Saunders in command in place of Brett, and the *Nottingham* again with Saumarez. There was also the new *Gloucester*.

The following is the list of ships under Hawke:

| Ship | Captain | Guns | Men |
|------|---------|------|-----|
| *Devonshire* (Flagship) | Moore | 66 | 550 |
| *Kent* | Fox | 64 | 480 |
| *Edinburgh* | Cotes | 64 | 480 |
| *Yarmouth* | Saunders | 64 | 480 |
| *Monmouth* | Harrison | 64 | 480 |
| *Princess Louisa* | Watson | 60 | 400 |
| *Windsor* | Hanway | 60 | 400 |
| *Lion* | Scott | 60 | 400 |
| *Tilbury* | Harland | 60 | 400 |
| *Nottingham* | Saumarez | 60 | 400 |
| *Defiance* | Bentley | 60 | 400 |
| *Eagle* | Rodney | 60 | 400 |
| *Gloucester* | Durell | 50 | 300 |
| *Portland* | Steevens | 50 | 300 |

The French convoy left Rochelle Roads on 8th October, and was sighted by the *Edinburgh* of Hawke's squadron at seven o'clock on the morning of 14th October, about three hundred miles north by west of Cape Finisterre. The convoy consisted of two hundred and fifty ships sailing to the southward, and the escort only nine ships of war compared with Hawke's fourteen, but the disparity in numbers was largely offset by the fact that the French ships were individually greater and more heavily armed. The wind was easterly. The French commodore, Monsieur de l'Etenduère, who was to windward of Hawke, at once sent his merchant ships ahead, escorted by frigates and one of his sixty-gun ships. With his remaining eight ships he formed line ahead and put them between the convoy and Hawke's squadron. Although inferior in number he considered himself a match for the British, and accepted battle, unlike his compatriot Monsieur Bois de la Motte who had fled to Brest and left his rich convoy for Fox to take. A tough and sustained battle was about to begin.

Hawke's action was very similar to that of Anson five months earlier, who, after a general chase formed line ahead, and then ordered general chase when he realized that there was a risk of not getting up with the ships in time. Again the same instructions prevailed, that the first ships to engage should cripple the enemy, and then pass on to the next ahead, leaving their victim to be dealt with by the slower ships coming up astern. The action is of particular interest to us because of the presence of Charles Saunders and Philip Saumarez, and the perpetuation of the Anson tradition in resolute behaviour. It is interesting too because of a newcomer, Rodney, in the *Eagle*, who was an officer after Anson's own heart.

Hawke's report says:

> Soon after [half past ten in the morning], I perceived the enemy's convoy to crowd away with all the sail they could set, while their ships of war were endeavouring to form in a line astern of them, and hauled near the wind, under their topsails and foresails, and some with top-gallant sails set. Finding we lost time in forming our line, while the enemy was standing away from us, at eleven made the signal for the whole squadron to chase.

At half past eleven, the first ship to arrive at a suitable range, the *Princess Louisa*, began the engagement. She and her captain, Watson, had both been at the first battle of Finisterre, and had won praise from Anson for determination.

The *Devonshire*, carrying Hawke, was soon in action, and was the first to take a ship.

In passing on to the first ship we could get near—says Hawke—we received many fires at a distance, till we came close to the *Severne* of fifty guns, which we soon silenced, and left to be taken up by the frigates astern. Then perceiving the *Eagle* and *Edinburgh* (who had lost her fore-topmast) engaged, we kept our wind as close as possible, in order to assist them.

This attempt was frustrated by the *Eagle* herself, who twice fell on board *Devonshire*, her steering wheel having been shot away. Hawke's ship thereupon sought out Monsieur de l'Etenduère in the *Tonnant*, once again to be foiled by an accident.

*Eagle*'s falling twice on board us ... drove us to leeward, and prevented our attacking *Le Monarche*, of seventy four, and the *Tonnant*, of eighty guns, within any distance to do execution. However, we attempted both, especially the latter. While we were engaged with her, the breechings of all our lower-deck guns broke, and the guns flew fore and aft, which obliged us to shoot ahead, for our upper and quarter deck guns could not reach her. Captain Harland in the *Tilbury*, observing that she fired single guns at us, in order to dismast us, stood on the other tack, between her and the *Devonshire*, and gave her a very smart fire. By the time the new breechings were all seized I was set almost alongside the *Trident*, of 64 guns, whom I engaged as soon as possible, and silenced by as brisk a fire as I could make.

Hawke makes it all sound so easy. *Trident*, his second capture, put up a gallant fight before being silenced. Hawke, however, was not satisfied with the behaviour of all his commanders.

Just before I attacked her [the *Trident*], observing the *Kent* at some distance astern of the *Tonnant*, I flung out Captain Fox's pendant, to make sail ahead to engage her, as I saw it was in her power to get close up with her, she having lost her main top-mast. Soon after I got alongside, within musket-shot of the *Terrible*, of 74 guns, and 700 men. Near seven at night she called for quarter.

By now it was very dark. Besides the three ships that had struck to *Devonshire*, three had struck to other ships. The remaining two French ships had, however, slipped away to windward, the damaged *Tonnant* being towed by the *Intrépide*, which, being in the van, had remained undamaged. Saunders, Saumarez, and Rodney chased them, undaunted by the great superiority of these two powerful ships, and a confused but abortive night battle followed.

Having observed that six of the enemy's ships had struck—Hawke says—and it being very dark, and our own ships dispersed, I thought it best to bring to for that night; and seeing a great firing a long way astern of me, I was in hopes to have seen more of the enemy's ships taken in the morning; but instead of that, I received the melancholy account of Captain Saumarez being killed, and that the *Tonnant* had escaped in the night by the assistance of the *Intrépide*, which, by having the wind of our ships, had receiv'd no damage that I could perceive.

This was sad news indeed. In spite of the gallant night chase by Rodney and the two old *Centurion*'s in their battle scarred ships (two of them mere cruisers opposed to battleships), the great *Tonnant* (carrying de l'Etenduère) and the *Intrépide* had got away: and Philip Saumarez was dead.

But Hawke had won a decisive victory, and his flagship had played a most prominent part. He selected his flag captain, Moore, who 'signalised himself greatly in the action', for the honour of taking home the news of the victory. The bulk of the convoy had escaped in the dark, but Hawke sent the sloop *Weasel* to the West Indies to warn of their approach, and they were captured on arrival.

As the enemy ships were large—Hawke says in his despatch—except the *Severne*, they took a great deal of drubbing, and lost all their masts, excepting two, who had their foremasts left: this has obliged me to lay by these two days past, in order to put them into a condition to be brought into port, as well as our own, which have suffered greatly.

Anson had already realized the great disparity between English and French ships, both in speed and armament, and had taken the first step for improvement in the future by his new rating classification and an attempt to standardize and strengthen the ships of each rating. The great feature of this new victory, however, was the display of that same determination and unswerving resolution and courage which Anson had always displayed and fostered. 'It reflects the highest honour,' says one historian, 'in that nobleman, that all officers formed under his example, and raised by his influence, appeared themselves, in all respects, worthy of the commands to which they were preferred.'

It needed no little courage to lie alongside a two- or three-decker within pistol shot for several hours until she struck. Amid the chaos of broadside blasts and the screams of the wounded, the blinding smoke, the splintering of wood, the crashing of masts, yards, and rigging, the thunder of distant guns, the crack of muskets and small arms, the ship had to be fought and navigated. Between decks covered with sand to soak up blood, men stripped to the waist would sponge, load, and run out the guns by means of side tackles. Round shot for muzzle loading would be handy to the men at each gun, but the cartridges had to be brought up from the magazines by powder boys running to supply each gun before the charge and ball were rammed down the muzzle and the gun run out ready for firing. In a long close battle the chances of being wounded were of the order of one in five, and the likelihood of death one in thirty or forty, much depending on one's action station. It is probable that mortality through poverty and sickness were of such a high order that fear of death in action was greatly offset by inspiring leadership and the great chance of rich prize money.

Hawke said in his despatch:

... commanders, officers, and companies behaved with the greatest spirit and resolution, in every respect like Englishmen. Only I am sorry to acquaint Their Lordships that I must except Captain Fox, whose conduct on that day I beg they would give directions for enquiring into at a court martial.

This was because Fox had allowed the damaged *Tonnant* to slip away, at the time that *Devonshire* had parted all her lower deck gun breechings when firing at *Tonnant* at long range. The period of leniency still existed, for this was before Anson had had the Articles of War tightened up. Fox, though dismissed his ship, was acquitted of cowardice, and there was some concern that his acquittal would do much harm to the reputation of the Service and allow further neglect of duty in future actions. Fox's defence was that he had mistaken Hawke's signal ordering him to attack *Tonnant* for one asking for assistance for the hard pressed *Devonshire*. In this he had relied on the advice of his first lieutenant and master who may or may not have been mistaken over the signal. One of Anson's old *Centurion*'s, no less than Keppel, was at the court martial, and in a letter to Anson said that the first lieutenant and master of the *Kent* were 'two damned bad fellows' out to do all they could to ruin Fox.

Hawke arrived at Portsmouth on 31st October with his squadron and prizes, and soon afterwards was received by the King, and honoured with the Order of the Bath and the accolade of Knighthood. The King, who had been impressed by Hawke's singular initiative in the Toulon fiasco of 1744, was fond of him, and had been greatly amused by his reference to the enemy ships taking a great deal of drubbing.

Anson must have been very pleased that he had permitted the command of the Western Squadron to go to Hawke in spite of his being so junior. He received a letter of congratulation from Lord Sandwich which said:

You may easily believe me when I tell you it is with the utmost pleasure that I congratulate you upon the fresh success of our fleet under the command of Rear-Admiral

Hawke; besides the advantage this great stroke will give to us in our public affairs, the credit and reputation it will give to our mariners cannot but afford me a most thorough satisfaction; for it is impossible for anyone to have the prosperity of a profession more sincerely at heart than I have of that which you are so deservedly considered as the chief director; and to whose knowledge and ability the world is very ready to attribute the different figure that the English fleet has made in the last years from what it did in the beginning of the war.

The English fleet was certainly making a different figure, and the result in public affairs was that the French were beginning to tire of this unprofitable war in which they had promised Spain that they would remove the British from Gibraltar and Minorca. Everywhere, except in India, the British flag flew unchallenged. Towards the end of 1747 Anson, in consultation with the First Lord, the Duke of Bedford, obtained approval for an expedition to India under the command of Rear-Admiral Boscawen who had fought so gallantly in command of the *Namur* at Anson's victory at Finisterre in May, and, with Hawke, had been promoted in the following July. Everything had gone wrong for the British in India and this expedition was to be no exception. Although successful everywhere at sea, the British had suffered many reverses on shore. In May 1748, however, hostilities ended, and at the subsequent Peace of Aix-la-Chappelle there was a mutual restitution of all conquests that had been made since the beginning of the war. This meant that Louisburg was returned to the French.

The King in his speech on opening the session in November 1748 said, 'Our signal successes at sea must ever be remembered, to the glory of the British fleet, and entitle it to the particular attention and support of this nation.'

The naval successes went far beyond the signal victories of Anson and Hawke, for it was the general exercise of sea power so well foreseen by Anson that rendered it impossible for either France or Spain to reinforce their colonial possessions in either Canada, India, or the West Indies at this time. The successful duels and the decisive victories were the contributions that appealed to the British nation and weakened the enemy, but it was the command of the sea which brought the war to a conclusion and was to pave the way for the years of victory that lay a little way ahead in the Seven Years War of 1756–1763.

In the peace celebrations in May 1748 there was a promotion of flag officers, and Hawke was promoted to Vice-Admiral of the Blue. Anson was Promoted Admiral of the Blue. His position in the Navy and at the Admiralty was now well established, and his national prestige high.

# CHAPTER XVII

# An Uneasy Peace

ANSON's virtual rule at the Admiralty had not been without its difficulties. Bedford, the First Lord, was frequently away sick, and the Earl of Sandwich was absent abroad, first at The Hague, and later at Aix-la-Chappelle negotiating the peace. Anson, however, had the confidence of them both. But now an event occurred which changed matters.

On 12th February 1748, long before the end of the war, the Duke of Bedford became one of the Secretaries of State in succession to the Earl of Chesterfield, and the Earl of Sandwich then succeeded him as First Lord of the Admiralty. Bedford wrote to Anson as follows:

Feb 12 1748
Lord Anson                                    Admiralty Office
My dear Lord,
    The dye is at last thrown, and I have this morning kist the King's hand in the Closet for the Seals and the King puts Lord Sandwich in my place at this Board. The thing was going I was afraid to take so wrong a Turn, with regard to Lord Sandwich that I began to be afraid lest he should be passed over in the change Lord Chesterfield's resignation must have occasioned. . . . I hope when Peace is made to have as good success in getting Lord Sandwich appointed my Successor for the Seals, as I have now the satisfaction to see him established at the head of this Board. I am in great haste, My dear Lord most sincerely and faithfully
                                    Yours,
                                         BEDFORD

With the departure of Bedford and the continued absence abroad of Sandwich, Anson now suffered a setback in his virtual authority. In a letter to Lord Sandwich dated 14th February 1748, Anson writes:

> Your Lordship will easily conceive how disagreeable my situation must be, upon the Duke of Bedford's removal and your Lordship's absence, to act under Lord Vere, who, I find, is determined to continue at the Board, and seemed to be pleased with the change, as he imagines your continuance there will not be long.

Lord Vere Beauclerk was the son of the Duke of St. Albans, and stood above Anson on the list of members of the Board of Admiralty, having first become a junior lord of the Admiralty in 1738 when the old Sir Charles Wager was First Lord, and having been reappointed under Bedford in 1744. Although he had been made a captain at the early age of twenty-one he had seen very little naval service, and had never been in action.

On 15th February, Anson again wrote to Sandwich.

> I find from talking with Lord Vere, that he intends to continue till you return to take possession . . . in the meantime, he may make his continuance at the Board serve many good purposes of his own, which you will easily imagine must be very disagreeable to me, after the share the Duke of Bedford has allowed me in the direction of affairs afloat, and the success which has attended his Grace's administration of naval affairs in every branch of the department.

Anson goes on to describe how he and Bedford had been invited to dine with Newcastle.

> . . . being left alone with the Duke of Newcastle, I told his Grace I thought you would have great reason to complain of all your friends, if you were passed by on this occasion, and therefore proposed, if you could not get the seals, that they should be given to the Duke of Bedford, and your Lordship to take his place at the Admiralty.

Sandwich was young and ambitious, and regarded by every-one as able and cultivated. The King, however, disliked him for his reference to the 'little potentates of Germany'. His trust in Anson is revealed in letters of which the following are extracts:

The Hague<br>5th March 1748

My dear Lord

You will easily conceive my satisfaction in the receipt of the news contained in the last three mails from England. I am sensible how much I am obliged to your Lordship for the great weight of your friendship, and I readily perceive how much your support has contributed to make the way easy to the height of good fortune to which I am arrived, which I shall never forget to the last hour of my life.

. . . I would not lose a moment to desire that you would consider yourself as in effect at the head of the Admiralty . . . it is my meaning to throw my share of the power, and the direction of the whole, as much as possible, into your hands.

Aix-la-Chappelle<br>19th March 1748

I am sorry Lord Vere remains at the Board, if that is in any way disagreeable to you . . . In one of my letters to the Duke of Newcastle, I have told him that, in Admiralty business, he must consider you as one and the same thing with me, and that I intend to depend entirely upon your Lordship, and to throw the direction of the whole, as much as possible into your hands . . . I am sure it is what is most for the advantage of the Service.

This must have been very gratifying to Anson for he was about to introduce further reforms which a man of Beauclerk's limited experience would not have understood.

Anson's mind was very much on Admiralty matters in spite of the approach of a very important event in his life. This was his marriage on 25th April 1748 to Lady Elizabeth Yorke, daughter of his old friend Lord Hardwicke, the Lord Chancellor.

A portrait by Hudson of this attractive woman suggests a gay and charming character which accounts for the happy though short married life she and Anson enjoyed together. She was a loyal and proud supporter of Anson. Her father, the worthy Chancellor, adored her. Anson divulges his great happiness in a further letter to Sandwich.

> I shall say nothing of my marriage because all people in that state, think themselves extremely happy. I own I do. . . .

It is difficult at first to think of Anson as a happily married man. Hitherto he had been very much a man of single purpose, devoting all his energies and thoughts and resolutions on behalf of his country and the great Service in which he had served with growing distinction for thirty-six years. He was now fifty-one. There is ample evidence, however, in correspondence that the marriage was not only successful but that Anson regarded it as the happiest event of his life. The first part of their married life was spent at Carshalton, and it is probable that they enjoyed also a residence in London. In 1751 they moved into Admiralty House adjoining the new Ripley building in Whitehall. Here Anson lived, with one short break, until he died in 1762. Holidays were spent with brother Thomas Anson, at the family seat at Shugborough in Staffordshire, first built by William Anson, the Admiral's father, in 1695, and extended by Thomas Anson 1760–1770, in accordance with the designs of 'Athenian' Stuart. At the end of the century, the whole group of buildings was refaced and remodelled by Samuel Wyatt for the first Viscount Anson. The park at Shugborough is laid out largely to commemorate Lord Anson's naval feats, and includes a Chinese House which was put up in 1747, and follows fairly scrupulously, it is believed, designs made by Peircy Brett when at Canton.

It is apparent in letters from Thomas to the Admiral that they were always on good terms. The 'Dear Brother' becomes 'My dear Lord' after Finisterre; and it is about this time that the Chinese House was built. After the Admiral's marriage in April 1748 there are references to 'Lady Anson', no christian name, and to the furniture for the Chinese House which Anson is to provide and which Lady Anson will arrange when she visits Shugborough. Among the Hardwicke papers are many letters from Thomas Anson to Lord Hardwicke, indicating that Lady Anson spent much time at Shugborough. The letters give news of Lady Anson's health to the anxious father. Lady Anson is described by Mrs. Delaney as being 'a little cox-combical and affects to be learned'. Mrs. Delaney also says that 'Lord A., a most generous, good natured, amiable man, deserved a wife of more dignity.'

The affection for learning is certainly not evident in Lady Anson's letters, and she describes herself as lacking in fashionable graces. If this is true, she more than makes up for it by her wit and charm. She was certainly much admired, not only by her husband, but by her brother-in-law who lived and died a bachelor. It is interesting to reflect on these two brothers, one of whom married only late in life, and the other not at all, and to wonder whether this evasion of the most natural event in life was in any way due to the regard held by sons for a mother who was the dominant partner in a marriage, and who particularly influenced and inspired the male children of the union. The mother in this case, Isabella Carrier of Wirksworth, a coheiress, was known to be gifted in many ways. It was her sister Janet who had married Thomas Parker, made Lord Chancellor in 1718, and created Earl of Macclesfield in 1721. There are many cases of men who have been so influenced by and enamoured of their mother that they had but little time to be much concerned with other women. Walpole in his memoirs of the last years of George II implies that Anson's marriage was one of convenience.

Walpole's opinion of Anson generally was not high. That Anson was a friend of the Earl of Sandwich was itself a reason for Walpole's contemptuous remarks, but it is said that Walpole laid a scheme for marrying Anson to one of the Duke of Bedford's daughters, which was frustrated when Anson married a wife of his own choice. This may have been responsible for some of the cynical remarks concerning Anson.

'Lord Anson,' says Walpole, 'was reserved and proud, and so ignorant of the world that Sir Charles Williams said he had been round it, but never in it. He had been strictly united with the Duke of Bedford and Lord Sandwich, but not having the same command of his ambition that he had of his other passions, he had not been able to refuse the offer of the Chancellor's daughter, nor the direction of the Admiralty.' Walpole admits that 'Lord Anson, attentive to, and generally expert in maritime details, selected with great care the best officers.'

It is a strange fact that ambition is regarded by many as a failing. There is little doubt that Anson was ambitious in the best sense, and if we accept this to mean that he was desirous of excellence, Britain has every reason to be profoundly grateful.

In July 1746 Anson had become godfather to Peircy Brett's son who was to be christened Peircy Anson Brett. The following letter from Brett to Anson on the occasion of his marriage so late in life indicates the great regard in which Anson was held by his former lieutenant, now Captain of the *Yarmouth*. In spite of the delight and the formality of the letter, one also senses a mild and humorous reproach at this first step on the downward path from bachelor grace, as much as to say 'what now of your past assurances of freedom from entanglement?'

Yarmouth at Lisbon May 3rd 1748

Rt. Honorable
    Lord Anson.
My Lord,
    On my arrival at Lisbon I met with the agreeable news of your Lordships marriage and must beg leave to congratulate you on your happy choice, and shall please myself with hopes of having further occasion to give your Lordship Joy, which I am persuaded must make you compleatly Happy, if there is such thing as Perfect Happiness under Heaven.
    As I had so great and frequent Testimonies of your Favour and Goodness to me I flatter myself you will forgive me for using this freedom, and for desiring my Respects to your Lady Tho' I never had the Pleasure of seeing her Ladyship, yet I am not a Stranger to her Perfections, which I remember well to have had from your Lordship at a time when I believe you had no thoughts of

179

Marrying, I must once more beg your Lordships Pardon, and shall not increase your trouble beyond the assurances of my being with the greatest Respect

My Lord

Your Lordships most obliged

Humble Servant

PEIRCY BRETT

I beg my respects to Mr. Anson.

Brett was a frequent visitor to Mr. Thomas Anson at Shugborough. This friendship probably developed from the time when the idea of a Chinese House originated.

Anson and his wife moved from Carshalton to Moor Park in Hertfordshire, and with the assistance of 'Capability' Brown spent eighty thousand pounds on improvements. Moor Park in later years became a golf club. Shugborough became the seat of the first Earl of Lichfield in 1831, when the grandson of Anson's nephew Charles Adams was created Earl of Lichfield.

Lady Anson's father adored her, and was most solicitous for her health. In a letter of 28th August 1748 from his home in Wimple he writes to 'my dear Lord' concerning one or two political matters, and then informs Anson that 'As my wife writes to Lady Anson, I won't trouble Your Lordship with any Family Occurrences . . .' Nevertheless he ends: 'Give my Blessing to my Daughter, with an express Injunction to take care of her health.'

Two days later from his London house, Powis House, Lord Hardwicke writes again to Anson, expressing concern at the news that she had a feverish disorder.

Keep her from going to Lichfield Races, in case she should not be perfectly recover'd: or if she should appear to be so, to prevail with her at least not to dance, and to redouble caution. . . .

Anson replied on 3rd September:

Your Lordship's anxiety on your Daughter's account will be at an end. I am sure no one could suffer more than

I did during her pain and sickness. If she has any fault it is being too careless of her health thank God at present she is perfectly well and if she does not continue so she shall not go to the Races at all. . . .

In a letter of some three years later, the devoted father at Wimple expresses joy and the greatest pleasure at the 'good news of Lady Anson's having received so much benefit from her Sea-Bathing.'

The happiness of the marriage is probably best portrayed in a letter of 6th October 1748 written by Anson to Lord Hardwicke inviting him and Lady Hardwicke to stay with them at the Admiralty.

I esteem the Honour of being allied to your Lordship's Family as the most fortunate event of my life as indeed the principal happiness of it commenced at that time. Lady Anson joins with me in Duty and Affection to your Lordship Lady Hardwicke and all the Family.

The formality of these letters which may be seen at the British Museum leads one to believe that all letters were regarded as something to be kept, something to be added to the collection. Presumably, behaviour and conversation were conducted with the same decorum, and the propriety of polite conduct was an indispensable part of status and prestige.

Lady Elizabeth Anson writing to her father on 12th June 1753, more than five years after her marriage, is particularly formal though charming, and although she permits herself to refer to Mama rather than Lady Hardwicke she ends: 'I have the honour to be, with the Greatest Respect & Duty, My Lord, Your Lordship's most oblig'd and most obedient Daughter E. Anson.'

The year of Anson's marriage proved to be as arduous as earlier years, and with the conclusion of the peace of Aix-la-Chappelle in the autumn, the difficult question of economies and reduction of the Navy had to be tackled. The Earl of Sandwich wrote to Anson in October 1748 from Aix-la-Chappelle informing him of the favourable terms of the peace treaty, and stating that he looked forward to being back in England in a few weeks. His return, however, was delayed until the spring of 1749, and Anson continued to find Lord Vere Beauclerk a thorn in the flesh. With Sandwich still abroad, and Anson absent escorting his Majesty King George II across the English Channel to Holland, Vere appointed a Commander-in-Chief to Barbados: this was an appointment which was never intended in time of peace, and made Sandwich and Anson both very angry when they came to hear of it as an accomplished fact.

In the previous year, on 29th February 1747, Anson had received a letter from Henry Osborne, Rear-Admiral at Portsmouth, requesting an allowance for table money for Commanders-in-Chief when abroad. Mindful of expenses suffered himself when abroad, Anson was well disposed towards this request and supported it.

Ventilation in ships still did not exist, with the result that in rough weather with all lower deck ports closed, the air soon became foul and vitiated, with adverse effects on health and morale. There was a great conviction that this was a potent factor in the spread of scurvy. It is therefore interesting to read a letter sent to Anson on 31st March 1749 by a clergyman named Barlow, writing from Bath, and describing a device for evacuating foul air out of ships, consisting of an air bellows and a long 'canvas Hose-pipe hanging down through an opening in one of the Hatchways.' 'By this means the Air of the Hold and Decks will be kept sweet and cool and be even pleasant as well as healthful.'

Lighting in ships was as primitive as the ventilation, and for fear of fire, was accompanied by rigid regulations. Officers were forbidden to read in bed, and all candles had to be burned in lanterns.

The imminent reduction of the Navy which was to follow the peace treaty, raised the question of the disbanding or 'breaking' of the maritime regiments which were raised in war for service in warships. The duties of these sea soldiers or marines were many. Primarily they were embarked to carry out those functions which were traditionally best performed by soldiers trained under military discipline, and which also required familiarity with life afloat.

Such duties covered the formation of landing parties or boarding parties, the use of small arms by marksmen on the upper deck and in the tops during engagements, standing sentry, forming guards of honour, and acting as personal servants to the officers. Their high sense of military discipline and regimental training were often in marked contrast with the morale which prevailed on the lower deck, particularly when the press gangs had been active. Press gangs had two functions: one to 'press' men who were already seamen and who could be forcibly arrested, the other to take men who accepted the 'prest' or 'imprest' of one shilling thereby showing that they had enlisted in the King's service. The result was often a collection of miserable frightened men with no wish for service of any sort.

With the introduction of standing armies in the reign of Charles II, the first maritime regiment had been raised in 1664, giving service in naval engagements against the Dutch Fleet and being paid from Admiralty funds. It was disbanded in 1689 but two more marine regiments were formed in 1690. Between 1690 and 1748, marine regiments were raised and disbanded as required.

In August 1748 Anson received a letter from the Earl of Sandwich at Aix asking whether the marines were to be continued or not, and stating that the Duke of Cumberland had suggested that whenever they were to be re-formed it would be more appropriate for them to be under Admiralty jurisdiction. Sandwich felt that this was a principle which should be established before the existing regiments were broken, so that a precedent would be set up which would be impracticable for any subsequent ministry to change. Fox, the Secretary of State for War, appeared to be agreeable to the idea. The force was now totally disbanded with the signing of the peace, but the idea had gained ground that the resuscitation of the corps when required would rest with the Admiralty. Many of the officers were retained on half pay so that a measure of continuity as envisaged by Sandwich was made possible. The scheme was further assured of success when, in June 1751, Lord Sandwich was summarily dismissed by the King from the post of First Lord, and was succeeded by Anson himself, who had the confidence of nearly all, and was unlikely to be regarded as acting for political ends when pressing for reform. He was now generally accepted as a shrewd judge full of sound common sense. When war again became imminent in 1755, Anson considered that the time had arrived for the establishment of a permanent Corps of Marines to serve in warships, to be quite distinct from the army and to be administered entirely by the Admiralty. An Order in Council dated 3rd April 1755, and signed by twenty-four Lords Justices, authorized the raising of a corps of five thousand marines to be formed into fifty companies to which officers and non-commissioned officers were to be appointed, thus raising the strength to five thousand seven hundred. Headquarters were to be established at Portsmouth, Plymouth, and Chatham. From then on the Corps had a permanent and continuous existence. By 1759 their numbers had risen to eighteen thousand. In 1802 in direct recognition of their splendid and loyal service they received the style 'Royal Marines'. The benefits following the formation of a permanent corps under the Admiralty must have exceeded Anson's highest hopes, and perhaps the best testimony to his foresight and the finest tribute to the Corps, comes from one of Anson's successors, the Earl of St. Vincent, who said:

> There never was any appeal made to them for honour, courage or loyalty that they did not more than realise my expectations. If ever the hour of real danger should come to England, the Marines will be found the country's sheet anchor.

Between the wars, and beginning in 1749, a great drive was initiated by Sandwich and Anson to examine the administration of the dockyards and naval establishments, with the intention of eradicating corruption and neglect, and improving the execution of repairs and the availability of stores. This drive resulted in a system of annual or routine inspections by responsible authorities who were to report specifically on various points and on the general efficiency. The yards were full of idle men and incompetent supervisors. Regulations were ignored, stores were ill arranged, and accounts were falsified. This system of annual inspections brought to light many abuses which were quickly corrected, and is one which has continued ever since. Corruption and abuse may still be rife, but their practice continues only with difficulty and considerable retribution if apprehended.

During the respite afforded by the years of peace, Anson continued to do all he could for the improvement of the Navy, and resolutely refused to allow the Navy to be used for politics. The problems of manning even a few ships can be imagined when it is realized that the Navy was reduced from fifty thousand to ten thousand and later eight thousand. The hardships of the discharged men unable to find employment ashore are impossible to describe. Robbery and theft became common, and it was unsafe to roam the street unescorted. Newcastle was still in power, but owed his position to support derived largely from gifts of sinecures to pledged supporters. He was afraid of Anson, and in attempting to obtain the gift of certain positions which were under the control of the Admiralty, would ask Hardwicke to use his influence with Anson.

The following extracts of letters from Anson to Newcastle indicate Anson's determined action.

Moor Park Feb 15 1751

My Lord,

I had the honour of your Grace's letter, with an enclosure from my Lord Davis, recommending Mr. Whitemore to be Commissioner of Victualling. His Lordship might as well have asked for him to be made a captain of a man of war. . . .

This gives me an opportunity of observing to your Grace, that instead of adding to the useless people that are allowed in that office (if we should have a war with France), more people of business must be brought into it.

ANSON

Anson realized that the maintenance of peace was tenuous, and was determined to maintain what was left of the Navy as an efficient service, served by reliable commanders and able officers.

In another letter to the Duke, who had recommended

promotion of a certain officer in order to retain his support politically, he says:

Admiralty June 15 1751

My Lord Duke

. . . I must now beg Your Grace will seriously consider what must be the condition of your fleet if these Borough recommendations are complied with. . . .

My constant method since I have had the honour of serving the King in the station I am in, has been to promote the lieutenants whose ships have been successfully engaged on equal terms with the enemy, without having any friend or recommendation, and in preference to all others —and this I would recommend to my successors, if they would have a fleet to be depended on.

ANSON

How much England and his successors owed to Anson for this determined and enlightened stand became evident in the Navy's glorious records which were to follow.

# CHAPTER XVIII

# The Loss of Minorca

In June 1751, less than seven years after his appointment to the
Board of Admiralty, Anson became First Lord. This resulted
from a political quarrel in which he himself was not involved
but which concerned the King, the King's son, the Duke of
Cumberland, and the Pelham brothers; the two brothers were
Henry, the First Lord of the Treasury, virtually Prime Minister,
and Thomas, Duke of Newcastle, the Secretary of State.
Newcastle was keen to get rid of Bedford, but had no real
pretext for recommending his dismissal. He knew, however,
that if Sandwich were to be dismissed, Bedford would resign,
and therefore recommended to the King that Sandwich should
go. Sandwich had been imprudent in permitting the ceremony
of marriage at his private apartments at the Admiralty between
a Colonel Waldegrave and Lady Elizabeth Leveson Gower, a
sister of the Duchess of Bedford, against the wishes of Lord
Gower, the bride's father. Moreover, the King was not an
admirer of the Earl of Sandwich. His departure under apparent
disgrace was regrettable, but from the naval point of view
Anson's promotion into the vacancy was a gift. Although Anson
had been virtually at the head of the Admiralty for six and a
half consecutive years, first under Bedford and then under
Sandwich, the administration had not been free from politics.
Anson was now determined to serve the Navy efficiently and
promote the best officers. The French were already increasing
their Navy. One of Anson's first achievements on becoming
First Lord was to get a Bill passed authorizing an increase
from eight thousand to ten thousand men in the Navy. His

reforms in the administration of the Dockyards and in the standardization of equipment and rating of ships were already being implemented, and although the Navy was small, an efficient armed nucleus of ships, officers, and men, was being moulded. Admirals Boscawen and Rowley were appointed Lords Commissioners of the Admiralty.

The peace which followed the conclusion of the treaty of Aix-la-Chappelle was an unsettled one. It became obvious as the years passed, that France in spite of her professions of good faith, was disinclined to leave matters as agreed in the Treaty. Her intriguing at home and strengthening of possessions abroad showed that she was determined to retrieve all that she had lost. Piecemeal she was making encroachments on British colonial settlements. In the great ports of Brest and Rochefort, ships were preparing, and troops were assembling.

In March 1754, Henry Pelham died, and was succeeded as First Lord of the Treasury by his brother the Duke of Newcastle. The King on hearing of Pelham's death was reputed to say, 'I shall now have no peace.' The younger Pitt was at this time in the ascendency, but the King regarding him as a warmonger refused to accept his views or allow him office.

The Foreign Office was represented by two Secretaries of State, the Earl of Holdernesse and Sir Thomas Robinson, but neither was outstanding. Newcastle had for long favoured a defensive strategy and was determined to avoid an open breach with France. He was of the opinion that control of Britain's colonial territories, and the establishment of colonial frontiers, were matters which could be settled satisfactorily without becoming embroiled in a war which would involve Britain in military commitments on the Continent, the outcome of which was far from certain. Britain in supporting Hanover might find Prussia assisting France. The attitude of Austria and Holland, who might be counted allies, would depend very much on who was the aggressor. Spain and possibly the northern countries would support France.

Newcastle's private adviser in whom he placed much faith was no less than Lord Hardwicke, the worthy Lord Chancellor. He was as much at home with strategic problems as with those of equity, and at this time was against bringing matters to a head. The two men who perhaps had the greatest responsibility in advising the government, and who acted with such great competence in guiding the country's war strategy pending the accession to power of the younger Pitt, were the two service representatives, Lord Anson for the Navy, and Sir John Ligonier for the Army, acting on behalf of the Commander-in-Chief, the Duke of Cumberland.

Preparations for war accelerated. By April 1755, the order in council for five thousand marines had been signed, and British ships of war were being hurriedly fitted out. Nominally, France and Britain were still at peace, nevertheless in late April Vice-Admiral Boscawen was sent to Plymouth to take command of a fleet of eleven ships of the line and one frigate with the intention of proceeding to Newfoundland to intercept French reinforcements. Owing to thick fog, Boscawen missed most of the French fleet, but two French ships were apprehended and struck their colours, one of them, the *Alcide*, to Howe in the *Dunkirk*. No declared state of war existed, yet before the end of the year, three hundred French merchant ships and six thousand French seamen had been taken by British warships. The British public were clamouring for war, and though angry with Boscawen for missing the French fleet, regarded the capture of two French ships of the line as the beginning of hostilities, and were overjoyed.

The French were not yet ready for open war, as their encroachment on British settlements and erection of a line of forts were incomplete. They expressed astonishment and anger at the aggressive behaviour of the British fleet. Parliament had now voted thirteen thousand seamen and mobilization was active. (See map, page 233.)

Anson was wasting no time, and was determined not to allow the French any advantage. The fleet was placed on a war footing. Though war had not yet been declared, Anson ordered eighteen ships of the line to be manned and equipped to form a Western Squadron under Sir Edward Hawke. 'The best defence for our colonies, as well as our coasts,' Anson wrote, 'is to have a squadron always to the westward as may in all probability either keep the French in port, or give them battle with advantage if they come out.'

Hawke was directed to intercept French warships and merchants ships, and take them to Plymouth or Portsmouth. If he should hear that hostilities had begun, then he also was to act in a hostile manner by taking or destroying.

In June Anson visited Portsmouth to inspect the Fleet which had been fitting out under Hawke. He hoisted his flag, that of an Admiral of the Blue, in the *Prince*, a ship of ninety guns and seven hundred men, commanded by his old friend of *Centurion* days, Charles Saunders. As this was the anniversary of the accession of the King, a splendid entertainment in the form of a dinner was given, at which the Duke of Cumberland and many of the nobility and their ladies were present. At this time the press gang must have been particularly active, nevertheless it appears from a letter written by Lady Anson, that discipline and behaviour in Saunders' ship was of a high order. An extract of her letter is worth inclusion here:

> The whole passed *à merveille*: the admiration high (and we have the vanity to think, just). Our guest had seen ships before, but never till now saw a fleet; the condition of the ships and the discipline, men, Officers, all so totally different, so military, and above all things, astonished at the quietness at the time of the dinner on board the *Prince* when there must have been above 1200 people on board. No private house, the best ordered could have been quieter.

To the administration, the news of Boscawen's capture of two French warships was gloomy, and the feeling began to grow that half measures were worse than an outright declaration of hostilities. Two ships had been taken, but the French had been allowed to slip past and strengthen the Louisburg garrison by two battalions, and what was worse reinforce Quebec. French penetration in the rear of the British colonies was steadily growing and strengthening. On 14th July Hardwicke wrote to Newcastle:

> I have just received from Lord Anson the private letter which Admiral Boscawen addressed him under date

June 21st. We have done too much or too little. The disappointment this news causes troubles me greatly.

To Anson he replied:

It gives me much concern that so little has been done, since anything has been done at all. *Voilà*, the war begun!

But war was not to be declared until the best part of a year had passed.

So keen was Anson on a strict blockade of the French ports, that when Hawke put into Spithead in late September, he issued a rebuke from Their Lordships. Hawke had been unlucky through bad weather and unreliable information: the French squadrons had eluded him. Now his ship's companies were suffering from sickness and low morale. Anson, when in command of the Western Squadron, had been of the opinion that it was during the short days of autumn and winter that the enemy would choose to escape the blockade, and greater vigilance was all the more necessary. It is evident, however, in a letter written by Hawke that he was concerned about the state of his men, large numbers of whom had been pressed. Had Anson allowed similar concern to shake his resolution at any time during his famous voyage it is certain that he would never have completed it.

*St. George* at Spithead
Oct 1 1755

Sir,

I have received your letter of the 30th and am extremely sorry to find that their Lordships think any of my squadron could have stayed out any longer. I hope they will be of another opinion when they reflect that most of the men had been pressed, after long voyages, cooped up in tenders and ships at Spithead for many months, and the water in general long kept in new casks, which occasioned great sickness. . . .

I am ready and willing to resign my command to any one else in whose abilities they may have more confidence.

HAWKE

At this time France was courting support from Sweden, and in good faith informed her of her intentions. By some means the information found its way to Newcastle at the end of 1755: he handed it on to Hardwicke with a request that he would get Anson's opinion on the matter. Newcastle stood much in awe of Anson because of the latter's inscrutability and integrity, but he respected his refusal to play politics with the Navy, and valued his opinion.

Anson considered the declared French plan a weak one as it subdivided all available force in an attempt to cover every possibility. There appeared to be no concentration of force for a swift blow. His opinion was that England could cope with the situation.

About this time, however, France became aware of a treaty which had been negotiated between England and Prussia which would upset her war plans. All hope of attacking Hanover successfully was gone, and France's greatest hope of success now would be a concentrated crushing blow against England.

France's tone became somewhat belligerent, and while she continued to mobilize and arm and assemble transports and troops, she let it be known that not only had she designs on His Majesty's dominions beyond the seas but intended an invasion of Great Britain and Ireland. She was ready to take both Gibraltar and Minorca and restore them to Spain. Strong forces assembled at the Channel ports and at Toulon. Alarm began to spread through England, Scotland, and Ireland. Parliament voted fifty thousand seamen including nine thousand marines, and large bounties were offered to volunteer seamen.

The threat in the Channel was safeguarded by the existence of Hawke's powerful squadron. But the French plan now was to force Britain to extend her forces to cover all possibilities of invasion, and to include a blow at Minorca which would compel England to weaken her Western Squadron. It is important to realize the situation which now faced Anson as naval adviser to the Government, in view of the subsequent loss of Minorca. Anson and the government were later accused of sending an inadequate force to Minorca, and of paying too much concern to the threat of invasion of the British Isles. They cannot, however, be blamed, for the very threat to Minorca was itself a device intended to force Britain to divide her fleet and weaken her defence at home. Anson was well aware of this, and mobilization had scarcely begun. Ships, men, and money were still scarce. Military resources were far smaller than they had been ten years earlier when the Pretender's victorious march to Derby had thrown all England into a panic.

Confirmation of French intentions was received in England on 25th February 1756. Two days later, Hawke was ordered by Anson to blockade the French coast, and on 8th March Byng was warned to prepare a squadron of ten sail-of-the-line to be detached from Hawke's squadron for service in the Mediterranean. There were already one sixty and two fifties in the Mediterranean under Commodore Edgecombe, and Anson believed the combined fleet would be a match for anything the French could send from Toulon. Hawke was left with but sixteen sail-of-the-line and three fifties to cover the invasion of the British Isles.

If any criticism of Anson's action at this time is due, it would seem to rest in his choice of Byng, and not on the necessarily restricted size of the squadron allocated to him. Admiral the Honourable John Byng was the son of George Byng who became Viscount Torrington after his victory off Cape Passaro in 1718. His seniority and experience and the fact that he was already on active service in the Channel were appropriate to the appointment, especially in view of his intimate knowledge of Minorca and the Mediterranean where he had already held the principal command during the previous war. He was, however, no leader, was unpopular in the service, and though personally a brave man, as was shown in the manner in which he met his death, appeared to be too much aware of difficulties. Anson, with his outstanding capacity for determined resolution and fearlessness in the face of all difficulties, could hardly be expected to understand this characteristic that tended to meet failure half way. Wherever he had served he had inspired his officers with his own qualities of leadership and unswerving determination and his refusal to accept defeat. It is unfortunate that not one of his products was senior enough for such a command. It is also striking that only one of his officers from *Centurion* days, Patrick Baird, now Captain of the *Portland*, was present at Byng's action. *Portland* was one of the fifties already in the Mediterranean with Commodore Edgecombe.

Byng complained, before sailing, that his force was unequal to that of the enemy. He received his instructions at Spithead on 1st April, and sailed on 10th April, still short of his full complement of men. His instructions were to proceed with the utmost expedition to Gibraltar, and to enquire whether any French squadron had left the Straits for America, in which event he was to detach sufficient ships under the command of Rear-Admiral West to Louisburg. The instructions continue, and their clarity is important:

> If, upon your arrival at Gibraltar, you shall *not* gain intelligence of a French squadron having passed, you are then to go on without a moment's loss to Minorca. If you find any attack made by the French, you are to use all possible means in your power for its relief.

Byng was also instructed in a separate letter to land Lord Bertie's regiment, together with a battalion which he was to embark at Gibraltar. When he arrived at Gibraltar at the beginning of May he heard that the French were conveying sixteen hundred troops from Toulon to Minorca in two hundred transports escorted by a French squadron under Galissonière. In a short time the French were besieging the Fort of St. Philip at Port Mahón, stoutly defended by two thousand British troops under eighty-four-year-old veteran General Blakeney. The Governor of Gibraltar refused to let Byng have the battalion, on the grounds that 'the sending such a detachment would evidently weaken the garrison of Gibraltar, and be noways effectual to the relief of Minorca.'

Byng immediately wrote to the Admiralty complaining of his inferiority and anticipating failure:

> If I should fail in the relief of Port Mahon, I shall look on the security and protection of Gibraltar as my next object, and shall repair down here with my squadron.

Having been joined by Edgecombe, he sailed from Gibraltar on 8th May, and arrived off Minorca on 19th May. His squadron, now supplemented by Edgecombe's ships, consisted of thirteen ships, particulars of which are interesting because of Byng's complaint of inferiority:

| Ship | Guns | Men | Commander |
|---|---|---|---|
| *Kingston* | 60 | 400 | W. Parry |
| *Deptford* | 50 | 300 | J. Amherst |
| *Culloden* | 74 | 600 | W. Ward |
| *Ramillies* (Flag) | 90 | 750 | (Hon. J. Byng) |
| | | | A. Gardiner |
| *Trident* | 64 | 500 | P. Durell |
| *Princess Louisa* | 60 | 400 | Hon. T. Noel |
| *Revenge* | 64 | 500 | F. Cornwall |
| *Intrepid* | 64 | 500 | J. Young |
| *Captain* | 64 | 500 | C. Catford |
| *Buckingham* (Flag) | 68 | 535 | (Rear-Admiral West) |
| | | | Everitt |
| *Lancaster* | 66 | 520 | Hon. G. Edgecombe |
| *Portland* | 50 | 300 | P. Baird |
| *Defiance* | 60 | 400 | T. Andrews |
| | 834 | 6,205 | |

Galissionière had twelve ships of which two were fifties, five were sixty-fours, four seventy-fours, and the largest an eighty-four. They had a total of eight hundred guns and eight thousand two hundred and fifty men. The difference was not therefore so very marked, and could not be considered an inferiority of note.

Byng, on arrival off Mahón, endeavoured to send a message to the beleagured garrison, but Galissonière challenged his presence and on 20th May offered battle. The combatants approached each other from opposite points, the French in line ahead sailing to the north west, Byng in line ahead on a course to the south east. Each skirmished for the weather gage. The wind was at south west. The two forces passed each other on opposite tacks, Galissonière to leeward of Byng. It was now expected that Byng having won the weather gage, would tack all ships together as soon as his van was conterminous with the enemy's rear, thus reversing his line and proceeding on a parallel track, on the weather side of the enemy. In fact he proceeded beyond this point, his intention being to bring each of his ships into action on a slanting course to that of the enemy in order to allow his ships to use broadsides as they closed for engagement. After tacking, his leading ship, the *Defiance*, misunderstood his intentions for a slanting course and, followed by the next four, proceeded in line ahead. It was a long time before Byng was able to get the leading ships to join action, and when they did his plan for a slanting course was ruined. The leading five ships now engaged and did magnificent work, each forcing her opponent out of line. The sixth ship, however, the *Intrepid*, had so far to go under a raking fire, owing to the action of the first five in the line, that she suffered considerable damage, lost her fore-topmast and swung round in the path of the following ships, causing the utmost confusion. This created a gap in the British line which Galissonière was swift to realize. If he could penetrate this, he could, with the rear ships of his line, double the British van, and crush them between two fires. Byng, however, met the situation, filled the gap, and straightened his line. Galissonière, satisfied that he had given as good as he had received, now put before the wind and departed. His ships had clean bottoms and were faster, so there was no possibility of catching them. The casualties on both sides had been about equal; forty-three killed and 168 wounded on the British side, forty-one killed and 181 wounded on the French.

Byng claimed the victory, as Galissonière had declined to continue the action. Nevertheless, after four days, he held a council of war at which he presented a series of questions, so worded that the answers all indicated the desirability of a return to Gibraltar. In spite of the presence of the besieging force and the existence of Galissonière's squadron without which the besieging force could not rely on support, Byng sailed for Gibraltar. General Blakeney and his small garrison in Minorca, capitulated on 28th June, over a month later.

As soon as news of Byng's failure to relieve Minorca reached England, the people clamoured for his blood. His effigy was burnt in all the great towns, and his seat and parks in Hertfordshire were attacked by a mob. Injurious ballads and caricatures were sold in the shops which reflected not only on

Byng but on the administration. The latter realized that this fresh disaster would mean the fall of the ministry, but they acted swiftly, for Sir Edward Hawke was at once ordered to sail for Gibraltar in the frigate *Antelope* to relieve Byng and to send him home under arrest. The Governor of Gibraltar was also relieved.

Anson sent the instructions intended for Hawke to Newcastle, for his remarks, in a letter of which the following is an extract:

Admiralty. 5th June 1756.

Your Grace,

. . . if Galissonière is returned to Port Mahón and Byng returned to Gibraltar it must be lost and grievous it will be to this Nation.

ANSON

Newcastle in his reply shows that he is keen for the recapture of Minorca, but expresses concern for the junction of the French fleets from Toulon and Brest, and suggests that discretion must be left to Hawke, the new Commander-in-Chief in the Mediterranean.

The loss of Minorca was disastrous to the people's morale and fatal to the ministry, nevertheless from a strategic point of view the only drawback was that it rendered the British blockade of Toulon more difficult. It made no difference to the relative positions in America, provided the British continued to hold Gibraltar.

Byng had failed to carry out his instructions and had left the Minorca garrison to its fate, but in extenuation it must be asked whether in the long run he was guilty of anything more than an error of judgment.

For a month Hawke kept up a strict blockade of Minorca, intercepting supplies, and raiding the island to supply his own wants. The Toulon fleet remained in harbour and prepared for sea. Galissonière's squadron remained at Port Mahón. A deadlock ensued. At the end of October, Hawke was recalled with his squadron to resume his command in the Channel. About this time Galissonière died.

Early in November Newcastle resigned, and the Duke of

Devonshire formed a government. Newcastle wanted Pitt to succeed him, but the King was still opposed to Pitt. The latter however, became Secretary of State, with a special responsibility for the management of the war in India and America, and virtually formed the Government. On taking office he is reported to have said to the Duke of Devonshire: 'I believe that I, and only I, can save England.' With the fall of the Government, Anson was superseded as First Lord by Richard Grenville, Lord Temple. Boscawen remained on the Board as the senior Sea Lord. The arrangement was hopeless and was not destined to last long. Pitt had the backing of the people, but in both Houses of Parliament it was Newcastle who still had the influence and the majority.

On arrival in England, Byng was transferred from Portsmouth, under guard, to Greenwich Hospital, where he was closely confined in the Queen Anne Block in a garret unfurnished except for a deal table and chair, and in which both window and chimney were barred with iron. It is said that his ghost still roams the precincts.

On 28th December 1756, Byng's court martial began on board H.M.S. *St. George* in Portsmouth Harbour, under Vice-Admiral Thomas Smith. It lasted a month. Several officers of the fleet were brought home for the trial. Extracts from the verdict (Add. MS 15955 British Museum) read:

> At a Court martial assembled on board H.M.S. 'St. George' in Portsmouth Harbour upon 28 December 1756 and held every day afterwards Sundays excepted till the 27 January 1757 inclusive.
>
> . . . unanimously of the opinion that he did not do his utmost to relieve St. Philip's Castle . . . did not do his utmost to take seize and destroy the ships of the French King.
>
> . . . he falls under part of the 12th Article of an Act of Parliament . . . and as that Article positively prescribes Death without any alternative left to the Discretion of the Court . . . unanimously adjudge the said Admiral John Byng to be shot to Death . . . but . . . recommend him as a proper object of Mercy.

It is certain that the court that tried him never expected the extreme penalty. They had no alternative but to find him guilty of negligence, and the application of the newly worded 12th Article of War which imposed 'Death' as the penalty, without alternative, was inescapable, except by the implementation of the recommendation for mercy. To this recommendation were added those of Pitt, Voltaire, and Dr. Johnson. The whole country seemed to be divided into those who clamoured for a scapegoat and could see only Byng as the culprit, and those who considered that Byng was not guilty of an offence worthy of death. There is a tragedy itself in the long delay prior to the trial, and then the suspense of the month long court martial during this cold winter. From the comfort and security of Lord Hardwicke's house goes a letter written two days after the trial, and though it has no bearing on either Byng or the trial, it is worth recording as a background. By their silence, Anson and Hardwicke, the one no longer in office, the other no longer wanted for day to day advice by Newcastle, appear to accept the justice of the verdict. The contents of the letter are trivial, dealing with purgatives, health, and the weather. Hardwicke writes to his son in law:

> Powis House January 29, 1757.
> Saturday 6 o'clock.
>
> My dear Lord,
>
> I am extremely sorry that an accident has happened, which prevents my waiting on Your Lordship this Evening, as I full intended. I thought it necessary to take Rhubarb last night which has operated so much so late today, that my Lady Hardwicke will not give me leave to stir out this cold night.

And not so many miles away on this cold night sat Byng under close arrest, condemned to death. It appears from several letters by Lord Hardwicke that there was considerable effort to establish a justification of the previous administration which had recently fallen, and an opinion that Byng, and Byng alone, was responsible for the disaster of Minorca. His removal by execution would be a fair penalty. An inquiry into the loss of

Minorca had been called for in the House of Commons, in which the conduct of the Admiralty would be investigated. Much preparation was necessary to make out a case which would justify the actions of the fallen ministry.

The Court which condemned Byng sent a letter to the Lords Commissioner of the Admiralty, explaining that they had endeavoured to do the strictest justice, but implying that the sentence was too severe for something that might be regarded as an error of judgment, and recommending the prisoner to his Majesty's clemency. The Board of Admiralty, of whom Anson was no longer a member, submitted the letter to the King, but instead of supporting the recommendation for clemency, expressed doubts about the legality of the sentence, and asked for an opinion of the judges as to whether the sentence was legal. The answer was sent on 16th February 1757, and stated that opinion was unanimous that the sentence was legal.

On this day a warrant was signed for Byng's execution. A demand was also made that the offending 12th Article should be revised. It was not until twenty-two years later that an addition was made after the word 'death'—'or to inflict such other punishment as the nature and degree of the offence shall be found to deserve.'

It is unfortunate that Byng's court martial was composed wholly of officers who were junior to him.

On the day following the signing of the warrant, a letter was written to the Lords of the Admiralty by Mrs. Osborn, Byng's sister. The following are extracts from this pathetic letter:

17 February 1757.

My Lords,

The Judges having reported to His Majesty in Council that the Sentence passed on my unfortunate Brother is a legal one, permit me to implore your Lordships Intercession with His Majesty for his most gracious Mercy, and to hope your Lordship will not think an afflicted Sister's Application ill founded in a Case so hardly Circumstanced, and which the Judges, though by the severity of the Law they have thought themselves obliged to pronounce the fatal sentence have so earnestly recommended to your Lordships humanity.

The Court Martial, My Lords, seem to have acquitted my unhappy Brother of Cowardice and disaffection, and therefore it is presumed he stands sentenced under the Head of Negligence. It is not fitting perhaps that a wretched woman, as I am, should offer any arguments on my Brother's behalf.

I must submit to your Lordships whether it be the meaning of the Law that every kind of negligence, wilful or not, should be punished with Death.

I hope your Lordships will not think he ought to suffer either under a Law unexplained, or doubtful, or under a sentence erroneously passed. If the Law has been misunderstood, and if my unfortunate Brother has been condemned under the 12th Article, according to the Spirit and meaning of which he should not have been condemned I submit to your Lordships whether his life should be the forfeit.

I hope I shall stand excused if I beseech your Lordships immediate Intercession with His Majesty in his behalf.

I am

Your Lordships

Most obedient

Humble Servant

S. OSBORN

But all was in vain. On Monday 14th March, Admiral Byng met his death on the quarter deck of the *Monarque* in Portsmouth Harbour. He had suffered close imprisonment, indignities, and prolonged anxiety for more than seven months, but faced his execution with calmness and dignity. Shortly before his death he said: 'They make a precedent of me such as Admirals hereafter may feel the effect of.'

Voltaire, describing the scene, says that the shore was crowded with people eagerly watching. Four soldiers fired three bullets into the victim's head, after which the crowd dispersed with an air of satisfaction. 'In this country,' he said, 'it is found necessary from time to time to shoot an admiral, to encourage the others.'

How does Anson stand in this affair? He was out of office at the time of the trial and execution, but appears to have been convinced that Byng had failed to do his utmost and must suffer the consequence laid down in the Articles of War. It is fairly certain that, had he wished to plead on behalf of Byng, he could have used his influence with Hardwicke to plead for clemency by the King. Had he been in Byng's position off Minorca there was little doubt in his own mind that with determination and skill worthy of a British admiral the chances of a victory were high, and there would have been no question of withdrawing to Gibraltar until Galissonière had been defeated and Minorca relieved. By the time he had arrived at Minorca his thirteen ships would have reached such a pitch of training and mutual understanding that there could be no possibility of mistaking the intentions of the admiral.

Poor Byng; everything seems to have gone wrong for him, but there is little doubt that his execution must have acted as a discipline that spurred many failing hearts and doubtful minds to victory in later years.

# CHAPTER XIX

# The Struggle for Command of the Sea

WAR had been officially declared on the French King on 17th May 1756, on the grounds of 'the unwarranted proceedings of the French in the West Indies and North America since the conclusion of the Treaty of Aix-la-Chappelle, and the Usurpation and Encroachments made by them upon our Territory,' and all ships had been instructed by the Admiralty to 'act in a hostile Manner by taking, sinking, burning or otherwise destroying all Ships of War belonging to the French King or his Subjects.'

By the autumn of 1756, however, when Anson had resigned with Newcastle, things were not going well. Britain's ally, Frederick of Prussia, found himself faced by a formidable coalition which included Sweden, Saxony, Poland, Russia, France, and Austria.

In the Speech from the Throne on 2nd December 1756, Pitt's great war policy was announced. It at once swept away the vacillations and ill-defined plan of Newcastle's Government, and made it clear that 'the succour and preservation of America were to be the main object', and there were to be 'resolutions of vigour and despatch', and 'an adequate and firm defence at home'. Finally he made it quite clear that they were not to get too much embroiled in Europe and that any undertakings there must be subordinate to the main object. The soldiers of Hanover would defend Hanover.

Pitt's administration was, however, short lived, for he was dismissed by the King on 6th April 1757, in connexion with a disagreement concerning the appointment of the King's son, the Duke of Cumberland, to command in Germany. It proved impossible to form a government owing to a clash of personalities, and for three months the King himself appears to have been his own Minister. Temple had been relieved on the fall of Pitt's administration, and his place as First Lord was taken temporarily by Lord Winchelsea. Boscawen again remained as the senior Sea Lord. The need for strong and capable men was obvious, but negotiations were protracted. In the end it was Hardwicke, the ex-Lord Chancellor who had made up his mind never to take office again, who was instrumental in forming an administration which was agreeable to the King. This was to be a coalition with Newcastle as Prime Minister, because of his great following in both Houses, Pitt as Secretary of State for foreign affairs with control of the war, and Anson as First Lord of the Admiralty. Thus then was Lord Anson restored on the 5th July 1757, to his position as First Lord of the Admiralty, following a five months' administration by Lord Temple and a three months' administration by Lord Winchelsea.

Anson was now promoted Admiral of the White, the most senior rank but one in the Navy, and his promotion was back-dated to June 1757. His last promotion had been in May 1748, but in July 1749 he was given the honorary appointment of Vice-Admiral of Great Britain.

There is drama in Lord Hardwicke's letter to Anson describing the later negotiations, and in spite of its great length it is worth reproducing in full. It seems to cover every side of the pro-tracted negotiations, deals with the composition of the Board, reveals pleasure and confidence in the proposed administration, and hints at a faith in the future success that most certainly followed.

Powis House
June 18 1757
Saturday Night. 11 o'clock

My Dear Lord,

You will probably be surprised at receiving this letter from me by the King's messenger; but it will make me more happy than ever I was in my life, if the subject of it shall be as agreeable to your Lordship as it is to me. You have heard how the administration projected under

Mr. Fox failed this day se'ennight, in the very moment it was to have been carried into execution, and he was just going into the closet to receive the Exchequer-seal. On Tuesday night the King, by the Duke of Devonshire, ordered me to attend him on Wednesday morning. I have since had the honour of several audiences of his Majesty; some of them most uneasy and painful ones, though without any anger towards me. My first orders were, for the Duke of Newcastle and myself to negotiate some settlement of an administration with Mr. Pitt and his friends, under certain restrictions, from which his Majesty declared he would never depart. In the course of my audience, I told his Majesty that I could take no part at all, unless some honourable regard was shown to your Lordship, though I could not just then point out the particular thing; that I had told the gentlemen with whom we had conferred the same thing, and had previously humbly conveyed it to his Majesty.

In his subsequent discourse the King, in aggravating the inconveniences that would arise from this new plan, told me with warmth, that resignations had been talked of; that, in the way we were going, there would be resignations enough; that my Lord Winchelsea was in the next room, in order now to come into the closet to resign. The convenience of this struck me, but I reserved myself. Some minutes afterwards the King read over my list in heat— objected to Mr. Legge being made a peer and first lord of the Admiralty—was determined not to do two great things for one man at the same time; and in this he was peremptory. I then threw your Lordship in his way, but that I was far from knowing what the other persons would say to it. His Majesty answered quick—'I shall like it extremely.'

When I stated this to the Duke of Newcastle it made him most happy; and I reported it at the meeting of all four in the evening; I stated it, as it was in reality, the King's option. My Lord Bute and Mr. Pitt received it with the greatest politeness. Lord Bute first broke the ice; declared his particular respect for your Lordship, and did

great justice to your character, and merit in your profession;
and declared that he knew those to be the sentiments of
the place to which he belonged. Mr. Pitt said he only
waited to hear what Lord Bute would say, and most
readily concurred in the same sentiments. In short, it
ended so that all the four plenipotentiaries agreed that
your Lordship should be again at the head of the Admiralty,
if the King continued in the same mind, and Mr. Legge
has his old office of Chancellor of the Exchequer, which he
had professed to like better than any other place.

I have been negociating ever since upon other points, and
have led a most fatiguing life. However at last the whole
was settled, and I carried the King the plan in writing
this day at noon. The three things which the King had
made his *sine qua non* were—1. That he would perform his
promise to make Mr. Fox paymaster. 2. That there should
be no change in the Secretary-at-War. 3. That Lord Anson
should be at the head of the Admiralty. When I told his
Majesty that we had carried all this for him, and that all
those points were most dutifully yielded up to his pleasure,
I never saw such a change in man. He said at once, with a
gracious smile—'Then this thing is done; and, my Lord,
I thank you heartily.' He is in haste to carry it into
execution immediately, and indeed it must be in a few
days.

I can't send your Lordship the plan, for the King kept
the original, and I have yet no copy. The great lines are—
Mr. Pitt, Secretary of State; Lord Temple to have a
Cabinet Council place; the Duke of Newcastle, First Lord
of the Treasury; and Mr. Fox, Paymaster. Thus your
Lordship is once more called to this great office by the
King's earnest desire, the united voice of all parties, and
the concurrence of Saville House—though that must not be
talked of. In other circumstances you might possibly not
so well like the company you are to sit with, which are
those who were turned out at Easter. You know that Mr.
Pitt and friends always made restitution their point, and
wanted to provide for those friends who were of that Board,
so there was no possibility of altering that. But I hope, in

The Hon. Edward Boscawen
*From an oil painting by Sir Joshua Reynolds*

Richard, Earl Howe

*From a mezzotint by J. Watson after T. Gainsborough*

the present situation, you will make no difficulty or hesitation about it. Indeed, my dear Lord, this unexpected event, which I have used some honest dexterity in bringing about, is the greatest thing for the King's honour, for the credit of his old administration, and for your own honour. It does, by their own admission, give the lie to all the calumnies that have been raised; it contradicts all that had been said upon the inquiry; and confirms the issue of that inquiry to be a total justification. The King sees it in that light, and therefore is prodigiously pleased with it. This is the true light wherein it is to be seen; and the unanimity of the Royal family upon it is a most happy and inviting circumstance; and will, I am confident, induce your Lordship to overlook all other circumstances, which a little time and opportunity will correct. I have privately laid in with Lord Bute and Mr. Pitt that some one of their people may be changed upon being otherwise provided for, and they have agreed to the reasonableness of this. You know the Duke of Newcastle had formerly promised Mr. Stanley, who may be useful to you in the House of Commons; so will Elliot, who, I dare say, will in six weeks be as much yours as theirs. Besides, I am told that Admiral Forbes is likely not to accept, and, if so, it will make room for Sir Edward Hawke, or any other man we shall like.

This is the state of the case, and when I look back I stand amazed at the sudden change. All our friends are in raptures with it; the court in general pleased, and the town more so. It is looked upon as the strongest administration that has been formed many years, and by good conduct, may become so.

I am glad to hear that the waters have agreed with your Lordship, but you must interrupt them for a few days; and, in obedience to his Majesty's commands, set out immediately, and be in town as soon as you can without hurting your health in this hot weather. I am to see the King on Monday, who will ask me if I have sent for you.

The Duke of Newcastle sends your Lordship his most cordial compliments and congratulations. Both his Grace and I, and all your friends, entreat your Lordship to make

no difficulties, and to let us see you as soon as you can, in
health. The messenger waits, and will bring you a letter
from dear Lady Anson, who knew not one word of this
matter till I had settled it finally with the King this day.
Adieu, my dear Lord, &c., &c.,

HARDWICKE

It is a pity that no letter is available to show Anson's reaction.
He was not a man to write much about his thoughts and
opinions, but essentially a man of action. He realized that his
experience and judgment were invaluable to the country at this
vital moment, and accepted.

It is said that Pitt made it a condition of his accepting office
that Anson should 'not possess the correspondence', the idea
being that the Board should provide the advice, and that
instructions and orders would be issued by Pitt. There is no
reference to such a condition in Hardwicke's letter, and it is
likely that the story arose from the practice Pitt adopted of
issuing orders, particularly those for combined operations
involving both army and navy, direct to the commanders
concerned. Such orders were only evolved after they had been
settled in the 'Secret Committee' of the Council, and the
necessity for passing them direct was a good safeguard for
surprise and secrecy. Anson himself, during his expedition,
showed his concern for the preservation of security of information, and would have been the first to support a system which
ensured it. One of Anson's first actions on returning to the
Admiralty in July 1757 was to send a letter to all commanders-
in-chief enjoining care in the handling of papers with orders.

There is also a story that Pitt virtually became a despotic
ruler acting over the heads of various departments, but here
again it is probable that the story was caused through Pitt's
decisive way of handling affairs, which was so much in contrast
with the previous clumsy administration. He subsequently
declared solemnly from his place in the House of Commons that
he never acted except through the heads of the offices concerned.
It is clear, however, that there were times when his impatience
led to an overbearing manner and indiscretion, as in the
matter described later that caused Hawke to strike his flag.

Anson for his part proved to be a loyal supporter of Pitt, though he did not always see eye to eye with his schemes.

Boscawen was again retained as a member of the Board. Anson was also anxious to get Hawke appointed to the Board to serve with him, but although he had Pitt's support, failed to obtain the approval of Newcastle who was keen to offer a place to one of his political supporters. The occasion is well described by Lady Anson in a letter to her father addressed throughout in the third person:

Downing Street, August 10, 1757.

Lord Anson, with his respectful compliments to Lord Hardwicke, begs pardon for employing a secretary, to inform his Lordship of an incident which happened, and which embarrasses him a good deal. The occasion of it is the appointment of a successor at the Admiralty in the room of Admiral West, who died last night at Tonbridge. Lord Anson waited on the Duke of Newcastle this morning to acquaint him with it, and to express his strong desire that as this created a vacancy in the Admiralty, it might be filled up with Sir Ed. Hawke. His Grace insisting very warmly upon his engagement to Mr. Stanley, Lord Anson begged him at least to defer filling it up a little (as he said he must have made a vacancy for Mr. Stanley), to try if he could not accommodate both. The Duke declared at the end of the conversation that he would go into the Closet, and settle it for Mr. Stanley directly: or he would never go to the Treasury again. Whether he has settled it accordingly is not yet known to Lord Anson, who thinks that if he had not shown the attention he paid to the Duke of Newcastle, but had gone at first where his Grace said he was going, he should have found it no difficult point to have carried it for Sir Ed. Hawke. Mr. Pitt very civilly and reasonably says, as he did upon that subject when this Board was appointed, that as there was nobody on it whom Lord Anson had chosen, he thought it very proper he should recommend him now, and if Sir Edward Hawke was agreeable to him he thought it very right he should succeed. Lord Anson cannot help thinking the circumstances very hard, considering the merits of the two persons proposed, one of whom will in all probability be very troublesome, and very likely a spy for Doddington. It is certain the office is not very desirable at this time— nor would it be bad or a discreditable reason for quitting it, that he had not been able to obtain so reasonable a wish as desiring to have an officer of the character of Sir Edward Hawke at the Board, before Mr. Stanley. Lord Anson would not willingly take any further steps before he has the advice of Lord Hardwicke; but he is extremely dissatisfied, and beside 'the manner of doing it' not listening to any chance of delay, or accommodating. He very much doubts if he ought to submit to stay at the Board, and see it always filled up, by the Duke of Newcastle, with persons of no use there, and of no weight or abilities elsewhere. It is much to be wished Lord Hardwicke could induce the Duke of Newcastle to some scheme of accommodation, as in appearance there cannot be a worse addition to the Board than that proposed.

In spite of Pitt's aggressive attitude towards conducting the war and Anson's support in providing an efficient Navy charged with blockading the French ports, the year 1757 continued to bring disasters to the British, and encouragement to the French. French reinforcements for Louisburg managed to slip out of Brest and arrived safely at their destination. Admiral Holburne, with a British fleet of nineteen sail-of-the-line and some cruisers and frigates, in the course of blockading Louisburg, encountered on the night of the 24th September 1757, a hurricane, when he was in a position about sixty miles from a lee shore. His whole fleet was being forced towards the rocky shore of Cape Breton, twelve of his ships had been dismasted and one wrecked, when miraculously the wind veered to the north. His ships were saved, but were in such a shattered condition that most of the squadron had to proceed to Halifax for repair. The plan to take Louisburg and advance up the St. Lawrence to Quebec had been drastically thwarted for this year.

In the meantime Pitt's scheme to cause havoc in the French ports was already under way. The object was twofold. The primary reason was to create a diversion which would compel the French to send reinforcements to all their coastal towns, and so relieve pressure on the King of Prussia and Duke of Cumberland. The object was also to destroy harbour installations, docks, basins, arsenals, and ships, as a counter to the French threat to invade Great Britain and Ireland.

On 11th July 1757, a few days after taking over at the Admiralty, Anson summoned Hawke to London to inform him of his new command of a fleet which was to take part in a combined assault on the French port of Rochefort.

There were to be sixteen sail-of-the-line, with frigates, sloops, and bombs (small ships mounting mortars) in support. Land forces approaching a thousand strong under the command of Sir John Mordaunt were to be transported and landed while warships bombarded and reduced fortifications. Hawke's sixteen captains included Keppel, Byron, Rodney, Barrington, Denis, and Howe; four of them survivors of Anson's expedition. Mordaunt's Chief of Staff was James Wolfe, then a lieutenant-colonel of thirty years of age, and already an officer with a high reputation; he quickly contracted a friendship for Howe, captain of the *Magnanime*.

There was considerable delay in getting the force to sea, and it was not until 8th September that they sailed from Spithead. On the 22nd they anchored in the Basque Roads outside the approaches to Rochefort, having again been delayed, this time by fog and light airs. The whole expedition seems to have been prejudiced by poor intelligence and a false anticipation of difficulties and serious opposition. Protecting the estuary was the fortified Ile d'Aix. On the 23rd Howe, in the *Magnanime*, leading a division of six sail-of-the-line, sailed to within forty yards of the guns of Ile d'Aix, reserving his fire. To the astonishment of all, the fort surrendered. It was fully expected that troops would now be landed, but differences of opinion developed, and Sir John Mordaunt held a Council of War the result of which was to call off the whole expedition. By this time the French in Rochefort would be prepared for assault. Further councils, wrangling, and discussion followed, but the moment had passed, and by the end of the month, after an abortive attempt in bad weather, the expedition had been called off.

In a private letter to his father Wolfe said:

> We lost the lucky moment in war and are not able to recover it. The whole expedition has not cost the nation ten men; nor has any man been able to distinguish himself in the service of his country, except Mr. Howe who was an example to us all.

Here was a failure which caused further rejoicing in France and gloom in England. The lessons learned had, however, not been lost on Wolfe who realized that decisive and resolute action, surprise, and the elements of chance, must all be allowed their play. 'Lose no time in getting the troops ashore,' he said. 'Nothing is to be reckoned an obstacle which is not found to be so on trial; . . . something must be allowed to chance and fortune . . . the greatness of an object should come under consideration as opposed to the impediments that lie in the way.' These were great words and could well have come from Anson himself, had he been given to exposition. Here was an indication of the intelligence and character which were to prove so brilliantly successful at a later combined operation, notorious for its mutual service understanding and resolution.

Hawke returned to Spithead on 7th October 1757. In spite of the failure of the expedition he was received by the King, with whom he was a great favourite. To the King he had been 'My Captain' ever since the Battle off Toulon 1744. Mordaunt was later brought before a court martial, but was acquitted.

Almost immediately after Hawke's return, news was received that de la Motte's fleet which had eluded the British when outward bound to Louisburg, was now on its way home. Hawke, with a strong squadron, in which was also Vice-Admiral Boscawen, one of the lords of the Admiralty, was sent to intercept de la Motte. Again Hawke's luck was out, for he was driven off station by a gale at the critical moment, unknown to him, when de la Motte was approaching Brest. De la Motte once again reached Brest. This time, however, his ships were shattered by the gale, and his men went down with a fever which spread like fire through the town and paralysed the port for months.

Pitt had had little apparent success so far and there was much opposition to his direction of the war. Renewed effort was made to get him to send troops to the Continent, but he resolutely stuck to his plan, little swayed by momentary failure or success. Instead of troops, Frederick was given a subsidy of one million eight hundred thousand pounds, and a promise of further diversions on the coast. The blockade continued in the Mediterranean, where a sufficient squadron had been maintained by Anson under the command of Admiral Osborne and Anson's old friend and shipmate Saunders, now an admiral. So vigorous was this blockade that the French had been unable to carry out any effective preparation of a squadron of ships in Toulon, destined for the relief of Louisburg in the spring of 1758. In fact the French now possessed no active naval force which could seriously interfere with British naval plans. Pitt's 'system' was ripe for development.

The number of British seamen voted for 1758 rose to sixty thousand including nearly fifteen thousand marines. In the dockyards the slips and basins were alive with activity and strenuous preparations. The Admiralty now introduced a system of regular payment for seamen and an allotment scheme whereby money could be sent direct for the support of wives and families of seamen.

One of the first British successes in 1758 occurred off Cartagena. Osborne and Saunders were blockading a squadron of French ships that had taken refuge in Cartagena and which were about to be joined by a reinforcement of three ships from Toulon under the command of the Marquis Duquesne. One was quickly taken, a second was driven ashore on Spanish neutral territory, and the third, the famous eighty-four-gun *Foudroyant* which had worn Galissonière's flag in the engagement with Byng off Minorca, and was now wearing the flag of Duquesne, was taken after a long and determined engagement with the *Monmouth*, a small ship of sixty-four guns. *Monmouth*, commanded by Gardiner, who had been Byng's flag captain at Minorca, chased *Foudroyant* to the open sea, resolved to make amends for the shame of Minorca. A brisk single ship action developed unchecked by the approaching night. Gardiner was wounded in the arm by the first broadside. This merely added to his exertions and encouragement of his ship's company in the unequal contest. For four hours in the dark of the evening the action continued. About nine o'clock Gardiner was killed by a ball striking his forehead. With his dying breath he urged his first lieutenant to continue the fight. The first lieutenant, Robert Carkett, nailed his flag to the mast, and stubbornly clung to the *Foudroyant*, now a scene of carnage and wreckage.

For four more hours the action continued until, by one o'clock in the morning, each vessel had fought almost to a standstill. *Swiftsure* and *Hampton Court*, steering for the sound of guns, soon arrived, and Duquesne hauled down his flag. It was to Carkett that he surrendered his sword.

The French loss was a small one in ships, but the moral effect and the strategic consequences were great. The shame of Minorca had been avenged, and the plan to send French reinforcements from Toulon to Louisburg had been shattered. In the meantime active preparations were being made at Rochefort, and the Admiralty received early information of the fitting out of warships and assembly of transports destined to reinforce Louisburg and the French colonial possessions in North Africa.

Anson ordered Hawke to investigate with a division of seven sail-of-the-line. He was instructed to return for further orders after one month. Hawke sailed from Spithead on 12th March 1758 and was later joined by another sail-of-the-line and three frigates. On 4th April he sailed in line ahead into the Basque Roads, the scene of Mordaunt's abortive councils of war, and saw five sail-of-the-line, seven frigates and some forty transports and storeships. These, on seeing Hawke approaching, slipped their cables and made for the river in great confusion, where they stuck on the mud flats. With approaching night, and faced with shallows, Hawke came to anchor. The next morning revealed the French ships high and dry some miles away, industriously throwing guns, ballast, anchors, and stores overboard to enable them to gain the river mouth as the tide made. Thus they all escaped. Hawke sent in his frigates to cut away the buoys which had been left to mark the abandoned gear, and also destroyed the fortifications that were being reconstructed on the Ile d'Aix. He arrived at Plymouth on

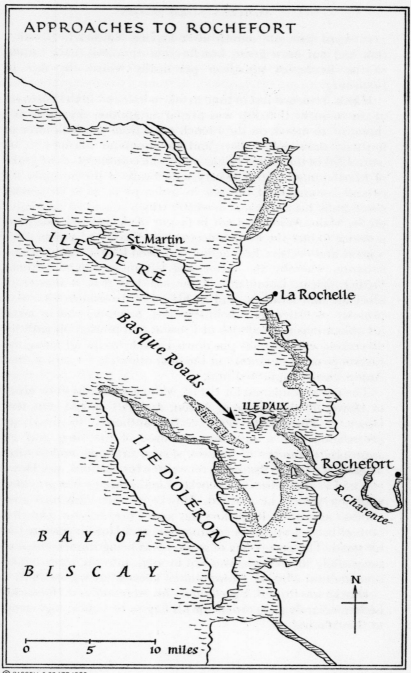

# APPROACHES TO ROCHEFORT

ILE DE RÉ

St. Martin

La Rochelle

Basque Roads

Shoal

ILE D'AIX

ILE D'OLÉRON

Rochefort

R. Charente

BAY OF

BISCAY

N

0    5    10 miles

© CASSELL & CO. LTD 1960

11th April just one month after leaving Spithead. Destruction had not been great, but the confusion and delay caused to the Rochefort squadron practically sealed the fate of Louisburg.

Hawke returned just in time to take command in the Channel at the moment that Pitt was preparing another diversion, the threat of an attack on the French coast from a British force of fourteen thousand soldiers and six thousand marines to be assembled in the Isle of Wight under the command of the Duke of Marlborough. Pitt was very well aware of the necessity for overall command of the sea in order to be able to launch successfully his particular diversion which was to be an assault on St. Malo. Anson was not in favour of the assault, except as a device to lure the French fleet to sea. Years had passed since a great and decisive fleet action had been fought resulting in a situation whereby the victor was left in command without further threat. Command of the sea was now a matter of blockade and strategy, and in his mind diversions without a primary objective were pointless. Pitt, however, had in mind his obligations to Frederick of Prussia, and pressed on with his diversions which would pin down French troops all along the French coast in ignorance of the next objective for attack, and Anson loyally supported him.

The naval command for the St. Malo assault was to be given to Howe, on the advice of Anson, and Pitt agreed. Pitt sent Howe to Portsmouth with verbal authority to speed up preparations for a squadron of three of the line, and an appropriate number of frigates, sloops, fireships, and bombs. There was delay in issuing secret written instructions, and Howe was told to apply direct to Hawke to make sure he was provided with everything he wanted. Hawke at once assumed that another assault on Rochefort was under preparation, and that he had been dropped as commander, and Howe appointed in his stead. The new policy of secrecy was being implemented so successfully that Hawke was not brought into the picture, and it is doubtful whether Howe himself knew what was on foot.

Hawke was furious. Egged on by his secretary and Holburne, he immediately gave orders for his flag to be struck, and wrote to the Admiralty:

Portsmouth
7 o'clock p.m. May 10, 1758.

Sir,

About four o'clock arrived here Captain Howe and delivered me their Lordships' orders of the 9th. In last September I was sent out to command an expedition under all the disadvantages one could possibly labour under . . . last cruise I went out on a particular service almost without the least means of performing it. Now every means to ensure success is provided, another is to reap the credit . . . He is to make his demands and I am to comply with them. I have therefore directed my flag to be struck. . . . For no consequence that can attend my striking it without orders shall ever out balance with me the wearing it one moment with discredit.

Here was a troublesome state of affairs and it was left to Anson to provide a solution. Hawke had proceeded in a most irregular manner in striking his flag and could not be reappointed in command. Such a reappointment would strike at discipline. Hawke, however, was an officer in whom Anson had great faith and whose services he was reluctant to lose. He therefore proposed to assume the command of the Channel fleet himself, though now sixty-one, and proceed to sea with Hawke as his second in command.

An extract from Anson's letter to his father-in-law says:

May 13 1758

Sir Edward Hawke came to the Board on Friday morning, and owned he had done a very wrong thing . . . he did not do it with any disrespect to the Board, but merely thinking it would appear a slur upon him to the world . . .

The Lords . . . came to the following resolution:

'That Sir Edward Hawke's striking his flag without orders is a high breach of discipline—therefore notwithstanding the acknowledgment contained in the minutes, the Lords do not think proper to restore him to the command of the ships in the Channel, although in consideration of that acknowledgment, and of his great services, they have not proceeded to any further closure. Whereupon, as the most proper measure upon this occasion, the Lords have ordered Lord Anson to take upon himself the command.'

On 19th May Lady Anson writing to her father says:

It gives him [Lord Anson] great pleasure to find your Lordship approves the step he has taken . . . Sir Edward Hawke had earnestly desired to serve under him . . . and has already set out for Portsmouth.

This must have been her first parting from her husband. She continues in the letter:

There seems no probability that my Lord should return from Portsmouth till the wished for hour of his return thither from the expedition.

By the 27th May the whole naval force had assembled at Spithead. Anson had hoisted his flag in the *Royal George*, a hundred guns, and was in command of twenty-two sail-of-the-line and eight frigates, a covering fleet for the expedition. Howe's detachment consisted of five small ships-of-the-line, ten frigates, five sloops, two bombs, two fireships, a hundred transports, and a number of storeships, cutters, and tenders. The total number of men embarked including seamen, amounted to thirty-four thousand. The army consisted of fourteen thousand. On 1st June Anson made the signal to weigh and sailed westward with his battle fleet. His plan was not to blockade, but to stand off the French coast in the hope that the French fleet would put to sea to attack the expeditionary force which had sailed under Howe for St. Malo. It is evident that he was disappointed with the low standard of efficiency in which he found his fleet. Gone were the pitch of readiness and degree of training which he had cultivated during his voyage and again when he was in command of the Western Squadron in 1747. He set about systematically exercising and drilling. He had his old shipmate Sir Peircy Brett as his flag captain in the *Royal George*, and made up his mind to get Saunders back from the Mediterranean to take over the disciplining and exercising of the fleet when he himself should return to Admiralty. Hawke had been taken ill soon after leaving, and had been sent ashore.

To his father-in-law Anson wrote on 22nd July, seven weeks after sailing from St. Helen's:

> I do assure your Lordship that when I began to exercise my fleet I never saw such an awkwardness in going through the common manoeuvres necessary to make an attack upon an enemy's fleet at all. What we now do in an hour, in the beginning took eight. . . .
>
> . . . most of them [the captains] declared they had never seen a line of battle at all.
>
> I should be glad to see Rear-Admiral Saunders in a fortnight or three weeks, if his health will allow of it, that I might have him with me some time before I leave the fleet, and that it might be kept in the plan of discipline I have formed for it, and which is in a great part new.

Howe's squadron met stormy weather but arrived off Cape La Hogue on 1st June. He immediately transferred to *Success*, twenty-eight guns, and proceeding inshore silenced a small battery in the harbour of Le Houle; disembarkation then proceeded. The following day the troops marched to St. Malo, destroyed ships, buildings, magazines, and storehouses, and then returned to embark in their transports. By this time vast numbers of French troops were pouring down the coast to St. Malo. Storms delayed Howe's departure, but on 21st June he arrived off Havre. Here, however, the French were ready for him, so he bore away for Cherbourg. A further storm nearly blew his squadron on to a lee shore, and it was with the greatest difficulty that they got away, this time to return to the Isle of Wight after an absence of a month.

On arrival at Spithead, they learned that Saunders had just come in from the Mediterranean with Duquesne a prisoner in his cabin, and the famous *Foudroyant* in his possession.

The expedition was resumed on 1st August and sailed on that day for St. Helen's, with Howe as commodore in command of the naval forces, and General Bligh in command of the land forces. This time Cherbourg was entered, and considerable demolitions carried out on the harbour installations and store-houses, and thirty ships were sunk. Batteries were rendered useless, guns and mortars thrown into the sea, and twenty-four brass cannon sent to England in a captured ship. By 15th August the destruction was complete, and on the 16th the whole force re-embarked and returned to Portland on the 17th to repair and replenish.

The twenty-four brass cannon were drawn through the city in ceremonial procession from Hyde Park to the Tower. Lady Anson, in a letter describing the scene, considered the whole thing a joke in comparison with her husband's achievements:

> To be sure—she said—war has its advantages, par-
> ticularly in the fine sights its triumphs afford, 300 dray
> horses with the 20 Cherburg cannon, which all the Johns
> and Joans in town, who have kept Hyde Park like a fair
> for some days, are convinced must be the first brass ones
> that were ever seen in England. I had a great mind to have
> them sent to Woolwich where there lies near 200 which
> my lord took and never showed to anybody.

By 31st August the diverting expedition departed again, this time to land troops at St. Lunaire to the westward of St. Malo. Weather and an expectant enemy proved their ruin, and mainly due to bad leadership the disembarkation at St. Cas proved costly, British casualties amounting to nearly a thousand.

St. Cas terminated the diversionary attacks. They had not been altogether successful but had produced the effect Pitt had intended. Howe had been outstanding as a naval commander, but it was obvious that the army commanders were in many cases old and useless. Wolfe had already summed up the requirements for success, and by implication shown how futile were the efforts of some of the army commanders. Anson had also referred to their incapacity in a letter written to Hardwicke after the first assault on St. Malo:

*Royal George* at Sea June 29 1758.

Certainly your army does not make the figure it ought to do.

. . . though you have changed your generals you have lost part of your possessions and forts, without even making any tolerable defence. At Rochefort your generals saw the enemy upon the hills, and although they knew there were no regular troops, they would not land.

Though I believe the men to be good and the generals brave, I account a want of experience which makes them fearful of coming into an action, or putting anything to the risk; which *must* be done in war.

Anson returned to Plymouth on 19th July for water and provisions, and sailed again on 22nd July, having been joined by Rear-Admiral Holmes for whom he had a great regard. Holmes hoisted his flag in *Ramillies*. About the end of August Rear-Admiral Saunders joined him and hoisted his flag in *Neptune*. Anson remained at sea with his fleet until the middle of September, when Howe had completed his expedition to France. He then returned to Portsmouth, leaving a division under Saunders to continue the blockade of Brest and endeavour to intercept a French squadron returning from Quebec.

Peter Denis, one of Anson's former lieutenants, and now captain of the *Dorsetshire*, fell in with a fine new French sixty-four, the *Raisonnable*, and captured her after an engagement lasting nearly two hours.

There is a letter written by Lady Anson to her father on 19th September 1758 from the Admiralty. She is daily expecting the return of her husband, and is concerned about his health after a strenuous cruise of sixteen weeks. The graphic description in her letter gives more than a suggestion of a whiff of the sea, and is a reminder of the prevalence of sickness in ships due to stale water, foul air, and monotonous food.

My lord has mentioned a visit he received from Captain Rodney and two or three more Captains returned from Louisburg (Mr. Rodney went to America only with General Amherst) whose company was so offensive from the state of their Health as to make it but just possible to bear the Cabbin with them, not even almost after they were gone.

I imagine that you heard that Sir John Armitage fell too at St. Cas. He was to have married Miss Howe immediately on his return and went a Volunteer.

St. Cas had been a tragic failure. Britain had once more obtained command of the sea, but was still in need of a decisive victory to bolster morale.

Commodore the Hon. Augustus Keppel
*From an oil painting by Sir Joshua Reynolds*

The *Royal Charlotte* with the future Queen of England embarking at Stade; Anson's last service at sea

*From a line engraving by P. C. Canot after T. Allen*

# CHAPTER XX

# The Eclipse of France's Naval Power

EVENTS in North America had hitherto been disastrous for British forces. In 1755 General Braddock's army had been cut to pieces when advancing on Fort Duquesne in the Ohio valley west of the Allegheny Mountains, and in 1757 Admiral Holburne had had his ships shattered in a hurricane while blockading the harbour of Louisburg. Nothing less than the conquest of North America would satisfy Pitt. In 1758 his resumption of attack began with land expeditions aimed at Fort Duquesne and Fort Ticonderoga, and an amphibious assault on Louisburg. If Louisburg were captured then a force was to proceed up the St. Lawrence for an attack on Quebec. Anson selected Boscawen for the naval command, and in February sent him with a large force of sixteen ships-of-the-line from the Channel squadron to join seven ships-of-the-line that had wintered in Halifax. These with six frigates and some smaller vessels were to blockade Louisburg as early as ice conditions permitted, and be prepared to meet any concentration of fleet warships that the French could provide at Louisburg. Troops from Portsmouth and Cork, and supplies and stores, all in different convoys, had to be escorted across the Atlantic. Of the land forces, General Amherst was in command and Brigadier Wolfe second in command.

The passage across the Atlantic was unduly prolonged. Rodney in the *Dublin*, seventy-four, carrying Amherst, stopped to take a rich prize carrying coffee, and spent a fortnight with her in Vigo bay. It was not until 8th June, a week after Anson and Hawke had sailed from Spithead to cover Howe's assault

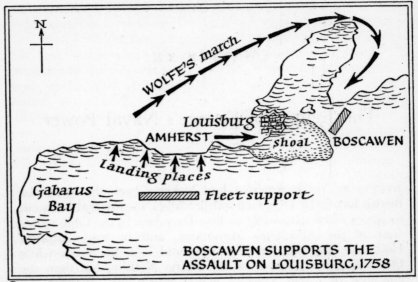

BOSCAWEN SUPPORTS THE
ASSAULT ON LOUISBURG, 1758

© CASSELL & CO. LTD 1960

across the Channel, that Boscawen assembled his fleet in Gabarus Bay outside the small Louisburg harbour. Under cover of naval guns, the soldiers landed at three different landing places against heavy shore fire, and under Wolfe's leadership pressed on, working their way right round the town to the land commanding the side of the entrance to the harbour opposite the town of Louisburg. Here Wolfe set up a battery of guns landed from Boscawen's blockading squadron, and silenced the enemy's guns erected on the island at the harbour mouth.

Inside the harbour were five French ships-of-the-line. They had promptly secured themselves in the harbour by sinking a frigate and two corvettes across the entrance, and fired their guns on the troops ashore. Mortars were now landed from Boscawen's ships, and by means of these, three of the French ships were set on fire and in a short time were blazing to the water line. In the meantime Amherst pressed home his troops. As soon as it was dark, Boscawen hoisted out all his boats and sent them into the harbour with six hundred seamen to capture the remaining two ships. The French General capitulated the following day, 20th July, and Louisburg was once more British. The gateway to Canada was open.

Anson's judicious choice of naval commanders and the improved conditions of ships, equipment, and administration, were beginning to play their part, and his reputation grew apace. Byng and Minorca were forgotten. From every church tower the bells pealed as the news of Louisburg was received. At a parsonage in East Anglia this autumn Horatio Nelson was born. It was at this moment that the efficient fleet foundations, essential as a basis for his phenomenal successes, were being laid.

The land expedition to Ticonderoga had received a fatal blow when its leader, Lord Howe, a brother of the naval captain, and regarded by Wolfe as the finest soldier in the world, had been killed leading his troops. The command had passed to an officer who led his troops frontally towards an impregnable position. This ended in disaster. For this reason the intention to proceed to Quebec this season was dropped, and reliefs were sent to the retreating troops.

Boscawen returned to England, and arrived at Spithead on 1st November 1758. He received the thanks of Parliament.

> Mr. Boscawen—wrote Wolfe—has given all and even more than we could ask of him. He has furnished arms and ammunition, pioneers, sappers, marines, gunners, carpenters, and boats, and is, I must confess, no bad 'fantassin' himself, and an excellent back-hand at a siege.

From such as Wolfe these were words of praise indeed.

The loss of Louisburg after the Rochefort fiasco was a great shock to the French, who now decided to retaliate by an invasion of England, Scotland, and Ireland. This, they reckoned, would throw Britain into a panic, and paralyse further aggression in America and put a stop to assaults on the French coast. An army began to assemble in Normandy, and transports were built and concentrated at Havre. At the same time it was intended that the Brest fleet under Conflans should be joined by the Toulon fleet under de la Clue. Anson's policy as usual was to tackle the danger at its source: Hawke was therefore to blockade Brest, and Boscawen in the Mediterranean was to blockade Toulon.

Anson was one of the first to realize that to confine the enemy's fleets in their ports was not sufficient to gain command of the sea. This alone might deny command of the sea to the enemy, but Anson realized that it was also necessary to have cruiser forces which would be free to protect lines of communications. He regarded the function of the battle fleet to be that of preventing the enemy's battle fleet from interfering with the role of the cruisers. In addition to Hawke's and Boscawen's blockading forces therefore, he arranged for flotillas to be disposed in strategic positions; one stationed at the Downs was under Commodore Sir Peircy Brett. Anson also initiated what was later referred to as Anson's project: this was to be the destruction of enemy transports in Havre, and was strongly supported by Pitt, who with Anson was confident that the French invasion was not yet imminent. Newcastle on the other hand, in possession through private sources of secret information of French intentions, was most concerned at the absence of the British battle fleet.

At the end of June 1759, Anson began to strengthen his light squadrons by taking up privateers for service and by arming transports.

In July 1759, after long delay through bad weather, Rodney, recently promoted Rear-Admiral, sailed to Havre with a small squadron of ships and six bomb-ketches, and bombarded the town for fifty-two hours without pause, destroying transports, magazines, and stores. Rodney blockaded the port for the rest of the year.

In August 1759, de la Clue slipped out from Toulon while Boscawen's squadron was at Gibraltar refitting and repairing; Boscawen had come to the conclusion that the French would not leave while he remained before Toulon. Three hours after de la Clue's squadron of twelve ships had passed through the Straits at night, Boscawen was out of port with his flag flying in *Namur* and seven ships in company. In a running action off Lagos, which lasted two days, three ships-of-the-line were captured, the *Centaur*, *Téméraire*, and *Modeste*, and two destroyed, the *Ocean* and *Redoubtable*. The remaining French ships escaped into harbour. Boscawen left his second in command, Broderick, to blockade the French ships, and sailed for England in response to an order from Anson to bring home ten ships.

Opinion was now daily growing that invasion was imminent. In one thing, however, was Pitt adamant, and that was the maintenance of strength for the attack on Quebec. Not a man or ship must be recalled from the West.

When the reassuring news of Boscawen's victory off Lagos reached England in early September, there was great rejoicing. The church bells of England pealed once again.

'I own,' said Newcastle in a letter to Hardwicke, 'I was afraid of invasion till now.'

Hawke's task of blockading Brest was as usual made difficult by frequent gales. The weather in the summer of 1759 was unusually bad. By August, Hawke's fleet was beginning to show signs of strain both in men and ships. In succession, two at a time, ships would be sent away for cleaning, storing, and rest. In the last half of August, he was compelled to extend his blockade to all the Breton ports as far south as the Loire, and a detachment of his squadron under Commodore Duff watched the Morbihan, a protected harbour leading off from Quiberon Bay, where the bulk of the invasion transports lay. He also sent a detachment to lie off Rochefort further south, but Anson disapproved of too much dispersing of the blockading squadron and said that 'the particular object of attention at this time' was 'the interception of the embarkation of the enemy at Morbihan, and the keeping of the ships of war from coming out of Brest.' This was a clear directive. (See map, page 230.)

As soon as news of the disaster to the Toulon squadron arrived, Conflans with his fleet in Brest was told to wait no longer, but to get out of Brest and attack the British blockading squadron, and then send a division of ships to escort the Morbihan troops under the Duc d'Aiguillon for the great invasion of the Clyde.

Hawke was driven off his station to take refuge in Plymouth on 14th October in a gale from the west-south-west, and left Duff to keep watch on Quiberon Bay. The news reached London and caused further concern to Newcastle, but Anson was unworried, realizing that the gale that kept Hawke away would also prevent Conflans from leaving Brest.

A week later Hawke was back on his station. This in itself was a relief to the British, but all England was now jubilant over the news of the fall of Quebec, and momentarily fears of invasion were forgotten. Anson agreed to send Hawke every ship he could spare, and informed Hawke that Conflans would shortly emerge from Brest.

Heavy weather continued, and many of Hawke's ships developed dangerous leaks. On 10th November he was once again forced to withdraw his squadron from Brest, this time to Torbay. He put to sea again on the 12th. On the 13th he was driven back again, and now transferred his flag from the leaking *Ramillies* to the splendid new three decker, the *Royal George*, of a hundred guns. This was the first British three decker of a hundred guns and was the pride of Anson's heart. Hawke got to sea again on 14th November.

During Hawke's absence, a French squadron of seven sail-of-the-line, which for some weeks had been expected from Martinique, ran into Brest with the same westerly gale that had driven Hawke off. This provided Conflans with a reinforcement of experienced seamen. He put to sea on 14th November with a fleet of twenty-one ships-of-the-line, bound for the Morbihan. It was this same day that Hawke sailed from Torbay with twenty-three ships-of-the-line. Contrary winds, gales, calms, all caused considerable delay, so that it was not till the morning of 20th November that Conflans approached Quiberon Bay, and here sighted Duff's ships fairly and squarely trapped. Duff divided his squadron to work inshore. The wind was of gale force from the west-north-west with heavy squalls. The sea was very rough. At this moment Hawke's fleet was sighted to windward, bearing down in the very heavy weather for the approaches to Quiberon Bay. Conflans at once made for the entrance to the Bay to leave the Cardinals to port, and La Four Shoal to starboard. It was unlikely that Hawke without French pilots would risk his fleet in such shoal waters. Hawke, however, formed line abreast at eight o'clock to bring his fleet together and at a quarter to nine gave the order for the chase. Conflans hoped to get his ships inside before the enemy reached him, but he was much closer to the wind than Hawke who had a following wind. Hawke set his topgallant sails, and the rest following his example shook out their topsail reefs.

At half past two, Conflans leading in *Soleil Royal*, made the entrance and hauled the wind to clear the Cardinals. By now the leading British ships were overhauling the rear of the French line, and nine of them were doubling the four French rear ships to windward and to leeward. The sky was overcast, wind and sea were rising with the passage of every hour. In the leading nine ships were four of Anson's 1739 squadron officers, each captain of a ship: Howe in the *Magnanime*, leading the field, closely followed by Denis in the *Dorsetshire*, Keppel in the *Torbay*, and Baird in the *Defiance*.

The French Rear-Admiral Du Verger in the *Formidable* was soon a casualty, but had his wounds dressed, and sat on a chair on deck directing the fight until he died. *Formidable* continued a gallant fight, hard pressed by the *Resolution*, but surrendered as the *Royal George* came up. Hawke had been warned of the shoals by his master but replied: 'You have done your duty in pointing out the danger: now lay me alongside the *Soleil Royal*.'

Conflans had given the signal for ships to wear in succession with the idea of bringing help to his rear ships. In the gathering gloom the utmost confusion resulted.

The French *Thésée*, engaged first by Howe and then by Keppel, sank, followed soon afterwards by the French *Superbe*: in both cases heavy seas through their lower deck ports hastening their end. The *Hero* struck to Howe. *Soleil Royal*, in endeavouring to escape a broadside from the *Royal George*, fell foul of two French ships. It was now five o'clock and almost dark. Hawke made the signal for all ships to anchor.

Daylight the next day showed the *Soleil Royal* and *Hero* anchored among the British ships. They quickly cut their cables but ran aground, pursued by the *Essex* who also ran aground.

Hawke had won a decisive victory which at once put an end to fears of invasion. The French had lost six ships-of-the-line, and of those that escaped by throwing guns and stores overboard four broke their backs, and only three were fit for sea again. The remainder escaped to Rochefort. Keppel, who was

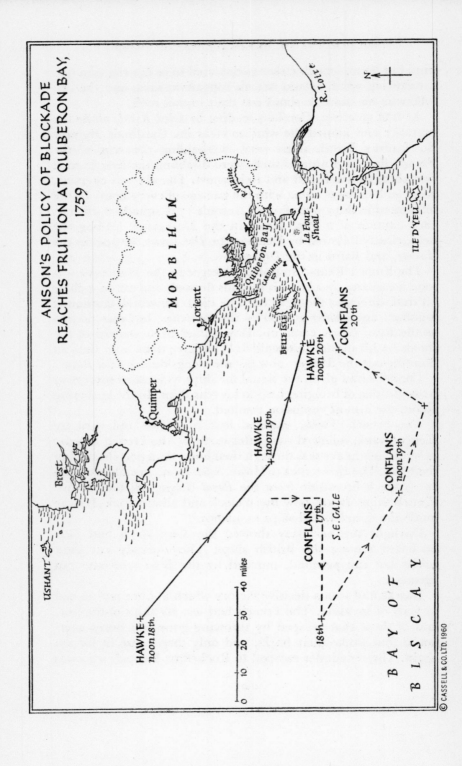

ANSON'S POLICY OF BLOCKADE
REACHES FRUITION AT QUIBERON BAY,
1759

N

R. Loire

MORBIHAN

Vilaine

Quimper

Lorient

Quiberon Bay

CARDINALS

BELLE ISLE

La Four
Shoal

ILE D'YEU

Brest

USHANT

HAWKE +
noon 18th.

HAWKE +
noon 19th.

HAWKE +
noon 20th.

CONFLANS
20th

CONFLANS
17th

CONFLANS
noon 19th

CONFLANS
noon 18th.

S.E. GALE

BAY OF
BISCAY

0    10    20    30    40 miles

© CASSELL & CO. LTD. 1960

sent after them, reported that they had been taken right up the River Charente. Conflans had fled ashore half naked.

Hawke was far from satisfied.

It was impossible—he said—in the space of a short winter's day that all our ships should be able to get into action. . . . Had we had but two hours more daylight, the whole had been totally destroyed or taken.

Smollett says:

One of the most important actions that ever happened in any war between the two nations. . . . it gave the finishing blow to the naval power of France.

What a change had been wrought since the time of Mathews' abortive action a short time before Anson had gone to the Admiralty.

# CHAPTER XXI

# Saunders at Quebec

SAUNDERS had relieved Anson in command of the Channel squadron in September 1758, and had set about disciplining the fleet in the way that Anson had recommended and found so necessary. Anson had the greatest confidence in his old friend and shipmate to whom he had given his first command, the *Tryal*. Saunders, however, was not to remain long with the Channel squadron. Pitt was already planning for 1759, and now that Louisburg was in British hands, preparations must be made for a push up the St. Lawrence in an amphibious operation to be launched against Quebec as soon as seasonal conditions allowed. Saunders, though little known at this time, was selected by Anson to be the naval commander of the operation, and was specially promoted to Vice-Admiral. Rear-Admiral Durell was to be second in command as he was already at Halifax, and Rear-Admiral Holmes, another of Anson's favourites, was to be third in command. Saunders had little to guide him in this great new expedition which was to carry regular troops hundreds of miles up the River St. Lawrence against unknown difficulties of navigation, but Anson knew that he was the man who would show initiative and determination to overcome all obstacles. He was a man who in many ways resembled Anson. Horace Walpole, seldom eulogistic, said of him: 'A pattern of the most sturdy bravery, united with the most unaffected modesty. No man said less or deserved more.'

Wolfe was to command the troops. Though only thirty-two, he had already captured the admiration of nations as a born

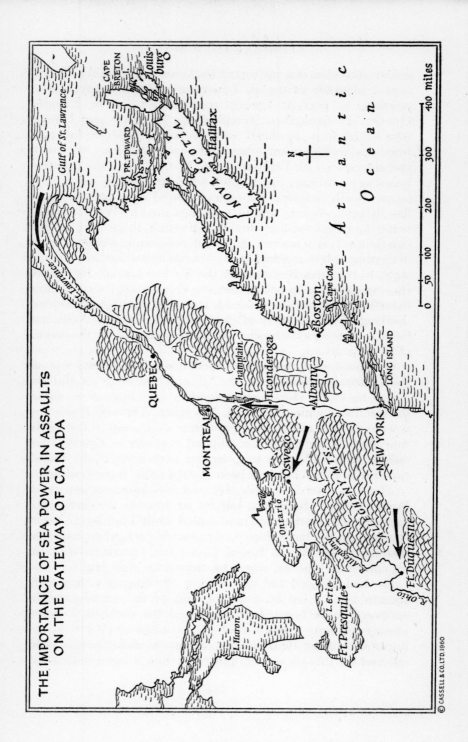

THE IMPORTANCE OF SEA POWER IN ASSAULTS
ON THE GATEWAY OF CANADA

© CASSELL & CO. LTD. 1960

leader. Saunders was instructed by Anson to ensure that Durell kept a blockade of the St. Lawrence as early in the year as possible, to prevent French reinforcements from reaching Quebec. To strengthen Durell's force, Saunders sent Holmes who sailed from Spithead with six sail-of-the-line and nine frigates, escorting twenty-thousand tons of transport, ordnance, and stores, on 14th February 1759. In the face of the expected invasion of Britain, this showed how determined was Pitt to secure North America. Saunders followed soon after, with his flag flying in *Neptune*, and was accompanied by Wolfe, his fleet being ten sail-of-the-line, three bomb vessels, three fireships, and two sloops. It is of interest that while proceeding along the coast of Spain, orders reached him to detach the *Stirling Castle*, a sixty, to reinforce Boscawen in the Mediterranean. He replied that he should keep her as 'she was very handy for rivers' and detached a seventy-four instead. It is clear that he was already thinking of the problem of close support. He and Wolfe had formed a strong attachment which augured well for the success of the expedition.

On arrival off Louisburg in April, it was found that ice made the approach impossible, so the Admiral bore away for Halifax. There he found Durell and promptly sent him off to watch for the first opening of the St. Lawrence. Through foul winds it was 5th May before Durell got clear away, and in the meantime French storeships had slipped through to Quebec, not only with considerable supplies but with news of the British expedition which Pitt had been at such pains to keep secret.

This was a terrible blow. Ice and fogs and contrary winds further delayed Saunders, but by 1st June he had embarked eighteen thousand troops and sailed from Louisburg. When *Neptune* and the large ships could proceed no further, Saunders transferred his flag to *Stirling Castle*, and continued with the expedition to Quebec, where he arrived on 26th June.

He had divided his vast throng of transports into three squadrons each led by a frigate, and by the aid of carefully anchored mark boats, had negotiated the dreaded Traverse passage without a single mishap. Saunders anchored at the upper end of the Ile d'Orleans, a narrow island twenty miles long which divides the St. Lawrence into a north and south channel immediately below Quebec. The north channel was full of shallows, but the south channel where Saunders anchored was navigable though exposed. How exposed and vulnerable Montcalm demonstrated the very next evening by sending down seven fireships. Saunders was, however, prepared for this, and his picket boats towed all seven of the blazing fireships ashore. (See map, page 238.)

Wolfe found that the French General Montcalm on receipt of the news of the British expedition had entrenched twelve thousand troops in a commanding position on the north-west bank, outside and below the city of Quebec, facing Saunders' anchorage in the south channel. It was here that Wolfe had hoped to land his own troops, and with Saunders engaging the fortress in a frontal attack, he had hoped to wrest the city by an encircling movement similar to that he had used at Louisburg. This was now out of the question. The guns of the city controlled the narrows of the river leading up stream. The position seemed impregnable. Wolfe divided his forces, however, and occupied points opposite Quebec and Montcalm's entrenchments: Pointe d'Orleans on the Ile d'Orleans, and Pointe des Pères immediately opposite Quebec, separated from it by the narrow neck of the river leading up stream. Wolfe, ever aware of the necessity for close support which only the Navy could give, and which happily Saunders was determined to provide, now laboriously and painstakingly erected a battery of siege guns and mortars at Pointe des Pères at the suggestion of Saunders, with the intention of neutralizing the guns of Quebec when required, and allowing passage up river for Saunders' ships. As a further diversion, Wolfe landed a force to face the lower flank of the French troops, separated only from them by a turbulent river, the Montmorenci. This required transports across the shallows of the north channel, and was accomplished as an amphibious operation. Covering fire was provided by the sloop *Porcupine*, to the command of which Saunders had just promoted John Jervis, the future victor of the Battle of Cape St. Vincent, an officer who had been given his commission in 1755 by Anson, and who had sailed from England with Saunders in the *Neptune*, impressing him with his zeal and efficiency.

Soon after arrival, Saunders had sent down to Durell, who

had been left with the heavy ships below the difficult passage, for reinforcements and the whole of the marines. These arrived with Holmes flying his flag in the *Captain*, sixty-four guns.

Wolfe, secure in the knowledge of the support of the fleet, had hoped to entice Montcalm to attack his divided force, but Montcalm was satisfied with his impregnability and superiority of numbers, and remained on the defensive. Time was also on his side, for summer was already on the wane. At the end of July, Wolfe, impatient and impetuous, made an abortive attempt, but soon realizing that it was hopeless, called it off. Soon he was down with fever. Depression and disappointment spread quickly.

As soon as the battery at Pointe des Pères had been completed, sailors and soldiers working happily together, the guns of Quebec were neutralized while ships specially selected by Saunders ran the gauntlet, and proceeded to the upper river. This not only provided the British with information concerning Montcalm's right flank, but produced a threat to the flank which caused Montcalm considerable concern. He was convinced that Wolfe would mount a frontal attack, if he had the temerity to attack at all, and believed this diversion of ships up river to be aimed at dividing his army by providing a threat to his flank. The attack would come frontally under cover of darkness and bombardment from ships. It is fairly certain that this was in fact Wolfe's intention right up to late August, with alternatives involving flank attack on the French left at Montmorenci. It was Saunders who insisted in late August that something definite must soon be done, as the season for naval operations was rapidly passing. He and Holmes both supported an idea that an assault should be made on the north shore above the town. Wolfe acquiesced. 'My ill state of health,' he wrote to Saunders from his position at Montmorenci, 'hinders me from executing my own plan. It is of too desperate a nature to order others to execute.' Not only did Wolfe agree, but decided that the plan would be put into force at once. Then followed considerable transport of troops and guns, feints, and threats, as Wolfe enjoyed to the utmost the superiority given to him of complete mobility. He daily continued his reconnaissance. Suddenly he decided that the moment had come. Montcalm, conscious of

the threats which now existed to both his flanks, yet still convinced that the final assault would be made at Beauport below
Quebec, had allowed a gap to appear in his front: his army was
divided in the middle. While Saunders bombarded Beauport,
Wolfe, in the evening of 12th September, landed his troops and
guns at the dead of night at a point on the shore just below the
western end of the Heights of Abraham. It was an extremely
difficult operation, with swift flowing tidal stream, inky darkness, and scores of transports, but was carried out successfully.
All troops were landed at the place where a goat track led up to
the heights above.

At daylight on 13th September Wolfe's army was arrayed
on the Heights of Abraham. This well disciplined force reserved
its fire until the French were within thirty paces. They then
opened fire, forcing the French to retreat, and quickly followed
with bayonets to achieve a decisive victory. Wolfe at the head
of his troops was brought down, and died soon afterwards.

'At 7.0', runs the log of the *Lowestoft*, 'anchored in 9 fathoms
low water. Distance of N. shore ½ mile. Landed all the troops.
At 11.0 was brought on board the corpse of General Wolfe.'

Quebec capitulated a few days later after Saunders had
brought his ships within range of the lower town.

General Townsend, who succeeded to the command, wrote:

> I should not do justice to the admirals and the Naval
> service if I neglected this occasion of acknowledging how
> much we are indebted for our success to the constant
> assistance and support received from them, and the perfect
> harmony.
>
> . . . in the immense labour in artillery, stores, and
> provisions, the long watching, and attacking in boats, the
> drawing up the hills of an artillery by the seamen, even in
> the heat of action. It is my duty to acknowledge how great
> a share the Navy has had in this successful campaign.

Saunders gave credit where it was due:

> Considering the darkness of the night and the rapidity
> of the current, this was a very critical operation very
> properly and successfully conducted. The difficulty of

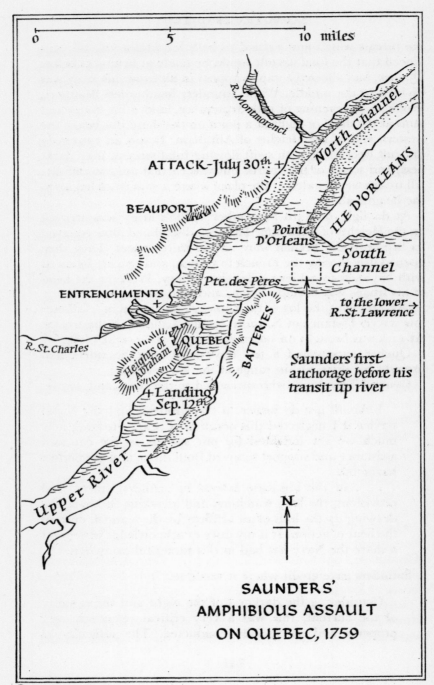

SAUNDERS'
AMPHIBIOUS ASSAULT
ON QUEBEC, 1759

gaining the top of the hill is scarce credible. It was very steep in the ascent and high, had no path where two could go abreast . . . during the tedious campaign there has continued a perfect good understanding between the army and navy.

Saunders, in his final despatch, apologized for having to leave before his work was finished. He was thinking of all the French ships up river, which could still operate against lines of communication. When he finally left in mid October, he detailed eight sloops to remain behind.

The credit for the capture of Quebec must go to Wolfe, but it is certain that a large share of the credit is due to Saunders for his determined support and inspiration which allowed the required flexibility in plan; and indirectly credit must go to Anson who passed on to Saunders so many of his ideas and who fostered his apprenticeship in seamanship during those tragic but dramatic years of the expedition to the South Seas.

Holmes and Durell reached Spithead with the bulk of the Quebec fleet the day after Hawke had been forced off his station into Torbay. They thought that they were closely followed by Saunders with the remainder of the fleet. Saunders had, however, fallen in with the *Juno*, and learnt that Hawke was on the trail of Conflans. Rest and honours awaited him in England but without hesitation he decided to join Hawke. In a laconic note to Pitt he said:

I have therefore only time to acquaint you that I am making the best of my way in quest of Sir Edward Hawke, which I hope his Majesty will approve of.

Quebec was now British but the French resistance had been so prolonged and Amherst's successful assault on Fort Ticonderoga so delayed that further progress this season was out of the question. Montreal was thus preserved for the French for another winter.

Anson confirmed Saunders' opinion of Jervis, and shortly afterwards promoted him to captain. Once again the country was indebted to Anson for his selection of one of its greatest and most successful admirals. As a mark of distinction for meritorious service, Anson obtained approval for the appointment of certain officers to honorary rank in the marines, with substantial emoluments. As a result, the following appointments were made: Admiral Boscawen, General of Marines; Vice-Admiral Sir Charles Saunders, Lieutenant-General of Marines; Sir Peircy Brett, The Honourable Augustus Keppel, and Viscount Howe, Colonels of Marines.

It is said that Wolfe, while embarked in a boat on the dark night of his landing below the Heights of Abraham, quoted Gray's Elegy, written a few years earlier, and said he would rather have written those lines than take Quebec. There is such beauty in the lines, and they are so appropriate to the moment, that they are worthy of reflection:

> The boast of heraldry, the pomp of power,
> And all that beauty, all that wealth e'er gave
> Await alike the inevitable hour:
> The paths of glory lead but to the grave.

# CHAPTER XXII

# Years of Glory

THE 'wonderful year of victories', 1759, had included other successes besides Lagos, Quebec, and Quiberon Bay, for Commodore Moore, after an abortive attempt against the island of Martinique, had taken Guadaloupe. Other West Indian islands capitulated soon afterwards.

Admiral Pocock had been successful in reducing French Naval opposition in the East Indies.

The British Navy was now back on its feet, and for the year 1760 the vote was for seventy thousand men, including 18,355 marines. The intention to maintain the command of the seas was now assured. The blockade of the French ports continued, so that French reinforcements for either India or Canada or the West Indies could be dealt with. Admirals, officers, and men were now experienced in their duties, and adequate measures were taken for the replenishment and maintenance of the ships.

There is little indication of Anson's health at this time, except for passing references to taking the waters in Bath. In April 1760 he was sixty-three, and must have begun to feel the strain of the critical years, the frequent threat of invasion, the need for speedy decisions requiring judgment and experience, the balancing of one pressing need against a conflicting one, the requirement to convince Pitt or the King about some professional point, the responsibility to the public, and the dedication to serve faithfully the needs of officers and men of his beloved Navy.

On the last day of May he wrote to Hardwicke about Lady Anson. He is obviously relieved at her recovery but the writing reveals a growing anxiety in spite of the reassuring words of the doctor:

Admiralty, the 31st May 1760.

I have the greatest satisfaction in acquainting your Lordship that Lady Anson is quite out of danger, and though her rash is not all out, she is easier, and to a degree has recovered her sleep and spirits, and desires me to make her dutiful acknowledgments and thanks for your Lordship's very kind and affectionate wishes; and she promises to be very careful of herself for the future.

How frequently had her adoring father pleaded for her to take things more easily. The letter continues:

Since I began this letter Dr. Wilmot thinks Lady Anson has rather more fever than she had in the morning, which, he says, is usual in these cases in the evening, and imagines there is more rash to come out. I don't understand their jargon, and always feel, when I have any of them in the house, as I always did when I had a Pilot; being ignorant myself, I always doubted whether my pilot knew as much as he ought to do; but in both cases there is nothing else to trust to.

I am, my dear Lord,

Your ever faithful and affectionate servant,

ANSON

At the foot of this letter, which is in the British Museum, there are two subscripts written by Hardwicke, which reveals the sad fact that the doctor's confidence had been misplaced. Lady Anson died on 1st June 1760.

This was a very unhappy affair, and a loss which could not be replaced. We thought Dr. Wilmot had not shown his usual sagacity in the illness.

H.

Till the death of this poor lady, our family had gone on in an uninterrupted flow of worldly prosperity: since that era we have had our share of private disasters. God's will be done.

H.

The Chancellor was to lose his wife in the following year.

There is little to indicate the effect which this sudden blow had on Anson. There is no doubt that the marriage had been one of great happiness and mutual affection. The loss of his wife must have been all the more severe to Anson because of his natural reserve towards most people, and his inherent shyness. Worn out with long hours of strenuous work, and with the consolation of his wife's genial company suddenly removed, it is certain that he himself began to ail. The deprivations and strain of his long voyage round the world were also beginning to catch up with him. There is a manuscript in the British Museum (34722) which gives a prescription for gout, for which Anson is reputed to have paid five thousand pounds. It reads as follows:

Lord Anson gave £5,000 for this receipt:

for the Gout or Rheumatic Gout
1 Drachm of Guinguineum
2    ,,    ,, Rhubarb
1 oz. of Cream of Tartar
2 oz. of Flower of Sulpher
1 pound of Clarified Honey
one Nutmeg or some Ginger grated into the above and the whole made into an Electuary.

take two Spoonfulls Night and morning fasting for 10 or 12 times if the Dose Operates too strongly on the Bowells the Quantity must be lessened the Patient may Drink any warm Liquor but should avoid Cold Drink.

News of the fall of Montreal in September 1760 to Amherst strengthened Pitt's resolve to mount an expedition against the coast of France as a further diversion. With his usual stress on secrecy, he led the public to believe that the attack was to be against the island of Mauritius, whereas he really had designs on Belle Isle, the possession of which he probably considered to be a good bargaining point in peace discussions. Anson, bearing in mind the disaster of the attack on St. Cas, instructed Hawke to detach Keppel for a detailed report on the feasibility of the scheme.

Anson wrote to Hawke:

9th October 1760.

The King reposing great confidence in you I have it in command to let you know that a very considerable body of troops, with a train of artillery, are collecting together, and transports getting ready to embark them, whenever it shall be thought proper.

Then followed detailed points which had to be answered concerning soundings and topographical details and local dispositions of enemy forces and fortifications.

I hope it is needless for me to repeat the confidence that is reposed in you on this occasion, and the necessity there is for the strictest secrecy.

ANSON

Sir Edward Hawke

Hawke's reply indicated that a landing was feasible, but criticized Pitt's strategy severely, questioning the need for occupying an island. Since Howe's expedition, Hawke was always jealous of a junior officer being appointed for a special mission which would bring the honour and fame that had so often eluded him. He was not the sort of man to rest on his laurels. George II had always liked him, but, apart from Anson, he had few other admirers. Pitt disliked him intensely, and the public soon forgot the momentary glory of the Quiberon Bay victory. In view of the time of the year, and the prospect of bad weather in the Bay, Anson was also lukewarm about the expedition. Pitt was resentful at growing opposition, and was particularly angry when Anson told him that the King considered the scheme impracticable. The whole episode came to an abrupt halt with the sudden death of the King on 27th

October 1760, in the thirty-third year of his reign, at the age of seventy-seven.

Keppel's expedition to Belle Isle blew hot and cold, remaining in readiness until 11th December when the whole thing was called off. In the following spring, 1761, Keppel's expedition was resumed, and by June 1761 the island had capitulated to the British.

Once again the bells rang. The country was ablaze with bonfires, and the people filled with jubilation. The news of the capture of Dominica in the West Indies which Pitt had ordered as a preliminary to an intended attack on Martinique, only served to strengthen Pitt's position. He was certain that an extension of the war was envisaged by France, and was determined to strike at Spain's colonial possessions if Spain entered the war.

In the meantime, negotiations for a separate peace between France and England were gaining ground, and received a powerful stimulus when the Duke of Bedford, one time First Lord of the Admiralty, joined the peace party. Bedford was reputed to be the only man who would face up to Pitt. His apparently logical and prophetic arguments indicated the danger that would follow if England entirely crushed France. He considered that 'a monopoly of all naval power would be at least as dangerous to the liberties of Europe as that of Louis XIV was, which drew almost all Europe upon his back.'

> Indeed, my lord—wrote Bedford to Newcastle—I don't know whether the neighbourhood of the French to our North American colonies was not the greatest security for their dependence on the mother country, which I feel will be slighted by them when their apprehension of the French is removed.

Pitt, however, was already aware of a potential alliance between France and Spain. Proposals from France were such that it became evident that she was anxious to preserve her sea power, and in particular was asking that she should retain the liberty of fishing off the coasts of Newfoundland. It was evident to Pitt that France was stalling. Although her fleets had been destroyed, and her colonies taken, she was hopeful of drawing Spain into the war. She still considered that the tide of Britain's successes would turn. The peace party in England were in favour of awaiting events. Pitt was insistent that immediate and decisive measures should be taken against Spain, and indicated his intention of resigning if he was not allowed to have his way. He was more afraid of Spain's benevolent neutrality towards France than her declared hostility to Britain.

As in 1757, Pitt regarded himself as the saviour of England, and said so.

> I was called—he said—to the administration of affairs by the voice of the people: to them I have always considered myself accountable for my conduct, and cannot therefore continue in a situation, which makes me responsible for measures I am no longer allowed to guide.

In September matters came to a head. Anson was against a declaration of war with Spain, on the basis that although he had ships available to reinforce Saunders in the Mediterranean and Holmes in the West Indies, the ships were nearly four thousand men short of their complements, and the fleet was not yet in readiness for any substantial operations against Spain. Pitt became more imperious as opposition mounted, and on 5th October resigned.

The remains of the administration which had opposed him, now continued the struggle with the same strategy that Pitt had always recommended. The attack on Martinique, set in motion earlier by Pitt, now came to fruition, and the island fell to an amphibious assault under Rodney and Monckton in February 1762, after a combined operation reminiscent of Quebec for splendid inter-service co-ordination. The lesser islands of Granada, St. Lucia, and St. Vincent fell into British hands shortly afterwards. The command of the sea was now undisputed. The understanding of the direct support which could be provided by the Navy for amphibious assaults, backed up by the continuous blockade of enemy ports, made it apparent that nothing was now impossible in offensive operations upon the enemy's colonial possessions.

Anson was nearing the end of his strenuous life, all of which, but for a few years of childhood, had been devoted to the service of his country. The Navy had been brought to a pitch of efficiency and success never excelled before. Administration was sounder, ships and equipment were more effective, and above all in importance, the officers and men were so well trained and disciplined that morale was universally high, not only in the service itself, but in the nation which now once again began to take an immense pride in its supremacy at sea.

Anson's last period at sea had been in the summer of 1758, when as an Admiral of the White, he had hoisted his flag in the *Royal George* at Spithead prior to blockading the French ports in the Bay. He was now to embark on his final commission at sea.

On 8th July 1761, the new King, George III, announced his intention of marrying Princess Charlotte of Mecklenburg-Strelitz, and ordered Anson to prepare a squadron of ships of war to proceed to Stade to receive and escort the Princess to England. At this same time Anson was promoted Admiral of the Fleet, the highest rank in the Navy, and passed over the head of the senior Admiral of the White, Sir William Rowley. He thus virtually became simultaneously First Lord of the Admiralty, senior Sea Lord, and the senior naval officer afloat. The yacht *Royal Caroline* was refitted and redecorated, and her name changed to *Royal Charlotte* in honour of the future Queen of England. The command of the ship was conferred on one of Anson's old *Centurion* lieutenants, Peter Denis, who had distinguished himself in command of the *Centurion* at Anson's victory off Finisterre. Anson hoisted his new flag, the union flag of an Admiral of the Fleet, in *Royal Charlotte*, and in company with the *Winchester*, fifty, *Nottingham*, sixty (the ship in which Saumarez had died in action), *Minorca*, thirty-two, *Tartar*, twenty-eight, and two sloops, sailed from Harwich on 8th August. On 24th August the Princess embarked in the Royal Yacht. The royal standard was hoisted at the main, the admiralty flag at the fore, and the union flag at the mizen. This colourful combination, not often seen, is well depicted in a topical painting. What a prize this would have been for the French: a future Queen of England.

On arrival at Harwich on 6th September, after a rough

passage, the Princess disembarked and set off for London. Anson struck his flag. This was the end of his career at sea. He now returned to Admiralty to continue the direction of the war at sea. Spain, spurred on by France, was acting in a belligerent manner, and as had been foreseen by Pitt, war with Spain now became inevitable. At the end of the year all ships and stations were ordered to 'act in a hostile manner against the Catholic King', and war was declared. Anson's first move was to extend the blockade of the French ports to those of Spain, in particular Cadiz and Ferrol where invasion armies were reported to be assembling. Sir Edward Hawke covered the Atlantic ports, while Sir Charles Saunders, assisted by Sir Peircy Brett, now a commodore, covered the Mediterranean. In the West Indies, Rodney, Swanton, Douglas, Pocock, and Keppel were all active. Commodore Lord Colville was vigilant on the North American station, and Vice-Admiral Cornish commanded in the seas of the East Indies. All these commanders were able to receive fleet reinforcements at will, the very life blood of continued success and the one necessity which through effective blockade was denied to the enemy, and in the end brought France and Spain to their knees.

In spite of the rigid blockade, France again made vast preparations in the spring of 1762 for an invasion of Britain, assembling fifty thousand troops in channel ports and planning a diversion towards Gibraltar in the hope of keeping the now extended British fleet occupied in that direction. Anson, however, had been prepared for such a diversion and the disposal of Hawke's and Saunders' fleets coped with the situation.

As soon as war had been declared on Spain at the turn of the year, Anson, though now a sick man but with recollections of 1739, conceived a plan for an attack on Havana in the Spanish West Indies. The plan received open opposition from Bedford who was averse to continuing the war at all, and there was no great support from Newcastle who was keen to send an expedition to support Portugal, regarded in the eyes of France and Spain as a British colony ripe for plucking.

At the same time a plan was developed for an attack on Manila, the intention being to paralyse Spanish trade at two main sources. In spite of Bedford's opposition, both plans were approved by the administration, who, although they had lost Pitt, now appeared to pursue his policy with enthusiasm. Anson forged ahead with great energy, though aware of the greatly increased demands which would be made on the fleet. His plan for the attack on Havana was somewhat novel, and embodied both speed and surprise by making the approach to the city through the relatively unknown Bahama Channel off the north coast of Cuba. This was much more direct than the normal approach via Jamaica and the south of Cuba, followed by the long haul to windward against the north-east trades as soon as the western end of Cuba had been rounded. The plans were most involved, since arrangements had to be made for reinforcements from England to rendezvous with the West Indies fleet in the Windward Passage between Cuba and San Domingo, and for a homeward bound convoy to be released at an appropriate moment. Care was to be taken that the Spanish fleet based on Havana, was not joined by the French fleet based on San Domingo. The scheme was brilliant in conception, and as a campaign is worthy of study in detail, for it is typical of Anson's great grasp of the essentials for success and thoroughness in planning. The old Bahama Channel had never been used by the Spaniards except for small ships, but Anson possessed an old Spanish chart that convinced him that with proper safeguards, such as could be provided by checking the soundings on this chart, a fleet could pass through, running before the wind the whole way, and arriving speedily and unexpectedly with the certainty that there could be no combination of the allied enemy fleets. (See map, page 250.)

Anson appointed Sir George Pocock as the admiral in command of the naval operations, and his old shipmate the Hon. Augustus Keppel as commodore second-in-command. Pocock's final orders were issued on 18th February 1762, and these were the last that Anson ever signed. His health was rapidly failing, but in this time of great need, with the combined might of France and Spain to be opposed, he remained at his post, resolved that the Havana assault should succeed.

Troops were to be assembled from England, North America, and the West Indies, which would provide an assault force of

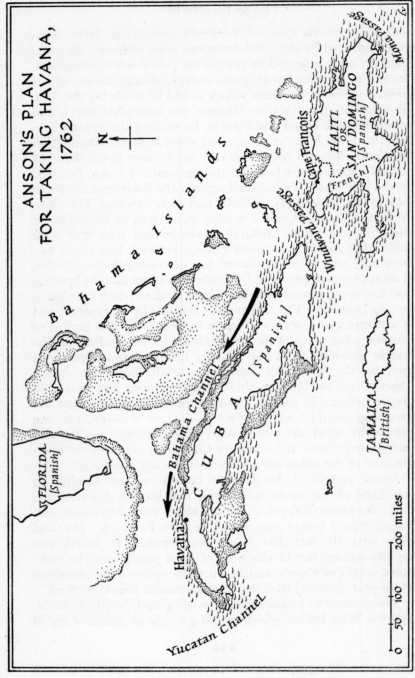

ANSON'S PLAN
FOR TAKING HAVANA,
1762

N

Bahama Islands

FLORIDA
[Spanish]

Bahama Channel

CUBA [Spanish]

Havana

Yucatan Channel

Cape François

HAITI
OR
SAN DOMINGO
[Spanish]

[French]

Windward Passage

JAMAICA
[British]

Mona Passage

0    50    100    200 miles

© CASSELL & CO. LTD. 1960

fourteen thousand men for the main attack under Lieutenant-General the Earl of Albemarle, Keppel's eldest brother. A third brother, William Keppel, was in command of a division of troops.

Pocock sailed in early March with five ships-of-the-line and a convoy of transports and storeships. The expedition had only begun, but Anson's work was done. There is little to record of his private thoughts as he now began to face worsening health. His devoted wife had died less than two years earlier, and he must by now have been a very lonely man with little interest outside his devotion to his country and the Service of which he was still head. We know from records of enquiries and replies that there was much concern from his friends. His reputation for devotion and integrity had never suffered, and his fame was nation-wide.

A reply to an enquiry from the Duke of Newcastle, sent from the Admiralty on 9th March 1762 says:

> Lord Anson returns many thanks to the Duke of Newcastle for his kind enquiry. He is better, and sincerely congratulates with his Grace upon the good news from Martinique.

And a further one a few days later says:

> March 18th 1762.
> My Lord Anson is somewhat better this evening, has had a little sleep, and his pains are easier, and his Pulse something better, but his breathing is still much opphrest, upon the whole his Lordship appears better but is by no means yett to be thought out of danger.
> Admiralty Thursday night eight o'clock.

In the meantime the Havana expedition was progressing. The Spanish admiral at Havana had been told to remain in the port. The French admiral at St. Domingo was more concerned about the defence of the French islands than the Spanish. And so the allied fleets remained separated, playing into the scheme which Anson had planned, while Pocock towards the end of April arrived at Martinique recently captured from the French, and awaited the concentration of his own forces. A squadron under Commodore Hervey meanwhile kept watch on the French fleet in Cape François, St. Domingo.

On 6th May Pocock sailed for his next rendezvous and the passage of the Old Bahama Channel. Anson at this time was receiving treatment from the Bath waters, and appeared to be improving. Pocock organized his convoy into seven divisions and divided his fleet into seven escorts, himself leading in the first, and Keppel following in the second. The channel had been well surveyed by Elphinstone, and by the 5th June, Pocock's whole fleet was through the Channel and less than a hundred miles from its objective. The following day, 6th June, Pocock's sails were sighted from the top of Moro Castle, and surprise was such that the Spanish officer who reported the news was reprimanded for spreading false alarms. They were certain that it must be the Jamaica convoy, homeward bound.

Pocock with thirteen ships-of-the-line and bomb vessels, proceeded to the blockade of the city, while Keppel, with six ships-of-the-line, bombarded two forts guarding the bay, and covered the troop landings. By 30th July, after a long siege, a breach had been made in the fortress, hitherto regarded by the Spaniards as impregnable, and the city capitulated soon afterwards.

Spain had entered the war with the hope of recovering Gibraltar, the gateway to the Mediterranean, but had now lost one of the gateways to the West Indies. This was a death blow from which she never recovered. Peace negotiations soon began again, and by November of this year, 1762, preliminaries for a peace were signed at Fontainebleau, ratified in February of the following year by the Peace of Paris. News of further British victories poured in while the peace negotiations continued, among which was the capture of Manila. Anson would have been particularly pleased at this. He was destined not to live to hear of the peace. On 6th June 1762, on the day that Pocock was reported off Havana, Anson while walking in his garden at Moor Park was suddenly taken ill, and died very shortly afterwards.

At no time had the prestige of Britain stood higher. She had begun the war suffering insults and encroachments on all her possessions abroad. At the conclusion of the war, with Anson recently interred in the family vault in Staffordshire, she now possessed a mighty Empire which with the passage of centuries was to develop into self governing countries where English laws and language would be respected.

What part Anson had played is perhaps best left to the praise of his contemporaries.

Newcastle, writing to Thomas Anson three days after the First Lord's death, said:

> There never was a more able, a more upright, or a more useful servant to his King and Country, or a more sincere or valuable friend.

Pitt, speaking in the House of Lords in 1770, said of Lord Anson:

> To his wisdom, to his experience and care the nation owes the glorious successes of the last war.

# Index

# Date Due

| NOV 1 '65 | | | |
|-----------|---|---|---|
| | | | |
| | | | |
| | | | |
| | | | |
| | | | |
| | | | |
| | | | |
| | | | |
| | | | |
| | | | |
| | | | |
| | | | |
| | | | |
| | | | |
| | | | |
| | | | |